WITHDRAWN

Adobe®

After Effects® CS5
Digital
Classroom

Adobe®
After Effects® CS5
Digital
Classroom

Jerron Smith and the AGI Creative Team

Wiley Publishing, Inc.

Adobe® After Effects® CS5 Digital Classroom

Published by
Wiley Publishing, Inc.
10475 Crosspoint Boulevard
Indianapolis, IN 46256

Copyright © 2009 by Wiley Publishing, Inc., Indianapolis, Indiana
Published by Wiley Publishing, Inc., Indianapolis, Indiana
Published simultaneously in Canada
ISBN: **978-0-470-59524-4**
Manufactured in the United States of America
10 9 8 7 6 5 4 3 2 1

For general information on our other products and services or to obtain technical support, please contact our Customer Care Department within the U.S. at (800) 762-2974, outside the U.S. at (317) 572-3993 or fax (317) 572-4002.

Please report any errors by sending a message to errata@agitraining.com

Library of Congress Control Number: 2010928470

About the Authors

Jerron Smith is an editor, animator and educator. He is a multi-faceted artist and video producer with nearly two decades of experience working with a wide variety of media. He has worked in both digital video/television production and post-production, and also in multi-media and print design. He teaches professional development classes at American Graphics Institute and serves as an adjunct instructor in the Communication Arts department at the New York Institute of Technology, where he instructs courses in computer graphics, animation and video editing. He holds undergraduate degrees in Art and Education and a Masters degree in Communication Arts where he specialized in Computer Graphic technology.

The AGI Creative Team is composed of Adobe Certified Experts and Adobe Certified Instructors from American Graphics Institute (AGI). They work with many of the world's most prominent companies, helping them use creative software to communicate more effectively and creatively. They work with design, creative, and marketing teams around the world, delivering private customized training programs, and teach regularly scheduled classes at AGI's locations. The Digital Classroom authors are available for professional development sessions at companies, schools and universities. More information is available at agitraining.com.

Acknowledgments

Thanks to our many friends at Adobe Systems, Inc. This book would not be possible without their valued input. Thanks also to the many clients of AGI who trust us to provide After Effects training. Many of the tips and suggestions found in this book come from teaching these classes. A special thanks to the instructional team at AGI for their input, assistance, and editorial guidance in the review process, truly making this book a team effort.

Thanks to the following for permission to use their content in this book:

Tony Billz, producer, Creating FreeForm Masks.

Natalee Shale, editor, Creating Shape Masks.

Zeenal Thakare, editor, Creating Track Mattes.

Credits

Contents

Starting Up

About Digital Classroom 1

Prerequisites 1

System requirements 1

Starting Adobe After Effects CS5 2

Fonts used in this book 3

Resetting Adobe After Effects CS5 preferences 3

Loading lesson files 4

Working with the video tutorials 6

Setting up for viewing the video tutorials 6

Viewing the video tutorials 7

Additional resources 8

Lesson 1: Understanding Motion Graphics

Starting up 9

Defining motion graphics 10

Digital video basics 11

Understanding video formats 11

Understanding frame rate and resolution 13

Understanding transparency 14

Self study 15

Review 15

Lesson 2: Understanding the After Effects Interface

Starting up 17

Understanding and working with menus 18

Opening an existing After Effects project 18

Understanding the After Effects panel system 20

After Effects panels 21

Primary panels 21

Understanding the workspace 32

Viewing and hiding panels 32

Docking and undocking panels 33

Resizing panels 35

Saving a custom workspace 37

Resetting the workspace. 37

Setting After Effects Preferences 38

Changing the default undo levels 39

Enable Auto-Save 39

Self study. 40

Review 40

Lesson 3: Media Management—Images, Video, and Audio

Starting up 41

What is Media Management? 42

Projects, compositions, and layers: an overview 42

Creating a new project 43

Importing media files 44

Organizing the Project panel 46

Modifying the column displays. 46

Creating folders and subfolders 47

Previewing footage 49

Previewing stills and video. 50

Previewing audio 50

Trimming a video clip 51

Importing multiple files 54

Importing Photoshop and Illustrator files 55

Importing image sequences 58

Importing After Effects compositions. 60

Locating missing files. 61

Using the Interpret Footage dialog box 62

Looping an audio or video file. 62

Using Remember Interpretation. 63

Using the Collect Files command to consolidate files . . . 64

Self study. 66

Lesson 4: Animation Workflow

Starting up 67

Understanding the animation workflow 68

Creating and working with compositions 68

Creating a new composition 68

Understanding composition settings 70

Importing compositions
from Photoshop and Illustrator. 72

Working with layers 73

Understanding the layer switches 78

Understanding layer stacking order 80

Changing layer names. 81

Creating Kinestasis by animating the Anchor Point 83

Animating rotation. 86

Using layer parenting to ease repetition 88

Animating position. 90

Understanding motion paths 95

Using layer motion blur. 97

Adjusting Motion Blur settings 98

Using blending modes 100

Applying layer styles 103

Understanding nested compositions
and precomposing 105

Adding nested styles 105

Pre-composing layers 108

Creating a fade-in by animating Opacity and Scale 110

Self study. 111

Review 111

Lesson 5: Working with Masks, Track Mattes, and Keys

Starting up 113
Working with masks 114
Creating masks with the shape tools. 117
Selecting and manipulating masks 118
Animating the position of masks 121
Creating freeform masks. 125
Animating the shape of masks 132
Understanding track mattes 135
Creating track mattes 135
Creating mattes from animated Photoshop files. 137
Creating a chroma key. 140
Creating a garbage matte. 142
Creating a chroma key 144
Refining the matte 147
Self study. 150
Review 150

Lesson 6: Working with Text

Starting up 151
Creating text. 152
Setting text properties globally 155
Formatting individual characters 158
Animating text properties 164
Saving an animator as a preset 169
Working with text animation presets 170
Modifying animation presets. 172
Creating custom text animators 175
Creating a typewriter effect. 175
Creating text on a path 178
Self study. 180
Review 180

Lesson 7: Working with Audio

Starting up 181

Audio in After Effects 182

Previewing audio 183

Adding audio files to the Timeline 183

Viewing audio file metadata 186

Looping audio files. 188

Animating audio levels 190

Working with audio effects 191

Using composition markers to set the beat. 193

Naming composition markers. 196

Refining the position of composition markers 198

Syncing animation to composition markers 199

Creating keyframes from audio files 203

Self study. 207

Review 207

Lesson 8: Working with 3D in After Effects

Starting up 209

Previewing animation with RAM preview 210

Working the 3D capabilities of After Effects 211

Creating 3D layers. 211

Using multiple viewports 213

Understanding 3D Transform properties 215

Understanding Material Options 216

Animating 3D layers. 217

Creating and using lights 221

Understanding light options 227

Animating light properties 227

Creating and using cameras 231

Understanding camera options 234

Animating camera properties. 234

Creating the depth-of-field effect 243

Creating a Rack Focus shot. 245

Working with Live Photoshop 3D. 248

Importing Live Photoshop 3D effects 248

Animating Photoshop 3D compositions 250

Adding a Glow and Lens Flare effect. 254

Self study. 257

Review 258

Lesson 9: Advanced Animation

Starting up 259

Animating with effects 260

Applying effects to layers 260

Animating effect properties. 264

Saving animation presets 268

Applying and modifying effects presets 268

Time-reversing a layer 270

Using the Motion Sketch panel to capture motion. 272

Controlling layer orientation 275

Using the Smoother panel to soften movement 276

Using the Wiggler panel to add frantic motion 277

Create acceleration and
deceleration using Easy Easing. 281

Changing spatial interpolation 281

Adding easing to keyframes 283

Using squash and stretch to enhance the animation. . . 285

Animating with the Graph Editor. 287

Create a strobing effect using hold interpolation 291

Automating animation with expressions. 292

Finding expressions 293

Adding expressions to properties 293

Using the LoopOut( ) expression 294

Using the Random( ) expression. 295

Using the Time property with expressions 297

Using the Wiggle( ) expression 298

Working with scripts 300

Installing and running scripts 300

Creating scripts 300

Finding additional scripts 301

Using and applying scripts 301

Self study 305

Review 305

Lesson 10: Outputting After Effects Projects

Starting up 307

Rendering files for output 308

Understanding the Render Queue 309

Adding compositions to the Render Queue 309

Adjusting render settings 311

Duplicating jobs in the Render Queue 314

Creating render templates 317

Exporting a project file 319

Trimming and cropping compositions 320

Rendering an individual frame 324

Self study 325

Review 326

Appendix A

After Effects Secondary panels 327

Appendix B

Importable media formats 335

Still images and image sequences 336

Project formats 337

Appendix C

Understanding formats and codecs 339

Understanding bit rate 340

Understanding spatial and temporal compression 340

Appendix D

Understanding Video Displays 341

Understanding aspect ratio and pixel aspect ratio 341

Progressive display versus interlacing 343

Starting up

About Digital Classroom

Adobe® After Effects CS5 lets you create artwork for a variety of uses. The animation and compositing tools of After Effects are second to none; allowing you to manipulate text, images, audio and video. After Effects provides you with the tools to express your creative ideas for video, film and broadband production. After Effects CS5 is also tightly integrated with other Adobe products such as Photoshop® CS5 , Illustrator CS5 and Premiere Pro®.

Adobe After Effects CS5 Digital Classroom is like having your own personal instructor guiding you through each lesson while you work at your own speed. This book includes 10 self-paced lessons that let you discover essential skills and explore the new features and capabilities of After Effects CS5 on either a Mac OS or Windows computer. Each lesson includes step-by-step instructions, lesson files, and video tutorials, all of which are available on the included DVD. This book has been developed by the same team of Adobe Certified Experts and After Effects professionals who have created many official training titles for Adobe Systems.

Prerequisites

Before you start the lessons in *After Effects CS5 Digital Classroom,* you should have a working knowledge of your computer and its operating system. You should know how to use the directory system of your computer so that you can navigate through folders. You need to understand how to locate, save, and open files. You should also know how to use your mouse to access menus and commands.

Before starting the lessons files in *After Effects CS5 Digital Classroom*, make sure that you have installed Adobe After Effects CS5. The software is sold separately, and not included with this book. You may use the 30-day trial version of Adobe After Effects CS5 available at the *adobe.com* web site, subject to the terms of its license agreement.

System requirements

Before starting the lessons in *After Effects CS5 Digital Classroom*, make sure that your computer is equipped for running Adobe After Effects CS5, which you must purchase separately. The minimum system requirements for your computer to effectively use the software are listed on the following page.

System requirements for Adobe After Effects CS5:

Windows OS

- Intel® Pentium® 4 or AMD Athlon® 64 processor (Intel Core™2 Duo or AMD Phenom® II recommended); 64-bit support required
- 64-bit operating system required: Microsoft® Windows Vista® Home Premium, Business, Ultimate, or Enterprise with Service Pack 1 or Windows® 7
- 2GB of RAM
- 3GB of available hard-disk space plus 2GB of space for optional content; additional free space required during installation (cannot install on removable flash-based storage devices)
- 1280x1024 display with OpenGL 2.0–compatible graphics card
- DVD-ROM drive
- QuickTime 7.6.2 software required for QuickTime features
- Broadband Internet connection required for online services

Macintosh OS

- Multicore Intel processor with 64-bit support
- Mac OS X v10.5.7 or v10.6
- 2GB of RAM
- 4GB of available hard-disk space plus 2GB of space for optional content; additional free space required during installation (cannot install on a volume that uses a case-sensitive file system or on removable flash-based storage devices)
- 1280x900 display with OpenGL 2.0–compatible graphics card
- QuickTime 7.6.2 software required for QuickTime features
- Broadband Internet connection required for online services

Starting Adobe After Effects CS5

As with most software, Adobe After Effects CS5 is launched by locating the application in your Programs folder (Windows) or Applications folder (Mac OS). If necessary, follow these steps to start the Adobe After Effects CS5 application:

Windows

1 Choose Start > All Programs > Adobe After Effects CS5. If you have the Creative Suite installed, you may have to select Adobe After Effects from within the Creative Suite folder.

2 Close the Welcome Screen when it appears. You are now ready to use Adobe After Effects CS5.

Mac OS

1 Open the Applications folder, and then open the Adobe After Effects CS5 folder. If you have the Creative Suite installed, you may have to select Adobe After Effects from within the Creative Suite folder.

2 Double-click on the Adobe After Effects CS5 application icon.

3 Close the Welcome Screen when it appears. You are now ready to use Adobe After Effects CS5.

Menus and commands are identified throughout the book by using the greater-than symbol (>). For example, the command to print a document would be identified as File > Print.

Fonts used in this book

After Effects CS5 Digital Classroom includes lessons that refer to fonts that were installed with your copy of Adobe After Effects CS5. If you did not install the fonts, or have removed them from your computer, you may substitute different fonts for the exercises or re-install the software to access the fonts.

If you receive a Missing layer dependencies warning dialog when you open a file, the is usually due to not having a necessary font installed on your system. If this occurs, press OK and After Effects will substitute a default system font. You can then change the default font to one similar to the one used in the lesson..

Resetting Adobe After Effects CS5 preferences

When you start Adobe After Effects, it remembers certain settings along with the configuration of the workspace from the last time you used the application. It is important that you start each lesson using the default settings so that you do not see unexpected results when working with the lessons in this book. Use the following steps to reset your Adobe After Effects CS5 preferences.

Steps to reset Adobe After Effects CS5 preferences

1 Quit After Effects.

2 Locate and rename the Adobe After Effects 10.0 MC Prefs, as follows.

- In Windows: Rename the Adobe After Effects 10.0 MC Prefs (for example to Adobe After Effects 10.0 MC Prefs-old) in the Documents and Settings/*(user)*/Application Data/Adobe/After Effects /10.0.

- In Windows Vista: Rename the Adobe After Effects 10.0 MC Prefs (for example to Adobe After Effects 10.0 MC Prefs-old) in the Users/*(user)*/AppData/Roaming/Adobe/ Adobe After Effects CS5 Settings/*(language_location)* folder.

- In Mac OS: Rename the Adobe After Effects 10.0 MC Prefs file in the Users/*(user)*/ Library/Preferences/After Effects/10.0 folder.

3 Start After Effects. It creates a new preferences file.

You can also reset preferences using a keyboard shortcut. When starting the application, press and hold Command + Shift + Option (Mac OS) or Control + Alt + Shift (Windows). When the dialog box appears asking if you are sure you want to delete the preferences file press OK.

Loading lesson files

The *After Effects CS5 Digital Classroom* DVD includes files that accompany the exercises for each of the lessons. You may copy the entire lessons folder from the supplied DVD to your hard drive, or copy only the lesson folders for the individual lessons you wish to complete.

For each lesson in the book, the files are referenced by the file name of each file. The exact location of each file on your computer is not used, as you may have placed the files in a unique location on your hard drive. We suggest placing the lesson files in the My Documents folder (Windows) or at the top level of your hard drive (Mac OS).

Copying the lesson files to your hard drive:

1   Insert the *After Effects CS5 Digital Classroom* DVD supplied with this book.

2   On your computer desktop, navigate to the DVD and locate the folder named aelessons.

3   You can install all the files, or just specific lesson files. Do one of the following:

   • Install all lesson files by dragging the aelessons folder to your hard drive.

   • Install only some of the files by creating a new folder on your hard drive named aelessons. Open the aelessons folder on the supplied DVD, select the lesson you wish to complete, and drag the folder(s) to the aelessons folder you created on your hard drive.

Unlocking Mac OS files

Macintosh users may need to unlock the files after they are copied from the accompanying disc. This applies only to Mac OS computers and is because the Mac OS may view files that are copied from a DVD or CD as being locked for writing.

If you are a Mac OS user, and have difficulty saving over the existing files in this book, you can use these instructions so that you can update the lesson files as you work on them and also add new files to the lessons folder

Note that you only need to follow these instructions if you are unable to save over the existing lesson files, or if you are unable to save files into the lesson folder.

1   After copying the files to your computer, click once to select the aelessons folder, then choose File > Get Info from within the Finder (not After Effects).

2   In the aelessons info window, click the triangle to the left of Sharing and Permissions to reveal the details of this section.

3   In the Sharing and Permissions section, click the lock icon (🔒), if necessary, in the lower right corner so that you can make changes to the permissions.

4   Click to select a specific user or select everyone, then change the Privileges section to Read & Write.

5   Click the lock icon to prevent further changes, and then close the window.

Working with the video tutorials

Your *After Effects CS5 Digital Classroom* DVD comes with video tutorials developed by the authors to help you understand the concepts explored in each lesson. Each tutorial is approximately five minutes long and demonstrates and explains the concepts and features covered in the lesson.

The videos are designed to supplement your understanding of the material in the chapter. We have selected exercises and examples that we feel will be most useful to you. You may want to view the entire video for each lesson before you begin that lesson. Additionally, at certain points in a lesson, you will encounter the DVD icon. The icon, with appropriate lesson number, indicates that an overview of the exercise being described can be found in the accompanying video.

DVD video icon.

Setting up for viewing the video tutorials

The DVD included with this book includes video tutorials for each lesson. Although you can view the lessons on your computer directly from the DVD, we recommend copying the folder labeled *Videos* from the *After Effects CS5 Digital Classroom* DVD to your hard drive.

Copying the video tutorials to your hard drive:

1   Insert the *After Effects CS5 Digital Classroom* DVD supplied with this book.

2   On your computer desktop, navigate to the DVD and locate the folder named Videos.

3   Drag the Videos folder to a location onto your hard drive.

Viewing the video tutorials with the Adobe Flash Player

The videos on the *After Effects CS5 Digital Classroom* DVD are saved in the Flash projector format. A Flash projector file wraps the Digital Classroom video player and the Adobe Flash Player in an executable file (.exe for Windows or .app for Mac OS). However, please note that the extension (on both platforms) may not always be visible. Projector files allow the Flash content to be deployed on your system without the need for a browser or prior standalone player installation.

The accompanying video files on the DVD use the Adobe Flash Video format to make universal viewing possible for users on both Windows and Mac OS computers.

Playing the video tutorials:

1   On your computer, navigate to the Videos folder you copied to your hard drive from the DVD. Playing the videos directly from the DVD may result in poor quality playback.

2   Open the Videos folder and double-click the AEvideos_PC.exe (Windows) or AEvideos_Mac.app (Mac OS) to view the video tutorial.

3   Press the Play button to view the videos.

The Flash Player has a simple user interface that allows you to control the viewing experience, including stopping, pausing, playing, and restarting the video. You can also rewind or fast-forward, and adjust the playback volume.

A. Go to beginning. *B*. Play/Pause. *C*. Fast-forward/rewind. *D*. Stop. *E*. Volume Off/On. *F*. Volume control.

Playback volume is also affected by the settings in your operating system. Be certain to adjust the sound volume for your computer, in addition to the sound controls in the Player window.

Additional resources

The Digital Classroom series goes beyond the training books. You can continue your learning online with training videos, or at seminars, conferences, and in-person training events.

Book series

Expand your knowledge of creative software applications with the Digital Classroom training series which includes books on Photoshop, Flash, Dreamweaver, Illustrator, and more. Learn more at *digitalclassroombooks.com*.

Training & Professional Development

The authors of the Digital Classroom seminar series frequently conduct in-person seminars and are available for in-person training and professional development for your organization, company, school, or university. Learn more at *agitraining.com*.

Resources for educators

Visit *digitalclassroombooks.com* to access resources for educators, including instructors' guides for incorporating Digital Classroom into your curriculum.

What you'll learn in this lesson:

- What types of content you can create in After Effects

- The properties of the video files you will be creating and importing into After Effects

- About the various broadcast and broadband standards that you can create content for

Understanding Motion Graphics

This lesson provides an overview of various types of motion graphics and digital video. It's filled with important information that you need to know to work effectively with After Effects. If you can't wait to get started using the program, skip over this lesson for now and jump ahead to Lesson 2, "Understanding the After Effects Interface." If you jump ahead, make sure you come back to review this lesson later.

Starting up

This lesson includes useful background information. If you'd prefer to jump right into working with After Effects, you should move to the second lesson, which gets you hands-on right away.

See Lesson 1 in action!

Use the accompanying video to gain a better understanding of how to use some of the features shown in this lesson. The video tutorial for this lesson can be found on the included DVD.

Defining motion graphics

Adobe After Effects is a standard tool for creating motion graphics that are used for broadcast television, film, and other video productions. After Effects is used to create content that appears in presentation graphics and on mobile devices. It is a tool for storytelling, creating visually appealing motion graphics that integrate into any medium to enhance a presentation, story, image, or mood.

Television and video graphics

After Effects is a principal tool of broadcast-design professionals. After Effects is used to create original content for interstitial, lower thirds, bumpers, and show openings. Many video professionals consider it an essential tool in their daily work. In fact, you can see it at networks such as MTV, Spike, truTV, and the Food Network, where it's used to produce stunning, high quality graphics and motion design packages quickly and affordably.

Internet and mobile devices

The Internet and mobile devices are becoming a major entertainment medium. After Effects high-quality motion graphics are being widely used for online and mobile content. Video sharing sites, such as *Vimeo.com* and *YouTube.com*, provide content creators with access to a wide audience, which creates additional distribution opportunities for individuals and organizations alike.

Desktop distribution and presentation graphics

Digital displays such as high-definition televisions, monitors, and projectors have created new venues for displaying motion graphics. After Effects adds impact to otherwise static slides, charts and graphs.

Regardless of how you plan to use After Effects, you will find it to be a powerful, well-rounded tool that, with a little practice, can serve you well.

Digital video basics

You could just open After Effects and start creating graphics without any understanding of how video works. If you really can't wait to get started, jump ahead to Lesson 2, "Understanding the After Effects Interface." However, successfully producing graphics for video and other media requires that you understand a few technical requirements. If you don't understand these, you'll merely be pushing buttons and clicking checkboxes, so you should take a few minutes to at least get a foundation in digital video.

When working in After Effects, you will want to consider the final destination for your project. Will it be used on television, in video, on a mobile device? Knowing this information allows you to accurately create your composition settings to match your intended destination. Projects for high-definition television differ from those for a portable device with a small-screen. Each of these media has its own standards for items, such as frame rate, aspect ratio, and bit rate. Understanding these items saves you time and effort in the production process.

Understanding video formats

Some video formats are common for professional video production, while others are suitable only for broadband or small-screen purposes. There are two main standards used for broadcast television, a handful of competing standards for desktop and web video, and a series of device-specific standards used in mobile handheld devices. Technical standards, such as the ones mentioned here, are very complex, and a full description of each one is beyond the scope of this book. In general, regardless of the platform for which you are creating video content, there are three main properties to keep in mind:

Dimensions: This property specifies the pixel dimensions of a video file—the number of pixels horizontally and vertically that make up an image or video frame. This value is usually written as a pair of numbers separated by an x, where the first number is the horizontal value and the second represents the vertical value, such as 720×480. Pixel is a combination of the words *picture* and *element* and is the smallest individual component in a digital image, whether it is a still image or a single video frame.

Frame rate: This property specifies the number of individual images that make up each second of video. Frame rate is measured as a value of fps, which is frames per second.

Pixel aspect ratio: This property specifies the shape of the pixels that make up an image. Pixels are the smallest part of a digital image, and different display devices such as televisions and computer monitors have pixels with different horizontal and vertical proportions.

When producing graphics for broadcast television, you have to conform to a specific set of formats and standards. You will need to know if your graphics are going to be displayed on high-definition or standard-definition screens. Similarly, you will want to know if you're in a region that broadcasts using the ATSC or PAL standards. If you are producing animation for the Web, you'll need to know what format the distributing site will be using.

ATSC

In the United States, the ATSC, or Advanced Television Systems Committee, has issued a set of standards for the transmission of digital television that replaced the older analog NTSC (National Television Standards Committee) formats. The standards embraced by the ATSC include both standard-definition and high-definition display resolutions, aspect ratios, and frame rates. All broadcast video and graphics must conform to one of the ATSC standards. Information on the various ATSC standards is available on their web site at ATSC.org.

High-definition television

While high-definition (HD) television technology has existed for decades, it wasn't until the beginning of the 21st century that it came to the attention of the average American television viewer. The term HD is used to describe video that has a higher resolution than traditional television systems, which are called SD, or standard definition. There are two main high-definition standards for broadcast television—720p and 1080i—while many televisions and Blu-ray disc players can support a third, 1080p.

720p: The 720p format has a resolution of 1280 pixels wide by 720 pixels high and supports a variety of frame rates, from the 24 fps used by film, through the 30 fps that was part of the old NTSC standard, all the way up to 60 fps.

1080p and 1080i: The 1080 formats come in both progressive and interlaced versions and, like other modern digital standards, they support a variety of frame rates between 24 fps and 30 fps.

You will learn more about the differences between progressive display and interlacing later in this lesson.

Standard-definition television

Prior to the invention of high definition, there was only one standard in the United States, NTSC (National Television Systems Committee), which includes settings for both 4:3 and 16:9 aspect ratios. While technically it has been replaced by the ATSC standards, the term NTSC is still used by most video cameras and editing and graphics applications when referring to standard-definition, broadcast-quality video.

NTSC and NTSC widescreen: Applications such as Adobe After Effects include pre-built settings for video projects called presets. The NTSC presets include settings for both a standard (4:3) and widescreen (16:9) aspect ratio. They use the same dimensions, 720 × 480, but different pixel aspect ratios, and this is what accounts for the difference in shape. Devices that comply with the NTSC standard use a frame rate of 29.97 frames per second.

PAL

PAL, or Phase Alternating Line, is the standard for broadcast television used throughout Europe and much of the rest of the world outside North America. PAL differs from NTSC in several key ways, including dimensions and frame rate. It uses a frame rate of 25 fps, which is closer to the 24 fps used in film and, like NTSC, it has both a standard and widescreen setting.

PAL and PAL widescreen: In applications such as After Effects, the PAL presets include both a standard (4:3) and a widescreen (16:9) aspect ratio. Much like their NTSC equivalents, they use the same pixel dimensions, in this case, 720×576, but each have different pixel aspect ratios.

Web and mobile device video: There is no single standard for video on the Web or on mobile devices, though there are only a handful of competing audio/video formats. QuickTime, Windows Media Video, Flash Video, Silverlight, and H.264 are the main video formats. The QuickTime format is controlled by Apple Inc., and for years was the de facto standard for web-delivered video. The freely available QuickTime Player is compatible with both Mac OS and Windows and is required to view QuickTime movie files. QuickTime format video is also supported on some mobile devices; most notably the Apple suite of phones, iPods and iPads.

Windows Media Video, often simply called WMV, is the Microsoft standard made by the creators of the Windows operating system. A variation of WMV is used for Silverlight video, which is widely used by many professional media organizations, including NBC Sports for their live Olympics coverage and Netflix for streaming videos. Windows Media is also a supported format on some multimedia players and mobile devices, such as Windows phones.

Flash video is the native video format of the Adobe Flash platform, and is used for distribution of video online. While the Flash player is widely installed on the desktop computers of Internet users, it is not as common on mobile devices. Many organizations and publishers are moving their video content away from Flash to other formats, such as H.264 and Silverlight. The dominance of Flash Video is being especially challenged by H.264. H.264 is a standard for video compression that is derived from the MPEG-4 standard. It really is a family of standards, and is intended to fit a wide range of different applications for displaying digital video content. Mobile devices such as the Apple iPod, Sony PSP and Microsoft Zune all support variations of H.264, as do many mobile phones and third-party video playback applications, such as the QuickTime Player, Flash Player and the VLC Media Player. H.264 is also the native video compression supported by the new iteration of the web page authoring language HTML 5.

Understanding frame rate and resolution

Video is essentially a series of individual still images that are displayed very quickly, one after the other. The frame rate of video is measured by the number of frames it contains in each second, denoted as fps or frames per second. Different video standards have different frame rates. Some video standards support a variety of frame rates. American television is broadcast at just below 30 fps, PAL uses 25 fps, and film uses a frame rate of 24 fps.

If you have a background in graphic design, you may be familiar with the term *resolution*, which refers to the pixel density or the number of pixels in a given space. As such, in North America, resolution is denoted in pixels per inch or ppi. For example, images created for printing in high-quality magazines are usually 300 ppi, while images created for use on a web site usually have a resolution of 72 ppi. When working with video, ppi is not used to address resolution. When discussing video, the term *resolution* is used to refer to the pixel dimensions of an image: the number of horizontal and vertical pixels that make up the actual image.

If you need to create graphics in Photoshop, the default resolution for video graphics is 72 ppi. The same is true for web graphics.

Understanding transparency

In video applications, transparency is referred to as alpha.

Graphics that are used in video are created using the RGB color mode. Each individual pixel is assigned a unique color value consisting of combinations of red, green, and blue. Each of these colors is saved to its own color channel. When the colors are combined together, the full color image is revealed. Some files are created using the RGBA mode, where the A represents an Alpha channel for the transparency of the image. If you also work in Photoshop, you may already be familiar with alpha channels, although the meaning of an alpha channel in video is somewhat different. In Photoshop, any saved selection is called an alpha channel, and you can have up to 99 alpha channels. In After Effects, the term alpha channel refers specifically to the transparency of an image or video file. Alpha channels use the 256 shades of gray to represent transparency. When looking at an alpha channel, black pixels represent those that are fully transparent, white pixels are fully opaque, and gray pixels represent semi-transparent areas. Only some image and video formats support saving alpha channels along with the other image information. Commonly used file formats that can include alpha channels are: Tagged Image File Format (.tiff), TARGA (Truevision Advanced Raster Graphics Adapter, .tga), QuickTime (.mov), and Flash Video (.flv and .f4v). Alpha channels are automatically created for the transparent areas of native Photoshop and Illustrator files when they are imported into After Effects.

You can create an alpha channel in Photoshop by creating a selection, saving it as an alpha channel in the Channels panel, and then saving the file in one of the image formats that support RGB and Alpha, such as PSD, TIFF, or PNG .

Self study

In this lesson, you learned about some of the technical details that affect decisions you make when creating your After Effects projects. As new video, image, and audio formats are developed and support for them is added to After Effects, you will also want tounderstand these emerging standards. Good sources to keep your knowledge levels up to date include the Adobe web site (*adobe.com*) and forums (*adobe.com/support/forums*). There are also a wide variety of print and online journals that serve all facets of the video and design market.

Review

Questions

1   What are the names of the two different standards that govern video for American and European broadcast television?

2   What are the frame rates for American television, European television, and film?

3   What are some of the areas where After Effects is used professionally?

Answers

1   ATSC (Advanced Television Systems Committee) is the name of the set of standards that govern American television and PAL (Phase Alternating Line) is the standard used in Europe.

2   American television uses a frame rate of 30 fps, European television uses a frame rate of 25 fps, and film uses a frame rate of 24 fps.

3   Television production, film, on-line video, mobile video, and presentation graphics are all areas where After Effects is used.

Lesson 2

What you'll learn in this lesson:

- Working with the key panels that are integral to using After Effects
- Previewing footage files and composition layers
- Customizing and saving panel layouts called workspaces

Understanding the After Effects Interface

The After Effects interface can seem daunting to the beginning user. In this lesson, you will gain an understanding of the key elements of the interface and how to work with the various application panels.

Starting up

You will work with several files from the ae02lessons folder in this lesson. Make sure that you have loaded the aelessons folder onto your hard drive from the supplied DVD. See "Loading lesson files" on page 4.

See Lesson 2 in action!

Use the accompanying video to gain a better understanding of how to use some of the features shown in this lesson. The video tutorial for this lesson can be found on the included DVD.

SPRING CREEK CAMPUS

Understanding and working with menus

After Effects has nine menus on Windows and 10 on Mac OS, located at the top of the application window that combine with various panels to form the interface of the program. Some of the menu names may be familiar to you from other applications, while others may be new and unfamiliar. You'll start with the File menu to open an existing After Effects project.

Opening an existing After Effects project

Opening a project in After Effects is much like opening a file in any other software program. In this exercise, you will work with an existing After Effects project to help you understand the organization and structure of the interface, and you will soon create your own projects.

1   Choose File > Open Project. Navigate to the ae02lessons folder that you copied to your hard drive and open the file named lesson02_StartingProject.aep.

    This project is composed of several different compositions that you will use to explore different aspects of the program interface.

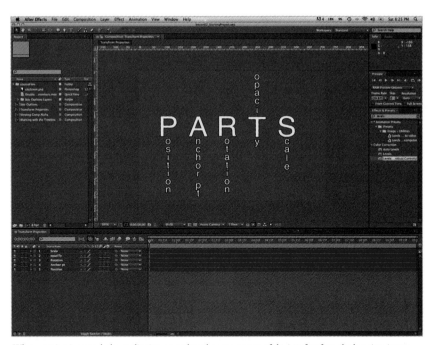

When a project is opened, the application remembers the arrangement of the interface from the last time it was used and saved.

2   Choose File > Save As and, if necessary, navigate to the ae02lessons folder on your hard drive. Rename this file **lesson02_StartingProject-working.aep** and press Save.

    Do not close this file, you will need it when working through the exercises.

After Effects menus

The Mac OS includes an Application-specific menu, for commands for hiding and quitting the Application. For Mac OS users, this is also used to access the After Effects Preferences dialog box. The remaining menus are consistent for MacOS and Windows users:

File

As in most other applications, you use the File menu for accessing key features of the program that deal mostly with creating new files, opening existing files, and importing or exporting files. In addition to these common commands, you will also find features for browsing files in Bridge, creating incremental saves and collecting files for output.

Edit

As in other programs, use the Edit menu to Copy, Cut, Paste, Delete, and perform other editing tasks with the content of your compositions. When working in Windows, this is where you can find the Preferences dialog box.

Composition

The Composition menu holds most of the commands you need to create, edit, and manipulate compositions. Each composition has its own independent timeline and is the space where all animation occurs. From this menu, you can create new compositions, adjust or preview comp settings.

Layer

After Effects places each separate media element on its own track, which is called a layer. You use the Layer menu to create new layers and edit the properties of existing layers.

Effect

After Effects is basically a motion graphics and compositing program. You use the Effect menu to apply layer effects in the application. These effects can be anything from simple color corrections and drop shadows to more advanced operations, such as chroma keying, particle generation or explosive simulations.

Animation

The Animation menu contains commands to accomplish both common animation tasks, such as adding property keyframes to create animation, and advanced tasks such as adding Easing to keyframes or Expressions to properties to automate animation tasks.

View

You use the View menu to control the Composition panel. From the View menu, you can zoom in and out, open new preview windows, and set the display properties for your composition.

Window

You use the Window menu to access the commands that control the After Effects interface. From this menu, you can choose your workspace and open or close the various panels found in the application interface.

Help

The Help menu gives you access to the help functions of After Effects. In addition to the standard After Effects Help command, you can also access specific references for the keyboard shortcuts and animation presets, as well as have After Effects check for program updates.

After Effects software versions

After Effects project files are not backwards compatible, and files created in a newer version of the application cannot be opened using an older version of the software. When you open an older After Effects project file in a newer version, you receive a warning message and you have to use the Save As command to save the file in the newer format. Once a file is converted to the latest file format, you are not able to return to using an older version of the software for additional edits. For this reason, if several people are working on an After Effects project, they all need the same version of the software.

Understanding the After Effects panel system

After Effects uses a docked, panel-based interface by default. The entire interface configuration is called a workspace, and After Effects includes a variety of pre-built workspaces to accommodate different working styles and tasks that you may need to accomplish. You can also set each panel to move or float, independently.

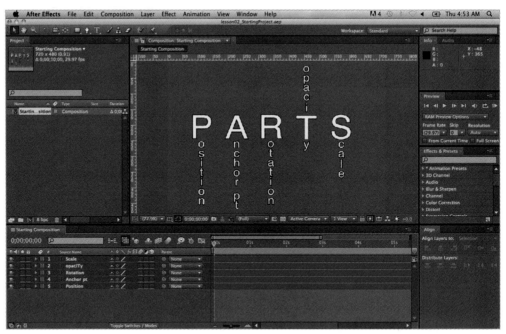

The After Effects workspace.

After Effects panels

The After Effects interface is divided into panels, where you will do most of your work. Some panels are for previewing footage or animation, and others set options for the tools, while others are for creating animation. All the panels in After Effects are accessible through the Window menu. To help you better understand the panels, we've divided them into two groups: Primary panels, which you will use more frequently, and Secondary panels, which you will use less often.

Primary panels

Composition

The Composition panel is one of the most important panels in After Effects. It is the preview window and the main animation space that you work in when building an After Effects project. You can build your animated projects in this panel, and it has features you can use to change how your composition previews. Perhaps you want to create, show, or hide guidelines. Or maybe you need to isolate the alpha channel of your composition so that you can see which areas are transparent and which are opaque. This can all be accomplished in the Composition panel. In this exercise, you will work with the Composition panel to change the preview resolution of the display and learn how to reveal a composition's alpha channel.

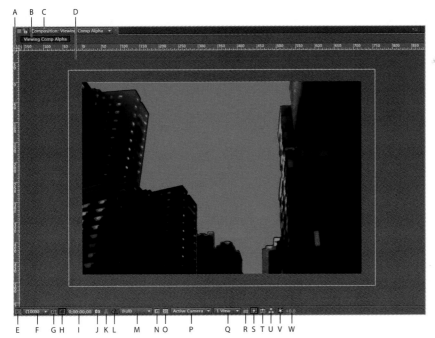

A. Rulers Composition. B. Flowchart Selector. C. Selector. D. Composition. E. Always Preview Toggle. F. Magnification. G. Guide & Grid Options. H. Toggle Mask & Shape Path Visibility. I. Current Time. J. Take Snapshot. K. Show Snapshot. L. Show Channel and Color Management Settings. M. Resolution. N. Region of Interest. O. Toggle Transparency Grid. P. 3D View Popup. Q. Select View Layout. R. Toggle Pixel Aspect Ratio Correction. S. Fast Previews. T. Timeline. U. Composition Flowchart. V. Reset Exposure. W. Adjust Exposure.

1   With the lesson02_StartingProject-working still open, look in the Project panel and double-click on the composition named Viewing Comp Alpha to make it active. This makes the composition visible in the Composition panel and also reveals the comp timeline in the Timeline Panel.

Double-clicking on any composition in the Project panel makes that composition active in both the Composition and Timeline panels.

This composition includes a single layer named cityScene.psd. It was created from a Photoshop document that contains transparent areas. The color blue that you can see behind the buildings is the background color of the composition itself. It is visible only in the area where the Photoshop document is transparent. In video programs, transparency is often referred to as Alpha, or the Alpha Channel. You can change the display of the Composition panel to confirm which areas are in transparent.

2 With the Viewing Comp Alpha composition active, click on the Show Channel and Color Management Settings button (![button]) located at the bottom of the Composition panel. From the list that appears, choose Alpha.

All the RGB color information has been hidden because you are showing only the Alpha channel of the composition. This leaves only a black and white representation of the comp. When viewing alpha information, the black area represents fully transparent sections while the white areas are fully opaque and gray areas are semi-transparent.

Viewing a composition's alpha information like this is a good way of confirming which parts of a layer are fully transparent and which are not.

3 Now that you have seen that the background of the image is fully transparent, return to the standard display by clicking on the Show Channel and Color Management Settings button and choosing RGB from the list.

4   Click on the Resolution/Down Sample Factor Popup button at the bottom of the Composition panel and choose Quarter from the list that appears.

You can use the Composition panel to vary the quality of the preview by changing its resolution setting. Down sampling can be necessary to create longer and faster previews when you are working with complex compositions that might otherwise take a long time to preview.

Notice that this preview appears much more pixelated, or blocky, than the original, which was displaying at full resolution. At the quarter resolution setting, the program only previews every fourth pixel. This allows it to build the preview much faster and can be helpful for reviewing complex animations. This lowered resolution is for preview purposes only; it does not affect the final output quality when you output your file.

At the Quarter setting, the original composition's resolution is reduced by three quarters, but is still displayed at its original size, which results in the image degradation you see here.

5   Click the Resolution/Down Sample Factor Popup button at the bottom of the Composition panel and this time choose Half.

The image appears to be a higher quality than when it was generated at quarter resolution in the previous step. This is because every other pixel is being previewed, resulting in double the quality of the previous setting, which was previewing every fourth pixel.

6 Click on the Resolution/Down Sample Factor Popup button one last time and choose Auto from the list that appears.

Notice that the menu now displays the setting of Full, but that it is surrounded by parentheses. The parentheses indicate that the display is currently using the Auto setting. The Auto setting adjusts the resolution of the Composition panel to render only the pixels necessary to preview the composition at the current zoom level.

The Auto setting gives the best image quality, and at the same time avoids rendering unnecessary pixels by actively adjusting the Composition panel's preview based on the Zoom percentage you are currently using. For example, if you are viewing a comp at 25%, the Auto settings will set the Resolution/Down Sample factor to Quarter to preserve processing power and provide a faster preview.

7 Choose File > Save, or use the keyboard shortcut of either Ctrl+S (Windows) or Command+S (Mac OS) on the keyboard. Do not close this file, you will need it later in the lesson.

You should quickly look at two other panels before getting into another exercise in the lesson.

Effect Controls

Use the Effect Controls panel to edit effects you have applied to layers in your Composition or Timeline panels. While this panel is not a part of the Standard workspace, however you can access it using the Window > Effect Controls. To access effects you have applied to a layer, you must select the layer in either the Timeline or Composition panels, or by using a keyboard shortcut. If you do not have a layer selected, or if the selected layer doesn't have any effects applied to it, this panel remains blank. While it is not a part of the Standard workspace, the panel will be added the first time you apply an Effect to any layer. You will use the Effect Controls panel many times throughout this book, but especially in Lessons 5, 7, and 9.

Flowchart

The Flowchart panel provides an organizational chart, or a graphical representation of the relationship between compositions and footage items in your After Effects project. The Flowchart panel is a passive tool that displays the relationship between elements in your project; you cannot use it to change that relationship. This panel comes in handy when working with very complex animations that may contain multiple nested compositions. You will not use the full flowchart panel in this book, but will instead work with a companion feature, the Mini-Flowchart view, in Lesson 7, "Working with Audio," when you begin working with audio files.

Footage

Use the Footage panel to preview individual pieces of footage. Double-clicking on any piece of imported media in your Project panel causes it to preview in the Footage panel. You can also use the drop-down menu at the top of the panel to choose footage to preview.

In this exercise, you will open a footage panel in order to use it to preview an imported video file.

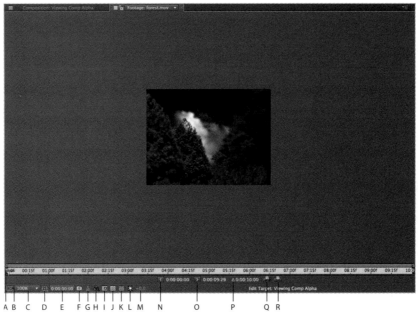

A. Time Ruler. B. Always Preview Toggle. C. Magnification. D. Guide & Grid Options. E. Current Time. F. Take Snapshot. G. Show Snapshot. H. Show Channel and Color Management Settings. I. Area of Interest. J. Toggle Transparency Grid. K. Toggle Pixel Aspect Ratio Correction. L. Reset Exposure. M. Adjust Exposure. N. Set IN Point to Current Time. O. Set OUT Point to Current Time. P. Duration. Q. Ripple Insert Edit. R. Overlay Edit.

1   With the lesson02_StartingProject-working project still open, locate the Forest.mov file in the Project panel. It is in the folder named sourceFiles.

2   Double-click the Forest.mov file in the Project panel. This opens the Footage panel allowing you to preview the video clip.

3   Press the spacebar on your keyboard to preview the animation in this video file.

Once it has played through one time, you can press the spacebar again to stop the playback. Notice that the Footage panel has many of the same buttons and menus that are present in the Composition panel.

You can also click on the Time Ruler to stop the playback as well. Once stopped, you can move the Time Marker, the yellow wedge on the Time Ruler, backwards and forwards to preview the animation.

4   In the Project panel, double-click on the footage item named cityScene.psd to open it in the footage panel.

An alternative method for viewing footage is to select the footage item from the pull down-menu at the top of the Footage panel.

From the Magnification ratio drop-down menu, choose Fit up to 100% to fit the footage item in the panel.

Fit up to 100% can be used with the Composition, Footage, and Layer panels to auto-adjust their magnification setting.

5   Click the Show Channel and Color Management Settings button located at the bottom of the Composition panel. From the list that appears, choose Alpha. You can view the individual channels for footage items in the panel the same way you did when previewing the composition.

6   Return to the standard display by clicking the Show Channel and Color Management Settings button and choosing RGB from the list.

Click the Composition panel's tab and choose the Transform Properties comp for the list that appears. Alternately, you can double-click on the Transform Properties composition in the Project panel.

7   Choose File > Save, or press Ctrl+S (Windows) or Command+S (Mac OS) on the keyboard. Do not close this file, you will need it later in the lesson.

Layer

Double-clicking a footage layer in the Composition panel opens it in the Layer panel. A footage layer contains a file that has been imported into the Project panel, as opposed to an item that is created in After Effects, such as text or a composition. Some effects, such as paint, motion tracking, and stabilization, cannot be applied in the Composition window but must instead be applied in the Layer panel. Here, you will explore the Layer panel.

Next, you will learn how to jump back and forth between your composition and layer panels.

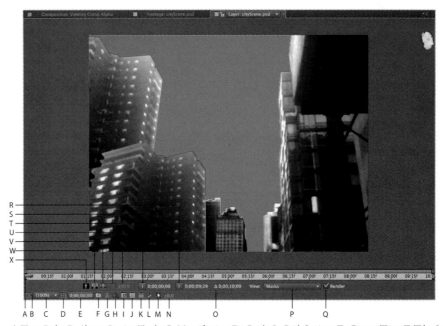

A. Time Ruler. *B*. Always Preview Toggle. *C*. Magnification. *D*. Guide & Grid Options. *E*. Current Time. *F*. Take Snapshot.
G. Show Snapshot. *H*. Show Channel and Color Management Settings. *I*. Area of Interest. *J*. Toggle Transparency Grid.
K. Toggle Pixel Aspect Ratio Correction. *L*. Comp Button. *M*. Reset Exposure. *N*. Adjust Exposure. *O*. Duration.
P. Effect/Layer Controls Editing drop-down menu. *Q*. Show rendered result for current view. *R*. Set OUT Point to Current Time.
S. Set IN Point to Current Time. *T*. Alpha Boundary/Overlay Opacity. *U*. Alpha Boundary/Overlay Color.
V. Toggle Alpha Overlay. *W*. Toggle Alpha Boundary. *X*. Toggle Alpha.

1 With the lesson02_StartingProject-working project still open, double-click the Viewing Comp Alpha composition in the Project panel.

2 In the Timeline panel, double-click the cityScene.psd layer to reveal it in the Layer panel.

   Like the Footage panel, the Layer panel is not a part of the Standard workspace, but is added to the interface when you double-click on a footage layer. This panel can also be opened by choosing Window > Layer.

   Notice that just like in the Footage panel, many of the buttons and menus here are similar to those of the Composition panel. From the Layer panel, you can preview the alpha or other color channels of a layer, or adjust a layer's duration.

When you double-click on a text layer, it allows you to edit the text, and when you double-click on a composition layer, it reveals the composition's timeline in the Timeline panel.

3 Click the Comp Button ( ) at the bottom of the Layer panel to return to the composition that is associated with this layer. This reveals the Composition panel by moving it in front of the Footage and Layer panels in the interface.

4 Choose File > Save or press Ctrl+S (Windows) or Command+S (Mac OS) on the keyboard to save the project. Do not close this file, you will need it later in the lesson.

Project

The Project panel contains references to all the footage files (video, audio, and images) and compositions that you have imported or created inside the After Effects project. These items are referred to as references because of the way the program treats imported files. These files remain in their original location on your hard drive, and After Effects simply creates a link to them. If the files are modified, After Effects simply generates a new preview and updates your project accordingly. This linking system is helpful because you can still manipulate imported objects in their original programs, such as editing an image in Photoshop. But it can also cause problems if you move, rename or delete your original media files. Keep this in mind as you work in After Effects, as your project files need to be able to locate the objects you import.

A. Thumbnail preview. *B*. Search text field. *C*. Columns. *D*. Interpret Footage. *E*. Create a new folder.
F. Create a new Composition. *G*. Color depth. *H*. Delete selected project items.

1   With the lesson02_StartingProject project still open, choose Window > Workspace > Reset "Standard."

Choose Yes in the confirmation dialog box that appears to confirm that you want to reset the Standard workspace to its original configuration.

2   Click on any part of the Project panel to select it and make it the active panel. You can tell that a panel is active when it has an orange outline around it.

Press the tilde (~) key on your keyboard. The tilde key acts as a full screen toggle, enlarging the active panel to full screen size or returning it to normal size if it has already been enlarged.

3   Notice that once expanded to full-screen mode, the Project panel reveals several previously hidden columns. Currently, the items in the panel are listed in alphabetical order, but this can be adjusted so that they are listed in a hierarchy determined by any of the columns.

Click on the title bar for the Type column and notice that the panel's content reorders so that similar file types are placed near each other.

By default, the content of the Project panel is organized into an alphabetical list, but you can change this to suit your preferences.

4   Again press the tilde (~) key on your keyboard to return the Project panel to its normal size in the workspace.

Changing the display size of the panel doesn't affect the project, so there is no need to save the file again, but keep the file open because you will need it again later in this lesson.

Render Queue

Once you have completed your animation, you use the Render Queue panel to produce, or render, your project for final output. Use this panel to add multiple compositions, set the render options and destinations for each, and then render the compositions sequentially.

Timeline

The Timeline panel is one of the main panels used for creating animations. Each composition has its own independent Timeline panel, where you can animate layer and effects properties, position layers in time, and change the layer blending modes.

When working with two-dimensional layers, the stacking order of the layers controls which layers appear farthest back, or behind, the other layers.

The Current Time Indicator, also called the playhead, is the red vertical line that runs perpendicular to the Time Ruler. It indicates the current frame that is being displayed, moving as the animation or composition is played.

The default display of the Timeline panel is the layer bar mode. It displays the composition time as a Time Ruler across the top of the panel, while layer names and properties are displayed to the left. The layer bar mode can also be switched so that the panel displays the Graph Editor, an advanced tool for animation that allows for more precise control of animated properties. Here, you will work with the Timeline.

You will reveal a composition in the Timeline and Composition panels, and change the stacking order of its layers to change the entire appearance of the composition.

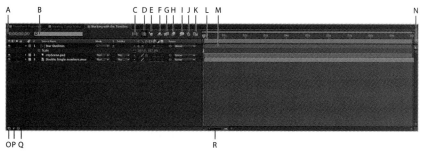

*A. Current Time. **B**. Search Field. **C**. Composition Mini Flowchart. **D**. Live Update. **E**. Enable Draft 3D.*
*F: Hide "Shy" Layers. **G**. Enable Frame Blending. **H**. Enable Motion Blur. **I**. Brainstorm. **J**. Auto-keyframe. **K**. Graph Editor.*
*L. Current Time Indicator (playhead). **M**. Work Area Bar. **N**. Add Composition Marker. **O**. Expand/Collapse Layer Switches Panes.*
*P. Expand/Collapse Transfer Controls Panes. **Q**. Expand/Collapse In/Out/Duration/Stretch Panes.*
R. Zoom In/Zoom Out Timeline.

1 With the lesson02_StartingProject project still open, double click the Working with the Timeline composition in the Project panel to make it active.

In the Timeline panel that is revealed, notice that this composition includes three different layers.

The first layer is named Star Outlines and has the same composition icon (🖼) that you see next to some of the items in the Project panel. This is a nested composition, or a comp that is placed inside of another comp. You will learn more about nested compositions as you progress further through this book. The second layer is named cityScene.psd and is composed of a single Photoshop document, while the third and final layer is named Double Single numbers.mov and contains a single imported video file.

The current layer stacking order makes it difficult to see the city and background video files because the white lines on top are so overpowering. You can fix this by adjusting the order.

2   Click and hold on the Star Outlines layer and drag-and-drop it below the Double Single number.mov layer.

Just like in graphics programs like Photoshop and Illustrator, layers can be dragged above or below each other in the display to change their stacking order.

Look in the Composition panel and notice that the cityScene.psd layer is now located above the white lines, leaving them visible only in the areas where the cityScene layer is transparent.

As you can see, the stacking order of layers in the Timeline panel is directly related to the way they display in the Composition panel.

3   Choose File > Save or press Ctrl+S (Windows) or Command+S (Mac OS).

4   Close the project by choosing File > Close Project.

Understanding the workspace

The organization and positioning of all the panels on screen is called the workspace. After Effects comes equipped with a series of preset workspaces that you can use. After Effects displays certain panels depending upon the workspace selected, and they are named based upon common tasks you might need to perform. Some of the workspaces are: All Panels, Animation, Minimal, Motion Tracking, Paint, Standard, Text, and Undocked Panels. When you run After Effects for the first time, the application displays the Standard workspace.

Viewing and hiding panels

To modify your workspace, you can open, hide, move, resize, float, or dock panels. This functionality makes the After Effects interface customizable to meet your preferences and working style. After deciding which panels you want to display, close any panels you will not need and open the ones you plan to use. Next, you will work with various panels to customize and then save the workspace.

1   Choose Window > Workspace > Animation to change the current workspace. The Animation workspace has several common tools that you can use when animating your work, and you can customize it to meet your needs.

2   If it is not already active, click the Info panel's tab to activate it and bring it to the front of its panel group. Click the x at the top of the Info panel to hide it. This leaves the Audio panel active in this group. Click the x icon to also close the Audio panel.

3   Choose Window > Align to open the Align panel. It appears in the bottom-right corner of the interface, directly below the Effects & Presets panel.

4   Click the x icon in the tab of the Effects & Presets panel to close it. This causes the Align panel to move. In the next section, you will reconfigure the workspace so the Align panel is placed in a more convenient area for your work.

Docking and undocking panels

After Effects panels are docked to the sides of the application window and also to each other. You can change this by docking and undocking panels to suit your work habits.

1   Click the tab at the top of the Align panel. Press and hold the Ctrl (Windows) or Command (Mac OS) key on your keyboard while dragging the Align panel to the center of the screen. This removes the panel from the docked interface, making it an undocked, or floating, panel.

If you are using a multiple monitors, you will need to use the Undocked Panels workspace to freely position the panels across your screens. When working with a single display, undocked panels often create more problems than they solve by obscuring the rest of the interface and hiding important areas of your compositions from view.

2   Click the Align panel's name tab drag the panel toward the Smoother panel at the top-right corner of your interface. Because you are no longer holding down the Ctrl (Windows) or Command (Mac OS) key, you will notice that a gray and purple overlay now appears as you move the panel around the screen. This is called a drop zone, and it highlights indicating areas where you can drag and drop your panel to dock it.

3 Position the Align panel towards the top of the Smoother panel. The top section of the drop zone becomes highlighted. The highlight appears when your mouse is hovering right below the Smoother panel's name tab. Release the mouse while this section is highlighted to position the panel between the Preview and Smoother panels as a separate, individual panel.

Dock the Align panel so that it rests above the Smoother panel.

Using drop zones

Drop zones are a unique feature of the After Effects panel interface. They make it easier to use the docked panels by providing you with visual cues as you drag panels to rearrange them.

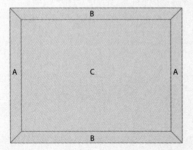

As you drag a panel around the interface, a drop-zone overlay appears above the current panel group that your cursor is hovering over. Different sections of the drop zone become highlighted to show you what your new panel configuration will be. If either section on the sides (labeled "A" in the figure) illuminates, the panel that you are repositioning will be placed to the side of the currently highlighted panel, creating a new, independent panel group vertically. The same is true for the top and bottom of the drop zone (labeled "B" in the figure), except this creates a new panel group horizontally. The third possibility is to release your mouse while hovering over the center of the drop zone (labeled "C" in the figure); this groups the panel that you are moving with the existing panel group, creating a new tab.

Resizing panels

In addition to hiding, opening, docking, and undocking panels, the After Effects interface lets you resize docked panels so they take up more or less space on the display.

1 Place the cursor on the dark-gray, vertical dividing line between the Composition and Project panels. The cursor changes to a double arrow (↔) when it is hovering over the dividing line.

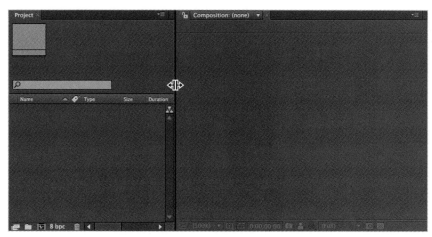

A double-arrow resize cursor appears between the panels enabling you to resize them.

2 Click and drag the dividing line towards the Project panel to increase the size of the Composition panel.

3 Position the cursor on the dark-gray, horizontal dividing line between the Composition and Timeline panels. Drag the dividing line down to shrink the Timeline panel and make the Composition panel larger.

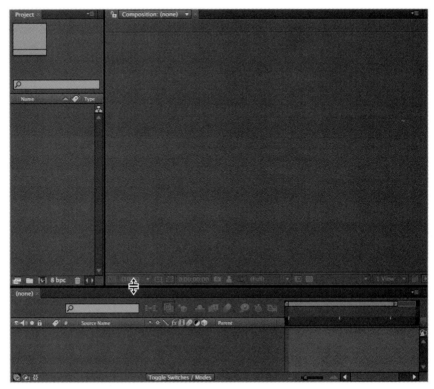

Resize the panels to make the Composition panel larger.

Saving a custom workspace

You can save modifications you make to a workspace and save them as a new, customized workspace. Custom workspaces allow you to show only the panels you require. Here you will save a custom workspace.

1 Choose Window > Workspace > New Workspace to open the New Workspace dialog box.

2 Name your workspace **Animation-Modified** and click OK to save it.

3 Choose Window > Workspace. You now see the name Animation-Modified among the list of available workspaces.

4 Click in any section of the After Effects interface to close the Window menu without changing the workspace.

Resetting the workspace

You can return to the original workspace and reset it to its default configuration.

1 Choose Window > Workspace > Animation to return to the Animation workspace.

2 Choose Window > Workspace > Reset "Animation" to open the Reset dialog box.

3 Confirm the reset by clicking Yes; the Animation workspace resets to its original appearance.

Confirm resetting a workspace.

Setting After Effects Preferences

Preferences control many aspects of After Effects, including things you can see, and the way it works with files and memory behind-the-scenes. Access Preferences by choosing After Effects > Preferences (Mac OS) or Edit > Preferences (Windows).

After Effects Preferences

The Preferences dialog box is divided into several categories. Understanding each section of this dialog will help you quickly modify the application to fit your specific needs.

General: Contains the commands that don't easily fit into any other group. In this section, you can control undo states, whether to show tool tips, and whether to use the operating system shortcut keys.

Previews: Specifies the settings for all preview operations. In this section, you can set Audio Preview duration, Adaptive Resolution quality, and whether to use hardware acceleration to aid in previews.

Display: Mostly used to set options for how motion paths are displayed, but you can also specify whether to use Project panel thumbnails and Info panel rendering displays.

Import: Contains options for setting the default image duration of imported still images and embedded alpha channels, and how to handle drag-and-drop import.

Output: Specifies options for segmenting files on output and whether or not to use a default filename and folder.

Grids & Guides: Specifies the color and style of grid and guide lines, as well as the screen size the action and title-safe grids should encompass.

Labels: Sets the default color and name for labels used in the Project and Timeline panels.

Media & Disk Cache: Enables and sets the location of disk and media cache folders. The cache is a storage area for conformed media files and other temporary files that are needed to optimize the After Effects workflow.

Video Preview: Specifies the external FireWire device, such as a camera or deck, to output video to during preview operations. Professionals generally use an external monitor to check color, motion, and safe margins during graphics or video work.

Appearance: Specifies the options for controlling the appearance of the interface and color highlighting of labels and masks.

Auto-Save: Allows After Effects to save a copy of your project file at set intervals. You can specify the interval for the Save command as well as the number of versions of your project file the application will create before it begins to overwrite them.

Memory and Multiprocessing: Sets a value for the amount of RAM to use for other applications. In general, the greater the amount of RAM that After Effects and the other applications of the Creative Suite can utilize, the better the applications perform.

Audio Hardware: When using a system with multiple audio input or output devices, you can specify which device is used by After Effects when playing back or capturing sounds.

Audio Output Mapping: Specifies how sound is played back or mapped to the system's selected audio devices.

Changing the default Undo levels

You can use the Undo command to take back, or undo, a mistake. In After Effects, you can step back through several errors one step at a time. By default, After Effects lets you undo the past 32 steps you performed, but you can modify this limit using your preferences.

1   Choose Edit > Preferences > General (Windows) or After Effects > Preferences > General (Mac OS) to open the Preferences dialog box.

2   Change the Levels of Undo from the default 32 to **50**.

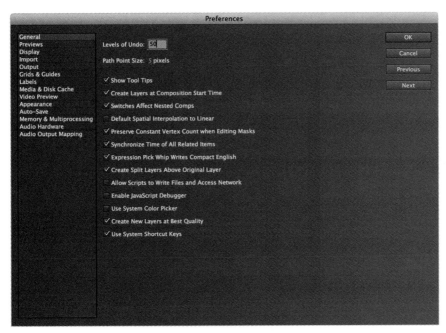

Change the Levels of Undo in the Preferences dialog box.

The Levels of Undo that your computer can support are based on the amount of RAM available on your system. The greater the value that you set, the higher the RAM requirements. If you are working on a computer with a limited amount of RAM memory, you should keep this at the default setting, or possibly lower it.

Enable Auto-Save

Unfortunately, computer programs can crash and you can lose your work. You should get in the habit of saving your projects frequently to avoid losing your work if your software crashes or power to your computer is interrupted. After Effects has an Auto-Save feature, which automatically saves a copy of your project file as you work. You can set how often the Auto-Save runs and how many copies of your file it saves.

1 If it is not already open, choose Edit > Preferences > General (Windows) or After Effects > Preferences > General (Mac OS) to open the Preferences dialog box.

2 Click the Auto-Save category on the left.

3 Click on the checkbox labeled Automatically Save Projects to enable the program to automatically create backups of your project file at its default settings.

The default value for Auto-Save is every 20 minutes and a maximum of 5 project versions. You can adjust these amounts to fit your personal needs. Because this feature is not saving over your original file, but instead making a copy, you can set the amount for Save Every to the minimum value you can tolerate. Keep in mind that when the Auto-Save function runs, it can disrupt your work.

Self study

Now that you have created a new workspace that emphasizes tools for animation, you can build one that focuses on the Timeline. Create an interface with only the Composition and Timeline panels and save it as a new custom workspace. Now that you are comfortable with opening and hiding panels, you can create new workspaces to accommodate your specific workflow.

Review

Questions

1 How do you reset the current workspace?

2 What is the advantage of saving a custom workspace?

3 How do you access the Preferences dialog box to make changes to the number of Undo levels in After Effects?

Answers

1 Choose Window > Workspace > Reset "Current Workspace Name."

2 Custom workspaces allow you to show only the panels you require for the specific task you are currently working on in After Effects.

3 You can access the Preferences dialog box by choosing Edit > Preferences > General (Windows) or After Effects > Preferences > General (Mac OS).

What you'll learn in this lesson:

- Creating and organizing projects
- Importing individual and multiple still images and video files
- Previewing files
- Locating missing assets

Media Management— Images, Video, and Audio

To be a successful After Effects artist, you need to understand the different types of media you will work with, and know how to keep them organized. You also need to know how to work with and manipulate a variety of media types . After Effect provides you with tools to import, organize, edit and preview almost any type of digital media.

Starting up

You will work with several files from the ae03lessons folder in this lesson. Make sure that you have loaded the aelessons folder onto your hard drive from the supplied DVD. See "Loading lesson files" on page 4.

See Lesson 3 in action!

Use the accompanying video to gain a better understanding of how to use some of the features shown in this lesson. The video tutorial for this lesson can be found on the included DVD.

What is Media Management?

A very important aspect of the design process that is also often overlooked is the concept of Media Management. Simply put, Media Management is how you organize or manage the media that you are working with in a project. There are two equally important aspects of Media Management. The first is how you manage the media that you are working with on your hard drive, and the second is how you organize the different media references that you import into After Effects.

You will look at how and where you need to store your original media files first. For the sake of portability, performance, and safety, it is usually best to store your media on an external hard drive. The two standard connection types for external hard drives are FireWire (400 and 800) and USB 2.0. Most video editors (especially those who work on the Mac OS) will probably recommend a FireWire drive due to its higher sustained bus speed, but because After Effects doesn't reference media in the same way as video editing applications, either connection type should work for you. What is more important than the type of connection that your disk drive uses is that you always keep it organized. There has long been a truism in the design and animation industries that the most important things to remember about working with files are where they are and what they're called.

Projects, compositions, and layers: an overview

The project file is at the heart of all the work you do in Adobe After Effects. The project file contains links to all the media that you are using in your compositions as well as the compositions themselves. While a project can contain many different media elements and compositions, only one project can be open at a time in After Effects. You can think of the project file as a container, a briefcase for carrying around the content of your animations. Project files in After Effects are kept very small because media are not embedded or added to the project file. Instead, the project file contains links or references to any piece of media (audio, video, or stills) that you import. This creates a situation where the project is dependent on the media files remaining unchanged and in the same relative location on your hard drive. So if you have a situation that requires you to move your projects from one computer to another, you must move not only the project file but also the original media that are stored on your hard drive. Not every element you will use is external, though; compositions, shapes, lights, cameras, and other content that you create in After Effects are stored as part of the project file.

Compositions, often called *comps* for short, are a unique feature of After Effects, though they are similar to sequences, which can be found in video editing and animation programs such as Adobe Premiere or Apple Final Cut Pro. They are one of the key program features that you will become used to working with as you begin to master After Effects. Each composition—you can have multiple compositions in each project—represents an independent Timeline and can contain any combination of video, audio, still images, shape layers, and other elements. Compositions can even contain other compositions (this is called *nesting compositions*), and this feature is the key to creating more complex animations and composites. When creating compositions, you want to set their properties for the format that you plan to output to.

If you have a video editing background, this is probably going to be completely contrary to what you have been taught, but it is actually the standard way of working in After Effects. So if you are creating graphics for standard-definition broadcast television, you will want to create your comps to the NTSC standard, and if you are creating graphics for display on a computer screen, you will want to build comps that match your expected screen resolution.

If you have used other graphics applications such as Photoshop, Illustrator, or Flash, layers may be a familiar concept to you. If you are new to the concept of layers, then, like compositions, they are a feature of After Effects that you will become more familiar with as you work your way through the lessons in this book. You cannot edit media in a composition directly; instead, each piece of media that is placed into a composition exists on its own track, called a layer. Each layer has properties such as position, opacity, and duration that you can adjust individually or in tandem with other layers. In addition to a layer's built-in editable properties, you have the ability to add a wide variety of effects from the Effect menu to any layer, and it is by manipulating the properties of layers and their effects that you can create your animations.

Creating a new project

Technically, every time you open After Effects, the program creates a new blank project for you. A project isn't a very impressive thing on its own; it's really just a container that stores the references to the media files you are working with, along with the compositions you create and any original content, such as cameras, lights, and shapes. A single project may contains links to dozens, perhaps hundreds of different files that reside on your hard drive.

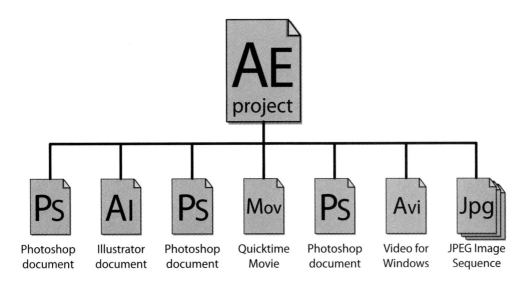

Example of an After Effects Project.

You will need to create a new project if you have closed either your active project or the default one.

Importing media files

One of the great strengths of After Effects is the wide variety of media that you are able to use with it. After Effects supports standard-format still images, audio, and video files. In this part of the lesson, you will create a new After Effects project and learn to import two very common media types: audio and video. In addition to common formats such as .tiff, .jpg, .aif, and .mp3, the program offers enhanced support for certain native file formats such as Photoshop (.psd) and Illustrator (.ai).

1   Create a new, empty After Effects project by choosing File > New > New Project, and reset your workspace to the standard layout by choosing Window > Workspace > Standard, then choosing Window > Workspace > Reset "Standard". Click Yes in the dialog box that prompts you to reset the workspace.

2   Choose File > Import > File to open the Import File dialog box.

There are many ways to open the Import File dialog box. You can use a keyboard shortcut, Ctrl+I (Windows) or Command+I (Mac OS); you can right-click in any empty area of the Project panel and select Import > File from the context menu that pops up; or you can double-click on any empty area of the Project panel to immediately open the dialog box.

3　In the Import dialog box, navigate to the ae03lessons project folder that you copied from the DVD included with this book. Continue to navigate to the video folder and click on the Double Single numbers.mov file. You can either double-click on the file or click the Open button to import it. Depending upon the speed of your computer, there may be a brief pause where a loading bar appears, then the reference to the video file appears in the Project panel.

The video file appears in the Project panel.

4　The Project panel is one of many panels that must share space on the screen, so after the video file has been imported into your project, it may be very difficult to see if the Project panel is small. To fix this problem, After Effects offers a toggle function that allows you to fit any panel to the full size of the screen. Click on the Project panel to make it active. The panel displays an orange highlight around it when it is active. Press the tilde (~) key on your keyboard to enlarge the panel to full-screen size.

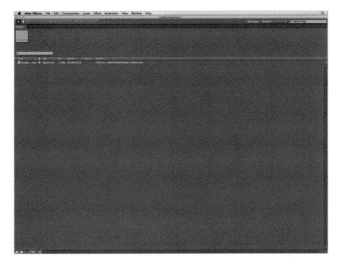

Press the tilde (~) key to enlarge any panel to full-screen.

Press the tilde (~) key again when you want to return to the standard workspace.

5 Choose File > Import > File. In the Import dialog box, navigate to the audio folder in ae03lessons and double-click on house beat.aif.

6 Open the Import dialog box again, navigate to the images folder in ae03lessons, and click on the file named distressedBG.tif. Hold down the Ctrl (Windows) key or Command (Mac OS) on your keyboard and click on Mini Cooper at Night.jpg and Washington City Street.jpg to select them as well, then click Open.

7 Choose File > Save As. Name your file **Lesson3-Working.aep** and save it in the ae03lessons folder on your hard drive.

The keyboard command for the Save As function is Ctrl+Shift+S (Windows) or Command+Shift+S (Mac OS).

Organizing the Project panel

Even with the Project panel at full-screen size, it may still need a few modifications. By default, the panel just displays all your imported files in alphabetical order, but this may not be the best approach to organizing your media.

Modifying the column displays

There are seven columns in the Project window: Name, Label, Type, Size, Duration, Comment, and File Path. The files are organized alphabetically by name as indicated by the arrow at the top of the panel. You can click on any other column header to reorganize the content in the panel. You can also hide or change the size of each column at any time.

1 Because you don't need the File Path column, you will hide it. With the Project panel highlighted, press the tilde (~) key on your keyboard to maximize the panel to full-screen size. Right-click on the File Path column and from the menu that appears, click on Columns > File Path. There is now an empty column to the right of the Comment column.

You can reveal the column in the same way by right-clicking on any label. You may have also noticed that there is another column on the list, Date, that is hidden by default.

2 You will now resize a column. Place your cursor at the dividing line between the Name and Label columns. Note that the label columns isn't identified by name but instead by a tag icon. It changes to a double-headed horizontal cursor. Click and drag the dividing line to the right to increase the size of the Name column.

3 Increase the width of the Type, Size, and Comment columns as well.

Increase the width of the columns.

Creating folders and subfolders

Folders are a very helpful tool for organizing the content of your Project panel, as well as for managing your media efficiently. Folders can be created in the root of the Project panel or nested inside of other folders.

1 Click the Create a new Folder button (⬛) at the bottom of the Project panel to create a new untitled folder.

Click the Create a new Folder button.

2 The folder name is highlighted, so rename it **Video**, then press Enter (Windows) or Return (Mac OS).

If you deselect the folder before naming it, you can always right-click on the highlighted folder and choose Rename from the context menu.

3 Click the Double Single numbers.mov file and drag it onto the Video folder. When the folder becomes highlighted, release your mouse button to add the video file to it. The folder should expand automatically, but if it doesn't, click on the arrow that now appears to the left of the Video folder name to reveal the folder's contents.

Click on the arrow to reveal the folder's contents.

4 Deselect the folder with which you have been working, then create two additional folders and name them **Audio** and **Images**. Make sure that the Audio folder is deselected before creating the Images folder.

5 Select all three image files—Washington City Street.jpg, Mini Cooper at Night.jpg, and distressedBG.tif—by first clicking on any one of them. Hold down the Ctrl (Windows) or Command (Mac OS) key on your keyboard and then click to add the other two files to your selection.

6 Click and hold any one of your highlighted files and drag it to the Images folder to move all the selected image files simultaneously. Click the triangle to the left of the Images folder to display its contents. Drag the house beat.aif file into the Audio folder and click the triangle to the right of the Audio folder to display its contents as well.

7 Right-click (Windows) or Ctrl+click (Mac OS) on an empty area of the Project panel and choose New Folder from the context menu that appears. Rename this folder **Background Images**. When you are finished renaming it, the folder jumps to the top of the panel, as it is still organized alphabetically by name.

8 Click on the Background Images folder and drag it into the Images folder. Then drag the distressedBG.tif file into this folder. This folder nesting is a useful way of providing even better organization in the Project panel and is probably very similar to the kind of structure you use with folders on your computer.

With the Project panel highlighted, press the tilde (~) key on your keyboard to minimize the panel and return to the Standard workspace layout.

Nesting files and folders keeps your Project panel organized.

9 Save your file by choosing File > Save.

The keyboard command for the Save function is Ctrl+S (Windows) or Command+S (Mac OS).

Renaming files

Renaming files in After Effects is a little different from other programs. In most programs you can just click on a highlighted file to rename it. Trying this approach in After Effects doesn't work. Here you will change the name of the Washington City Street.jpg file.

1 Click on the file named Washington City Street.jpg to highlight it.

2 Press the Enter (Windows) or Return (Mac OS) key on your keyboard. The filename becomes editable.

3 Change the filename by placing your cursor at the end of the word *Street* and adding **–daytime** at the end so that it now reads as Washington City Street-daytime.jpg, then press Enter/Return.

Changing the name of a file in the Project panel does not affect the actual file on your computer. Like all video editing programs, After Effects has a non-destructive workflow. Nothing you do in After Effects changes the original files on your hard drive. The one exception to this is when you use Edit Original commands, which are designed to open the original source files that you imported from external editing applications such as Photoshop and Illustrator.

4 Press the tilde (~) key on your keyboard to minimize the Project panel and return to the Standard workspace.

5 Save your file by choosing File > Save or by pressing Ctrl+S (Windows) or Command+S (Mac OS) on the keyboard.

Previewing footage

Media that has been imported into a project is often called footage. You can preview footage by using the Footage panel, which is hidden by default. You can simply display the Footage panel by choosing Window > Footage: (none).

1 Display the Footage panel by choosing Window > Footage: (none).

This will open an empty panel that is standing by to preview a piece of footage from the Project panel.

The Footage panel automatically opens when you double-click on any item in the Project panel. If you have previously used the Footage panel, the name of the last item you viewed is displayed next to the panel name in the Window menu.

Previewing stills and video

You preview still images and video files in almost exactly the same way. The only major difference between the two is that video footage has a time ruler so that you can adjust its duration.

1 In the Project panel, double-click on Double Single numbers.mov to load it into the Footage panel. The text on the tab of the Footage panel changes to "Footage: Double Single numbers.mov," to indicate that you are previewing a specific footage item.

2 With the Footage panel highlighted, press the spacebar on your keyboard to begin the video preview.

3 Once you see the animation begin to play, you can press the spacebar again to stop the preview.

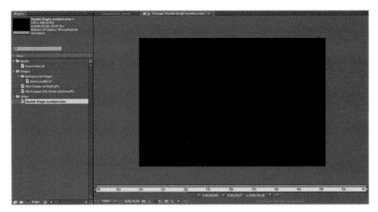

Press the spacebar to start and stop the animation.

If you click and drag the playhead through the time ruler, you move backward and forward through the video file. You can use this technique, called scrubbing the playhead, to navigate quickly to a specific time in the file. Remember that this is not a real-time preview; the speed at which you scrub the playhead controls the playback speed.

4 Double-click the Mini Cooper at Night.JPG file to see how easy it is to preview still images as well.

Previewing audio

You can preview audio files using the Footage panel. While an audio file is loaded into the Preview panel in the same way that any other file is (by double-clicking on it), pressing the spacebar does not cause the audio to play in the same way that video does. To preview audio files, you use a RAM preview.

1 In the Project panel, double-click on house beat.aif to load it into the Footage panel. Unlike when you previewed the video and image files, the Footage panel appears as a blank, gray screen.

The name of the audio file displays in the Footage panel tab and you see a time ruler for the duration of the audio file.

2 Locate the Preview panel on the right side of the workspace and click the RAM Preview button.

Click the RAM Preview button.

3 After a brief pause, the audio file begins to play. When you are happy with the preview, click anywhere in the interface to stop the playback.

4 In addition to creating a RAM preview of your composition you can also preview audio while scrubbing the playhead.

If it is not already there, move the playhead to the beginning (0;00;00;00) of the composition. Hold down the Ctrl (Windows) or Command (Mac OS) key on your keyboard and click on the playhead and drag it back and forth across the timeline to scrub it. You will now hear audio previewing as the playhead moves.

5 Save your file by choosing File > Save or by pressing Ctrl+S (Windows) or Command+S (Mac OS) on the keyboard. Do not close this file, you will need it in the next part of the lesson.

Trimming a video clip

Video clips often include a little extra padding at the beginning and end called handles, or sometimes you have a long video clip and only want to use a small portion of it. The process of shortening a video clip is called trimming, and you do it by adjusting the clip's IN and OUT points.

1 In the Project panel, double-click on Double Single numbers.mov to load it into the Footage panel. The entire clip is one minute long, but you are going to trim it down so that only a 20-second portion in the middle is used.

2   Click on the Current Time button () at the bottom of the Footage panel. The Go to Time dialog box appears.

The Go to Time dialog box.

3   Type the number **2000** into the time text field and click in any empty area of the Go to Time dialog box. After Effects automatically converts the number to its time code equivalent, so 2000 becomes 20 seconds (0;00;20;00). Click OK to go to the 20-second mark on the time ruler.

Understanding time code

Time code is used in video editing and motion graphics programs to keep track of your position along a Timeline, tape, or any time-based medium. It is easily identified as a series of four numbers separated by either colons or semicolons. As seen in the example below, starting on the left, the numbers represent Hours : Minutes : Seconds : Frames.

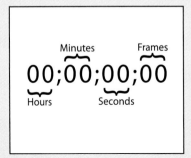

A time code.

Counting hours, minutes, and seconds is done the same way you would with a standard clock, except that the counting starts at zero instead of one. The one variable with time code is the number of frames that make up a second, which is based on the frame rate of the media you are dealing with. Depending on the Composition settings, you could be using the American television standard of 30 FPS (frames per second), the European standard of 25 FPS, or the film standard of 24 FPS. Time code is used to provide a discrete address to each frame of video.

4 Click the Set IN point to current time button (▣) at the bottom of the Footage panel. This moves the start of the clip to the current position of the playhead.

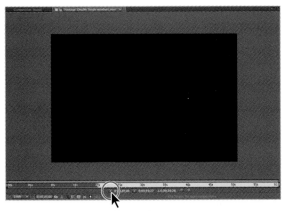

Click the Set IN Point Current Time button.

5 Click on the Current Time button and in the Go to Time dialog box, type **4000** and click OK to move the playhead to the 40-second mark of the time ruler.

6 Click the Set OUT point to current time button (▣) to finish trimming the clip.

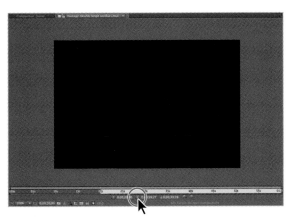

Click the Set OUT Point Current Time button.

The trimmed clip is added to the Timeline using the Ripple Insert Edit (▣) and Overlay Edit (▣) buttons in the Footage panel. If you drag and drop footage onto the Timeline directly from the Project panel, After Effects ignores any trimming that you have done on the video.

7 Save your file by choosing File > Save or by pressing Ctrl+S (Windows) or Command+S (Mac OS) on the keyboard.

Do not close this file, you will need it in the next part of the lesson.

Importing multiple files

Using the Import File command allows you to select multiple files simultaneously, but only if they reside in the same folder. To address this problem, After Effects uses a feature called Import Multiple Files.

1 Choose File > Import > Multiple Files to open the Import Multiple Files dialog box.

You can also use the keyboard shortcut Command+Option+I (Mac OS) or Ctrl+Alt+I (Windows) or right-click in any empty area of the Project panel and choose Import > Import Multiple Files.

2 Navigate to the images folder; press and hold down the Ctrl (Windows) or Command (Mac OS) key on your keyboard, and click on fountain.JPG and Washington Church.JPG to select them both. Click the Open button to import them. The files are imported and the Import Multiple Files dialog box opens again to allow you to select additional files.

3 Navigate to the audio folder and click on Subliminal.mp3 to highlight it. Click Open to import this file as well. Again, After Effects imports the file and the dialog box reopens.

4 Navigate to the video folder, hold down the Command (Mac OS) or Ctrl (Windows) key on your keyboard, and click on forest.mov and pingpongnode.mov to select them both. Click Open to import these files. The dialog box reopens.

5 Click Cancel to close the dialog box, as you no longer need it. The Project panel now shows that all the files that you imported have been added to your project.

— New files

The project panel shows that all five files have been added.

6 With the Project panel highlighted, press the tilde (~) key on your keyboard to maximize it to full-screen size.

7 Move the video files (forest.mov and pingpongnode.mov) into the Video folder. Move the audio file (Subliminal.mp3) into the Audio folder, and move the image files (fountain.JPG and Washington Church.JPG) into the Images folder. Your Project panel should now match the figure below. With the Project panel highlighted, press the tilde (~) key on your keyboard to minimize the panel and return to the Standard workspace layout.

Enlarge the Project panel, then organize your files for easier access.

8 Save your file by choosing File > Save or by pressing Ctrl+S (Windows) or Command+S (Mac OS) on the keyboard.

Do not close this file, you will need it in the next part of the lesson.

Importing Photoshop and Illustrator files

Adobe Photoshop and Illustrator are two industry-standard applications for creating pixel-based and vector graphics, respectively. While you can export a wide variety of file formats from either of them for import into After Effects, it is best to import the native file formats that they both produce. When importing Photoshop (.psd) and Illustrator (.ai) files, you can take full advantage of the integration between the applications. You can import layered Photoshop and Illustrator files either as footage or as compositions. If you import a file as footage, After Effects automatically flattens the layers; however, if you choose to import it as a composition, the file is converted into a composition and After Effects imports each layer as an individual layer so that they can be animated separately. The process is virtually identical for both types of files.

1 Choose File > Import > File. Navigate to images > photoshop & illustrator, and select the file Archaic Wheels.ai.

2   From the Import As drop-down menu, choose Composition – Retain Layer Sizes. Click the Open button to import the file.

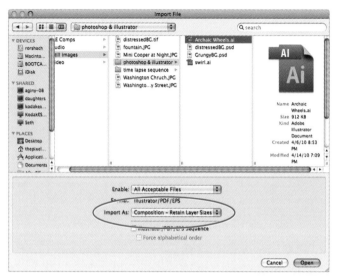

From the Import As drop-down menu, choose Composition - Retain Layer Sizes.

When you import a file as a composition, the Project panel has a new composition automatically added to it that is named for your file, and a new folder that holds the individual layers that make up the new composition. This always happens when you import an Illustrator or Photoshop file as a composition.

Composition versus Composition – Retain Layer Sizes

When you import native Photoshop and Illustrator files into After Effects, an often-misunderstood setting is the Import As feature. The difference isn't technically in how the file is imported, but actually has to do with how After Effects arranges the layers in the file when it converts the file into a composition.. Regardless of which one you choose (Composition or Composition – Retain Layer Sizes), you end up with a new composition and a folder that contains each individual layer from your file. The difference isn't in how After Effects brings in your files; it is in how it sets up the anchor point for each imported layer.

Composition.

When using the Composition setting, After Effects looks at the boundary of the layered file that is being imported and sets the anchor point for each layer to the center of the file, regardless of the content of each layer. When importing a Photoshop file, the center point is calculated based on the document size, while with an Illustrator file, the center point is set based on the contents of the file. This setting can be very helpful when you have a symmetrical composition and you want to transform every layer in relation to the image's central axis.

Composition – Retain Layer Styles.

When using the Composition – Retain Layer Sizes option, After Effects takes a different approach to assigning anchor points. With this setting, the anchor point of each layer is based only on the content of each layer. This setting is usually more beneficial when dealing with artwork that is asymmetrical or when you want to transform each layer separately on its own axis.

3   Click the Create a new Folder button (⬛) at the bottom of the Project panel to create a new folder. Name the new folder **Imported Comps**, then press Enter (Windows) or Return (Mac OS). Drag the Archaic Wheels composition and Archaic Wheels Layers folder into it.

4   Click on the Imported Comps folder to highlight it. Choose File > Import > File, navigate to images > Photoshop & Illustrator, and select the file GrungyBG.psd. Choose Composition in the Import As drop-down menu. Click Open to go to the secondary PSD Import dialog box.

5   In the dialog box, make sure that the radio button for *Editable Layer Styles* is enabled and that the checkbox for *Live Photoshop 3D* is disabled. Click OK to import the file. The imported Composition and Layers folder is placed inside the highlighted folder.

The Import options dialog box.

6   Save your file by choosing File > Save or by pressing Ctrl+S (Windows) or Command+S (Mac OS) on the keyboard.

Do not close this file, you will need it in the next part of the lesson.

Importing image sequences

Image sequences can be produced from a wide range of programs and also from devices such as scanners and digital cameras. While there is some variation in the naming convention for the images in a sequence, they generally begin with a filename followed by a number and then the file extension—for example, image01.jpg. When you select an image in a sequence, you can have After Effects search the folder for other images with similar names and import them as if they were part of a video file.

1   If necessary, highlight the Images folder and click the Create New Folder button at the bottom of the Project panel. Name the new folder **Image Sequences**, then press Enter (Windows) or Return (Mac OS).

2   Highlight the Image Sequences folder and choose File > Import > File or press Ctrl+I (Windows) or Command+I (Mac OS) to open the Import File dialog box.

3   Navigate to images > time lapse sequence and click on the first file in the folder, highway_0001.JPG, to select it.

4 Confirm that the *JPEG Sequence* checkbox is enabled at the bottom of the dialog box and click the Open button.

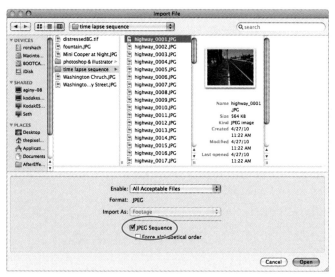

Make sure JPEG sequence is enabled in the Import file dialog box.

5 The files are imported and placed in the Project panel as a single entry named highway_[0001-0068].JPG. Double-click on the sequence to preview it in the Footage panel.

6 If necessary, click on the Magnification drop-down menu at the bottom left of the panel and choose Fit up to 100% from the menu.

Magnify the video picture.

7 Press the spacebar on your keyboard to preview the sequence. You can press the spacebar again at any time to stop the playback.

The preview created by pressing the spacebar is not a real-time preview—at least it isn't the first time it plays. A green bar appears at the top of the time ruler as you preview the file. This is an indication that the program is rendering the video file for playback. The second time you preview the footage, the rendering is complete and you experience the playback in real time.

8 Save your file by choosing File > Save or by pressing Ctrl+S (Windows) or Command+S (Mac OS) on the keyboard.

Do not close this file, you will need it in the next part of the lesson.

Importing After Effects compositions

So far in this lesson you have imported images, video, audio, and even image sequences. In addition to all these file types, you can import entire projects into other After Effects projects.

1 If necessary, press the tilde key (~) to enlarge the Project panel window. Highlight the Imported Comps folder in your Project panel and choose File > Import > File, or press Ctrl+I (Windows) or Command+I (Mac OS), to open the Import File dialog box.

2 Navigate to the AE Comps folder and select Spectral Background.aep. The Import As menu automatically sets itself to Project. Click Open to import the file.

The entire project, including all the links to its imported media, and everything else that was in the imported files' Project panel are now a part of your current project and are stored inside of a folder named for the project file.

3 Click the reveal triangle to expand the Spectral Background.aep folder. Double-click on the Spectral Background composition located in the folder to preview it in the Composition panel and Timeline.

Preview the Spectral Background composition by double-clicking the file in the Project panel.

4 Compositions must be rendered first before you can view them in real time. Click the RAM Preview button in the Preview panel to the right. The preview begins building, which is indicated by the green bar at the top of the Timeline. Once After Effects has finished building the preview, it begins automatically from the beginning. Depending upon the speed of your computer, it may take a few minutes. Faster computers with more RAM will speed your work with After Effects.

The duration of the composition preview is based on the amount of RAM on your system, which is why it is called a RAM preview. If you don't have enough RAM, you may not be able to preview the entire Timeline at once. If necessary, you can increase the duration of the RAM preview by reducing the resolution of the composition in the Resolution/Down Sample Factor drop-down menu at the bottom of the Composition panel.

5 Save your file by choosing File > Save or by pressing Ctrl+S (Windows) or Command+S (Mac OS) on the keyboard. Do not close this file, you will need it in the next part of the lesson.

Locating missing files

When you import a file, After Effects creates a link to the original media file on your hard drive. This link is what you see in the Project panel. These files are linked and not actually a part of the project itself. If anything happens to the original file, i.e., it is deleted, moved, or renamed, this will cause a problem. When you attempt to open a project, After Effects checks the media links to ensure that they are all still intact, and if it encounters a problem will display a warning dialog telling you how many files are currently missing.

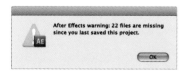

The number of missing files will vary depending on the project you are attempting to open.

To fix this problem you must relink the missing footage by replacing the original linked footage with itself. To find your missing files:

1 Click OK to close the initial warning dialog.

2 Locate one of the missing footage items in the Project panel. They will be easy to identify by the color bar icon (📊) to the left of the footage name.

3 Right-click on any missing footage item and from the menu that appears, choose Replace Footage > File.

4 When the Replace Footage File dialog box appears, navigate to the folder that contains the missing file that corresponds to this footage item. The name of the file should be visible in the dialog box's title bar.

5 Highlight the missing file and click Open. After a brief pause while your computer analyzes the folder's content and relinks the missing files it finds here, a confirmation dialog will appear informing you that previously missing files have be found.

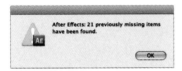

The number of recovered files will vary depending on the number of missing items After Effects was able to locate.

Click OK to close this dialog box.

If your files all still have the same names and are in the same relative locations as when they were imported this one operation may locate all the missing footage items. If not, you may have to repeat this process several times to locate all your missing files. In general, it is far easier to locate your missing media files when they are simply moved and not renamed or deleted.

Using the Interpret Footage dialog box

When you import a piece of footage, After Effects analyzes the file and uses a set of built-in rules to determine attributes such as pixel aspect ratio, alpha channel type, frame rate, and color profile, and it uses this information to determine how the file should be displayed. It uses these built-in rules to make a best guess, which is often correct, and you can happily go about the rest of your work. However, when the program interprets this information incorrectly, issues can occur with the appearance of your footage. The Interpret Footage dialog box allows you to set these footage attributes manually. The settings you have access to in the dialog box vary depending on the type of file and the information it contains. For example, one setting for audio files is how many times they loop, which wouldn't be an issue with still images.

Looping an audio or video file

The house beat.aif file that you imported earlier in this lesson is only 30 seconds long, which is actually not uncommon for audio that is intended for use as a loop. By default, all imported audio and video files are set to loop only once, but you can change that in the Interpret Footage dialog box.

1 Click on the house beat.aif file in your Project panel, and look at the file properties at the top of the panel. The duration of the file reads 0;00;30;00, indicating that it is thirty seconds in length.

2 Right-click (Windows) or Ctrl+click (Mac OS) on the house beat.aif file, and from the context menu that appears, choose Interpret Footage > Main. This opens the Interpret Footage dialog box.

The keyboard shortcut for the Interpret Footage dialog box is Command+Option+G (Mac OS) or Ctrl+Alt+G (Windows). Remember to highlight the file in the Project panel before using the keyboard command.

3   Locate the Loop property at the bottom of the dialog box. Type **2** as the new Loop property.

Set the Loop property to 2.

4   Click OK to close the Interpret Footage dialog box with your new settings. With the file still highlighted, look at the file properties at the top of the Project panel. The duration of the file now reads 0;01;00;00, double its former length.

5   Save your file by choosing File > Save or by pressing Ctrl+S (Windows) or Command+S (Mac OS) on the keyboard.

Do not close this file, you will need it in the next part of the lesson.

Using Remember Interpretation

At some point, you will want to apply the exact same type of interpretation to multiple files. This is easily accomplished by using the Remember Interpretation and Apply Interpretation commands.

1   Right-click on the house beat.aif file in your Project panel. Choose Interpret Footage > Remember Interpretation from the context menu that appears. This command stores the footage interpretation settings of the current file in memory.

2   Right-click on the Subliminal.mp3 file and choose Interpret Footage > Apply Interpretation. This command applies the currently stored footage interpretation settings to a new footage item.

3   Save your file by choosing File > Save or by pressing Ctrl+S (Windows) or Command+S (Mac OS) on the keyboard.

Do not close this file, you will need it in the next part of the lesson.

Changing Alpha Channel type

If you only use Photoshop to create your images, then you will probably never have a problem with the way After Effects reads your alpha channels. However, if you use other programs or rely on stock or royalty-free artwork, then you may run into a problem where the programs pick the wrong alpha channel type. This incorrect interpretation usually results in black or white halos around the transparent edges of your imagery, but you can use the Interpret Footage dialog box to fix this problem.

Because Photoshop was used exclusively to prepare the pixel-based artwork in the project files for this lesson, none of the imported images here require you to change the alpha channel type. However, the instructions below will help you if you ever run into this problem.

1   Right-click on the file for which you want to change the alpha channel type, and choose Interpret Footage > Main.

2   In the Interpret Footage dialog box, click the radio button next to the type you want After Effects to use.

Note that when switching to the Premultiplied – Matted With Color option, the two most common colors to matte with are black and white. Click on the color swatch to the right and use the Color Picker that appears to select the matte color.

Using the Collect Files command to consolidate files

Throughout this lesson, you have imported footage from different locations. Because of the nature of the lesson, everything came from the same root folder, but this isn't always the case. Many times you may find yourself importing from different folders and even different hard drives. You may also run into the problem of wanting to transfer an entire project and all the footage needed to recreate it to another designer or for archival purposes. This is a situation where you can use the Collect Files command.

1　Choose File > Collect Files to open the Collect Files dialog box.

The Collect Files dialog box.

2　Confirm that the Collect Source Files menu at the top of the dialog box says All, and click the Collect button to choose the destination of your new project folder.

3　In the Collect files into folder dialog box, the default folder name should be Lesson3-Working folder. Choose your desktop as the destination and click Save. As the Collect Files operation runs, you see a status bar on screen.

4　When the Collect Files operation completes, minimize or hide After Effects to view your desktop, and double-click the Lesson3-Working folder you saved there. Notice that the Collect Files operation created a copy of your After Effects project, a folder that stores copies of all the footage that was in the project, and a text file that stores information about the Collect operation, such as what footage and compositions were collected.

5　Double-click on the (Footage) folder and notice that the structure of your Project panel was used to set the order of files in this folder. If you double-click on the Images folder, you see that this organization carries through to the subfolders as well.

6　Close the folders and return to After Effects. Choose File > Save, then File > Close.

Congratulations! You have completed the lesson.

Self study

Create a new project and import a variety of different footage types. Create folders to organize the footage to make it easier to locate and use.

Review

Questions

1   What is the advantage of the Import Multiple Files command over the Import File command?

2   What does the Remember Interpretation command do?

3   What are the two most common colors to matte an alpha channel with when using a premultiplied alpha channel?

Answers

1   The Import Multiple Files command reopens the Import dialog box after every import operation so that you can import from different folders.

2   When you highlight a piece of footage, the Remember Interpretation command is used to store the settings for the Interpret Footage dialog box so that you can apply these settings to another footage item using the Apply Interpretation command.

3   The two most common colors to use for matting a premultiplied alpha channel are black and white.

What you'll learn in this lesson:

- Taking a project from a blank screen to a fully realized animation.
- Creating and adjusting composition settings.
- Animating layer properties, such as anchor point and rotation

Animation Workflow

Now that you understand the interface and how to organize your media, it's time to have some fun. In this lesson, you will animate your first compositions in After Effects.

Starting up

You will work with several files from the ae04lessons folder in this lesson. Make sure that you have loaded the aelessons folder onto your hard drive from the supplied DVD. See "Loading lesson files" on page 4.

See Lesson 4 in action!

Use the accompanying video to gain a better understanding of how to use some of the features shown in this lesson. The video tutorial for this lesson can be found on the included DVD.

Setting up

As you work in After Effects, you will inevitably open and close many panels, depending on the type of work you are doing. However, when working through the projects in this book, it is important to have an interface that matches the lessons. To this end, you should always reset your workspace to the preset Standard configuration.

1   Choose Window > Workspace > Standard to set your current workspace configuration.

2   Choose Window > Workspace > Reset Standard to reset the standard workspace in case you have modified it at some point.

Understanding the animation workflow

When working in After Effects it is important to understand that this program is usually used to animate or composite assets that are created in other applications. It's safe to say that most professional After Effects users are often expert users, of other graphic and design programs. They often make use of Adobe Photoshop, and sometimes Illustrator, along with a variety of packages that can create 3D graphics such as 3D Studio Max, Maya, or Cinema 4D to create the media they will work with in After Effects.

In order to speed the learning process, many of the lessons in this book have you start with a pre-built project. This lesson will be a little different, in that it will take you through the entire workflow, from creating a composition, to importing a variety of media content, and finally through the animation and previewing process. In this lesson, you will work with a variety of media assets to produce a logo animation for a fictitious corporation named Dison Worldwide.

Creating and working with compositions

In Adobe After Effects, compositions are where you do all your animation and compositing work. Inside a composition, each piece of media resides on its own layer. Think of each composition as an independent Timeline in your project. In addition to the assorted types of footage that you import into After Effects, compositions can also contain other compositions, allowing for both an organized design environment and very complex animation projects. Placing one composition inside of another is called nesting compositions, and you will learn more about it in this lesson. In this first part of the lesson, you will create the initial composition to hold the animated Dison Logo that you will create.

Creating a new composition

As mentioned previously, projects really don't have editable options; it is the compositions that set everything from frame rate to pixel dimensions to aspect ratio. Compositions can be imported from other After Effects projects, automatically created when you import a layered Photoshop or Illustrator file, or created from scratch.

1   Choose Composition > New Composition from the menus at the top of the After Effects interface to open the Composition Settings dialog box. You can also use the keyboard shortcut, Ctrl+N (Windows) or Command+N (Mac OS).

2 In the dialog box, change the default composition name to **Dison Intro**. From the Preset drop-down menu, select NTSC DV. Choosing the preset automatically sets the width, height, pixel aspect ratio, and frame rate.

The presets in After Effects will match most standard video projects. If you have a project with specifications that do not match an existing preset, you should choose the closest one and modify it.

3 Confirm that the Resolution is set to Full and change the duration to **0;00;15;00** (15 seconds).

4 Click on the background color swatch to open the Background Color dialog box. When it appears, notice that the Color Picker in the dialog box allows you to insert numerical values for color using HSB (Hue, Saturation, Brightness), RGB (Red, Green, Blue), and hexadecimal values.

5 Click on the R (Red) value and type in **141**. Repeat this for both the G (Green) and B (Blue) values as well. This produces a light–gray background color.

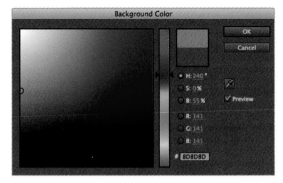

Whenever the RGB values are the same, you produce a grayscale value from black (R:0, G:0, B:0) to white (R:255, G:255, B:255).

You can also pick colors visually by selecting the hue from the vertical color slider and then clicking in the large color field to the left of the color formulas.

6   Click OK in the Background Color dialog box to return to the Composition Settings dialog box, and then click OK again in the dialog box to add the new comp to your project.

Understanding composition settings

The Composition Settings dialog box allows you to set and edit the properties of your compositions. The dialog box opens automatically when you create a new composition and can be opened manually by selecting a comp and choosing Composition > Composition Settings or by pressing Ctrl+K (Windows) or Command+K (Mac OS). The dialog box is divided into two sections, for basic and advanced settings.

Basic settings

A. Preset. B. Width and Height. C. Pixel Aspect Ratio. D. Frame Rate.
E. Resolution. F. Start Timecode. G. Duration. H. Background Color.

Preset: Video projects usually have to conform to an established standard such as NTSC or PAL. The presets menu contains a variety of prebuilt composition settings to match the most commonly used standards. Because most video projects will match one of the established video standards, the most efficient way to begin is to choose a preset from the drop-down menu and then modify any properties that do not fit your specific project. To the right of the menu are two buttons: one to save custom presets and the other to delete them.

Width and Height: This setting specifies the physical dimensions, in pixels, of your comp. This is comparable to document size in other applications.

Pixel Aspect Ratio: This setting specifies the shape of the pixels in your comp. Different video standards use different pixel aspect ratios to display content. An incorrect pixel aspect ratio will cause your work to appear distorted. The preset that you pick usually assigns this property for you.

Frame Rate: This setting specifies the number of frames per second (fps) that make up your composition.

Resolution: This setting specifies the quality of the Composition panel's display. Lower values require less RAM in order to preview.

Start Timecode: This setting specifies the timecode value at the beginning, or origin, of the Timeline. The After Effects default is 00;00;00;00 but if exporting your animations to videotape for broadcast, most stations require that the timecode origin be set to 01;00;00;00 (1 hour).

Duration: This setting specifies the length of the composition Timeline.

Background Color: This setting specifies the background color for the comp.

Advanced settings

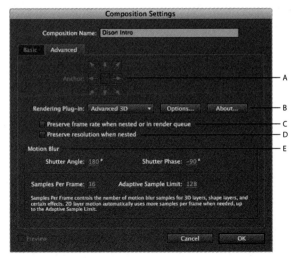

A. *Anchor.* B. *Rendering Plug-in.* C. *Preserve frame rate when nested or in Render Queue.*
D. *Preserve resolution when nested.* E. *Motion Blur.*

Anchor: This setting is not editable when creating a new comp, only when editing the settings of an existing one. If you are enlarging or shrinking its physical dimensions, the anchor settings specify how the transformation proceeds by locking a specific area in place.

Rendering Plug-in: This setting specifies the engine to use for rendering 3D layers. This setting is only available when you are using a supported video card and when supported third-party rendering plug-ins are available on your system.

Preserve frame rate when nested or in Render Queue: This setting specifies whether the comp's frame rate is preserved or converted when you place it inside of another composition.

Preserve resolution when nested: This setting specifies whether the comp's resolution setting is preserved or converted when you place it inside of another composition.

Motion Blur: This setting specifies the strength of the Motion Blur effect when it is enabled for layers. Using Motion Blur is covered in greater detail later in this lesson.

Importing compositions from Photoshop and Illustrator

If you are unfamiliar with them, Photoshop and Illustrator are two industry-leading applications for creating pixel-based and vector graphics, respectively. The fact that they are also Adobe applications allows them to have enhanced functionality when used as part of an After Effects workflow. When you import layered Photoshop and Illustrator files into a project, you have the ability to control whether they are either brought in as a flattened file (similar to when you import a JPEG) or converted into new compositions, which would maintain the integrity of the layers and the structure of the native files. For additional information on the benefits of using Photoshop and Illustrator files, refer to Lesson 3, "Media Management—Images, Video, and Audio."

1   Choose File > Import > Multiple Files. In the Import Multiple Files dialog box, navigate to the ae04lessons folder you copied to your hard drive earlier, and click on the file named globe.psd.

2   From the Import As drop-down menu, select Composition - Retain Layer Sizes. Click the Open button to gain access to the import options for the Photoshop file.

3   In the Import Options dialog box, confirm that the radio button for Editable Layer Styles is selected, and uncheck the Live Photoshop 3D checkbox if it is enabled. This file only contains two-dimensional artwork, so the 3D layer option isn't applicable, and making layer styles editable helps After Effects to match Photoshop's appearance attributes.

In general, enabling Editable Layer Styles from Photoshop ensures that your content in After Effects matches the Photoshop original.

Click OK to import the footage and reopen the Import Multiple Files dialog box.

4   In the Import Multiple Files dialog box, select the Archaic Wheels.ai file. From the Import As drop-down menu, select Composition. Click the Open button to import this file and reopen the Import Multiple Files dialog box.

In this instance, the Composition option works well because this file contains a series of concentric circles that are all centered on the Illustrator file's center point. The circles are also intended to be animated around a single central point at the composition's center.

5   In the Import Multiple Files dialog box, select the dison logo.ai file. From the Import As drop-down menu, select Composition – Retain Layer Sizes and click the Open button to import this file and reopen the Import Multiple Files dialog box.

6   In the Import Multiple Files dialog box, double-click on the Paper background.tif file to import it.

7   When the Import Multiple Files dialog box reopens, click the Cancel button to close it. Your Project panel should now look like the figure below.

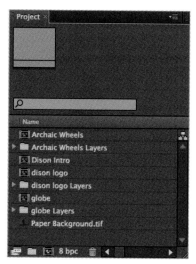

The advantage to using native Photoshop and Illustrator files is the ability to import compositions so that you can animate each layer.

8   Choose File > Save As. Navigate to the ae04lessons folder on your hard drive. In the Save As text field, name the file **Lesson4-working** and click Save.

Working with layers

If you are familiar with graphics programs such as Adobe Photoshop and Illustrator, then you may be familiar with the general concepts of using layers, though here they work a little differently. In After Effects, every piece of footage that you place in a composition resides on a separate and individual layer. These layers are visible in the Timeline panel and each layer contains its own properties that can be manipulated or animated independently of any others.

Now that you have created your main composition and imported the media assets you will work with, it's time to get a handle on working with the Layers panel. In this part of the lesson, you will add media to the timeline and work with the footage layers that are created to layout your composition.

1 If it is not already open, open your Lesson4-working.aep project that you saved at the beginning of this lesson. This project has the Photoshop and Illustrator compositions that were imported previously, along with the folders that were automatically created to organize each file's individual layers.

2 In the Project panel, double-click on the Dison Intro comp to preview it in the Composition panel and Timeline. This comp is now empty, but you are going to fix this in a moment.

It is important to note that when you double-click on a composition, it previews in the Composition panel and Timeline simultaneously. However, the ways that they preview are a little different. There is only one Composition panel by default, so double-clicking on a comp makes it active in the window and hides whichever one may have been visible previously. However, the Timeline panel is tab-based (just like your Internet browser), so you can see multiple comp tabs at the same time. As a result, double-clicking on a comp in the Project panel just brings its tab forward and makes it active.

Double-clicking on any composition immediately causes it to preview in the Composition panel and Timeline.

If you have multiple composition tabs on your Timeline, clicking on one makes it active in both the Timeline and Composition panels.

3 In the Project panel, click on the Paper Background.tif footage to highlight it, and drag it to the Dison Intro comp Timeline.

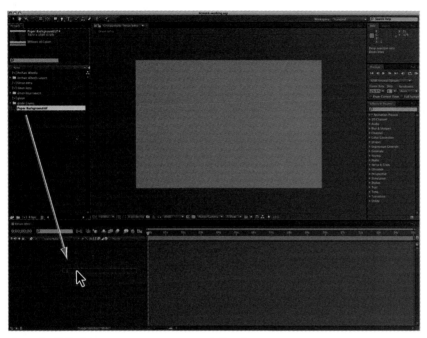

As you drag it, the footage appears onscreen as a gray wireframe box.

4   When the footage is over the comp's Timeline, release your mouse button. The footage is
added to the comp and becomes visible in the Composition panel.

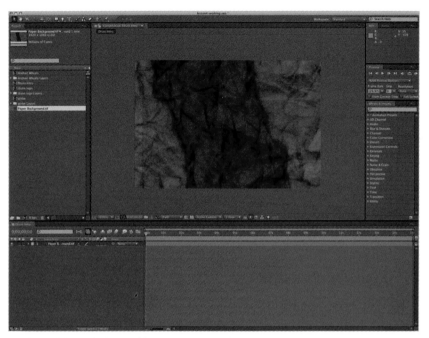

The drag-and-drop method is one of the easiest ways to add footage to a composition.

5   Again, in the Project panel, click on the globe composition, then drag and drop it below
the Paper Background.tif layer in the Dison Intro Timeline.

A composition can contain any type of footage: images, video, audio, and other comps.

Instead of dragging and dropping your footage into the Timeline, an alternative method is to drop it into the Composition panel. The difference between the two destinations is in how the layers are positioned. When targeting the Composition panel, the position of the layers is based on where you drag the footage; when placing footage directly into the Timeline, it is always centered on the composition.

If you look at the Composition panel, you will notice that the globe comp is not visible. This is because the paper texture is in front of it. You will fix this in the next exercise.

6 Save your file by choosing File > Save.

Understanding the different types of layers

In After Effects, the footage you import is added to a layer when you place it into a composition, but what about other objects, such as lights, cameras, or other shapes? They are layers as well; in fact, in addition to the standard layers you will create from your imported content, such as video, images, and audio, there are seven other types of layers that can be created entirely within After Effects:

Text layers can be animated using the standard layer transform properties (such as position or rotation). Additionally, text layers have unique properties (called *text animators*) which give you more control over the text. An example of when you would use text animators is if you wanted to rotate each character in a word. Text layers are used frequently to create credits, lower thirds, or kinetic typographic effects.

Solid layers, also called *layer solids* are single color layers that are created directly in After Effects. They are often used as color fields, rectangular shapes, or for effects which generated internally within After Effects such as the lightning grid effect, or beam effect.

Light layers are used to illuminate 3D layers and cast shadows. As an aesthetic tool, lights are used to enhance the sense of depth and volume in a scene.

Camera layers are designed to simulate the performance and behavior of video cameras in real life, and can be panned, tilted, and moved to create a sense of movement through space.

Null Object layers are invisible layers (which are visible in the composition and timeline panels, but do not render) that have all the transform properties of other visible layers. They are useful as helper objects, they require you to parent the properties of one layer to another, and they are often used as controller objects for cameras and three dimensional layers.

Shape Layers are vector shape objects created with the shape tools (rectangle, ellipse, polygon, etc.) in After Effects. Similar to text and solid layers, they have both layer transform properties and custom shape properties that are native only to shape layers.

Adjustment Layers are invisible layers that can be the target of effects, which are similar to adjustment layers in Photoshop. They are used when you want to apply a specific effect or series of effects to multiple layers simultaneously. Since any layers below the targeted adjustment layer will display as if the effect is applied to them, it avoids the trouble of having to apply the same effect multiple times.

Understanding the layer switches

If you have worked with design or graphics programs before using After Effects, then the idea of having switches to hide or lock a layer is not new to you. But in addition to these standard controls, the Layer area of the Timeline contains several other specialized switches used to enable or disable various layer features. In addition to being able to show, hide, and lock layers, you can solo, shy, or enable features such as motion blur or frame blending. If those terms are new to you, this section should help you understand them. Each layer switch corresponds with a label above it that details its name and usage.

*A. Video On/Off. **B.** Audio On/Off. **C.** Solo. **D.** Lock. **E.** Label. **F.** Number. **G.** Layer/Source Name. **H.** Shy. I. Collapse Transformations/Continuously Rasterize. **J.** Quality. **K.** Effects. **L.** Frame Blend. **M.** Motion Blur. **N.** Adjustment Layers. **O.** 3D Layer. **P.** Parenting.*

Video On/Off (⊚): Click this switch to toggle the visibility of the video on a layer. This switch is only available when working with a layer containing video; otherwise, the space is blank. In After Effects, this setting applies to both still images and actual video. When a layer's video track is disabled, it doesn't preview in the Composition panel and is not included when you render the composition for final output.

Audio On/Off (◀): Click this switch to mute the audio of a layer. This switch is only available when working with a layer containing audio. In this case, the audio can either be on its own layer, as when you add an MP3, WAV, or AIFF file to a composition, or embedded in a video file. When you disable a layer's audio track, it doesn't preview in the Composition panel and is not included when you render the composition for final output.

Solo (•): This switch hides all layers that do not have the Solo switch enabled. Often you will want to preview only a single layer in a much larger composition. In situations like this, toggling the video and audio off for many layers can be very time-consuming. This switch allows you to isolate only the layers that have Solo enabled. When a track is soloed, its audio and video don't preview in the Composition panel and are not included when you render the composition for final output.

Lock (🔒): This switch prevents any editing to a layer's content. When enabled, the layer cannot be selected or transformed at all. Use this switch to prevent accidental changes to content that you want to isolate, but want to remain visible in the composition.

Label ( ): This is a drop-down menu used to apply a color label to each layer. The color is used in two places: as the color of the border around highlighted content in the Timeline, and also as the layer's highlight color in the Timeline. While you can modify the colors, they default to specific colors based on the type of footage on the layer. You can change this default in the Preferences dialog box by editing the contents of the Labels category.

Number (#): This is a numerical value assigned to show the stacking order of layers in a composition. The first layer is on top of all other layers, followed by the layer numbered 2 and then 3 and so on. If you are using a keyboard with a number pad, you can select layers by pressing their corresponding keys.

Layer/Source Name: This column can be toggled to display two different values. The Source names option displays the names of the footage items from the Project panel, while choosing layer names displays the custom name (if any) that you have assigned to layers in the Timeline panel. New compositions default to the Source name display, in which they use the footage name from the Project panel. When edited, the column automatically switches to the Layer name mode, which allows you to mix custom names changed in the Timeline with Source names.

Shy ( ): The Shy switch is a tool for optimizing the display of the Composition panel. You can enable a layer's Shy mode, then use the Hide Shy Layers composition switch at the top of the Timeline panel to hide all Shy layers in the comp. This can be a helpful alternative to maximizing the Timeline panel to full-screen mode, because it removes Shy layers from the layer display but not the Composition panel. Shy layers still preview in the Composition panel and are also included when rendered for final output.

Collapse Transformations/Continuously Rasterize ( ): The function of this switch changes, depending on what the layer's footage type is. When applied to a composition, it collapses transformations on that layer, effectively changing the order in which effects and transformations are rendered in the nested composition. Continuously Rasterize applies only to vector-based content imported from programs such as Adobe Illustrator. When enabled, the layer is continuously rasterized, which produces a better result in animating properties, such as scale, but it does so with an increased performance cost.

Quality ( ): The Quality setting of a layer specifies how precisely it is rendered. This setting is applied to the appearance of the layer in previews, but is also applicable when rendered for final output. When you switch the layer quality, you can choose Best, Draft, and Wireframe modes. The Best quality mode displays the render at its highest quality, but takes a longer time to render than Draft or Wireframe modes. The Draft mode is a lower-quality preview than Best, and is intended to show your layers, but some effects are not rendered or may be applied inaccurately. Wireframe quality displays only the outline of a layer, discarding its appearance and all effects. The ability to change quality is helpful because a lower-quality display previews and renders faster, and this feature can be very useful when syncing the position or timing of elements.

Effects (*fx*): This switch is disabled unless an effect has been applied to a layer, when it is automatically enabled. You use this switch to disable effects on the layer, resulting in quicker previews.

Frame Blend (⊟): This switch is usually enabled when using time-remapping effects to speed up or slow down video footage. These effects can lead to jerky motion, which frame blending is designed to compensate for by combining multiple frames together.

Motion Blur (⬤): This switch enables motion blur in the layer, helping to create the impression of motion that viewers are familiar with from watching video and film.

Adjustment Layers (⬤): When enabled, this switch converts the layer into an adjustment layer. When using adjustment layers, the content of the layer is ignored and instead, effects applied to the targeted layer affect only the layers below it.

3D Layer (⬤): When enabled, this switch converts a two-dimensional layer into a three-dimensional layer.

Parenting: This column contains controls for setting the layer as a child, thus allowing the parent layer to control its position, rotation, scale, and anchor point.

Understanding layer stacking order

When a composition consists of multiple layers, the arrangement of those layers, called the *stacking order*, is very important. When a layer that is fully opaque is placed on top of other layers, the result is that only the top layer is visible. If, however, the top layer has transparent areas, you can see through those transparent areas to the layer or layers beneath. You can easily modify the arrangement of layers in the Timeline panel.

1   In the Dison Intro timeline, locate the Source Name column and place your cursor on the dividing line to the right of the column.

The panes of the Timeline panel can be expanded or contracted depending on your needs.

2   When your cursor changes to a double arrow, click and drag the dividing line to the right to enlarge the Source Name column.

Any column in the Timeline panel can be contracted or expanded, though this is most often used on the name column to accommodate longer filenames.

3 Click on the globe layer to highlight it, and drag it above the Paper Background.tif layer.

As you drag layers in the Timeline, a black line appears to show you a preview of the new stacking order.

4 You should now be able to see the globe composition as in the figure below. Save your file by choosing File > Save or by pressing Ctrl+S (Windows) or Command+S (Mac OS) on the keyboard.

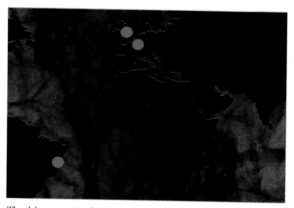

The globe composition has transparent areas that reveal the background beneath.

Changing layer names

In the Timeline panel, layer names are taken directly from the name of the source footage, but this is not always in your best interest. Many people prefer to have layer names that describe their content, because this makes them easier to locate when quickly scanning through or searching a composition.

1 Click on the Paper Background.tif layer in your Timeline panel to highlight it.

2 With the layer highlighted, press the Enter (Windows) or Return (Mac OS) key on your keyboard. This makes the layer name editable.

3 Change the layer name to **background**. Press the Enter/Return key again to exit this editing mode.

There are a couple things that have changed in the Timeline panel. The pane name is no longer called Source Name but is now instead titled Layer Name. Additionally, the globe layer is now enclosed in brackets, indicating that it is still being referred to by the Source Name.

4 Save your file by choosing File > Save or by pressing Ctrl+S (Windows) or Command+S (Mac OS) on the keyboard.

Understanding Layer Properties

Every visual layer has five built-in properties that can be animated: Position, Opacity, Rotation, Anchor Point, and Scale. Each of these properties can be animated either individually or in combination with other properties to create animations.

Position: This property specifies the X, Y, and Z (when the layer's 3D switch is enabled) coordinates of the layer. The units of measure used by the Position property are pixels, and are relative to the composition's origin point (0.0, 0.0) located in the upper-left corner. It is important to note that this property is for the anchor point of a layer, not its actual content.

Opacity: This property specifies the transparency of a layer as a value between 0 (zero) and 100 percent, where 0 percent would be fully transparent, and 100 percent would be fully opaque.

Rotation: This property specifies the amount that a layer turns around its central axis. When dealing with a two-dimensional layer, all rotation is around the z-axis. Once the 3D layer switch is enabled, however, the Rotation property is split into three: X Rotation, Y Rotation, and Z Rotation. Whether for two dimensions or three, the Rotation property is displayed as a series of numbers, 0x + 0.0°, where the first value is the number or times of complete rotations to make, and the second number is the ending degree value. So a value of 1x + 0.0° would mean to rotate one full time and stop at 0°, while a value of 2x + 45° would mean to make two full rotations, then stop at 45°.

Anchor Point: This is the reference or registration point of a layer. This is the point that all transformations (rotation, movement, scale, and so on) occur around, so it is sometimes called the *transformation point*.

Scale: This property specifies the relative horizontal and vertical size of a layer as a value that defaults to 100 percent. Values above 100 percent make the layer larger, while values below 100 percent make it smaller.

Specialized layers, such as cameras and lights, have a slightly different set of properties. For example, they both lack an Anchor Point and instead have a property named Point of Interest, which defines the target onscreen area that the light or camera is pointing at.

Any layer property can be animated independently from all the others. Once animation is enabled, any change to that property, either by using the Transform tools in the Composition panel or by editing its values on the Timeline, produces a new keyframe at the playhead's current position. If there is an existing keyframe at the playhead's current position, then you will instead modify its value when you change the properties.

Creating Kinestasis by animating the Anchor Point

Kinestasis is a very popular technique when working with still images. It is also sometimes called the *Ken Burns effect* or *Pan and Zoom*. Traditionally, before the advent of modern software, the effect was created by panning a video camera over a still image. In modern motion graphics, this effect is most often recreated in After Effects by animating a layer's anchor point.

This is what all your preparation up to this point has been for. You will now animate the layers that you have added to your composition to create a kinestatic effect.

Properties such as Anchor Point, Position and Scale have multiple values stored for each keyframe. These values are numerical and correspond to objects on your screen, which in turn can be animated. For example with Position, you will have an X value (horixontal) and a Y value (vertical). By setting two keyframes with different values you can animate an object horizontally, vertically or both.

While a three dimensional layer will have a third value for the Z-axis position.

1   If it is not already open, open the Lesson4-working.aep project that you saved at the beginning of this lesson. This project has the Photoshop and Illustrator compositions that were imported previously, along with the folders that were automatically created to organize each file's individual layers.

2   In the Project panel, double-click on the Dison Intro comp to preview it in the Composition panel and Timeline. In the previous exercises, two layers were added to the comp: globe and background. The layers must be modified a little before you can apply the Kinestasis effect. Both layers are much larger than the actual comp and must be scaled down to be useful, and the globe layer must be moved into the proper position for the effect.

3   In the Timeline panel, click on the globe layer to highlight it. Hold down the Shift key and click on the background layer to add it to your selection.

4   Click on the reveal triangle to the left of the globe layer's name to view the Transform properties for the layer. Because both layers were selected, two Transform properties are revealed.

The reveal triangles are used to display hidden layer properties.

5   Click on the reveal triangle for the globe layer's Transform properties to view the five individual properties that are inherent to all visible layers.

Many layer and effects properties are hidden in subgroups that you must reveal in order to access them.

6   Click on the Scale value to make it editable. Type **70** in the numerical text field and press the Enter (Windows) or Return (Mac OS) key on your keyboard. Because multiple layers were selected when you did this, both layers scale down to 70 percent of their original size.

7   Press Ctrl+Shift+A (Windows) or Command+Shift+A (Mac OS) to deselect all layers. Then click on the globe layer to select it.

8   For the globe layer, in the Position category, click on the value for X Position (the first value listed for the Position property) and change it to **146**. Then click on the value for Y Position (the second value listed for the Position property) and change it to **254**. Press Enter or Return to accept settings.

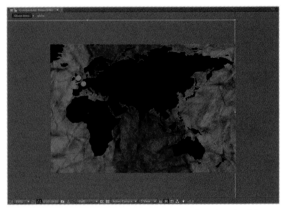

The position of the globe layer should line up with the right side of the composition.

Up to this point, you have been changing the layer properties globally. This changes them to the same value for the entire duration of the composition. Now you will animate the Anchor Point property to create movement.

9   If your cursor is not at the origin (0;00;00;00) of the Timeline, click on the Current Time field on the top-left corner of the Timeline to highlight it, type in the number **0** (zero), and press the Enter (Windows) or Return (Mac OS) key to move the playhead back to the beginning of the Timeline.

10   Click the Time-Vary Stopwatch (●) to the left of the Anchor Point property to enable animation for this property. This creates a keyframe at the current position of the playhead.

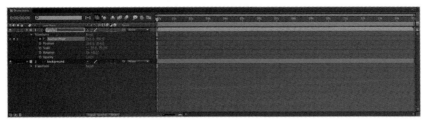

Keyframes are always created at the playhead's current position.

Keyframes store property values. In order to create animation, you will create a second keyframe farther down the Timeline with different values. The program will then animate the change for you.

11   Click on the Current Time field to highlight it, type **1000** into the numerical text field, and click on any empty area of the Timeline to move the playhead to 10 seconds.

12   Click on the X value of the Anchor Point property and change it to **185**. This creates a second anchor point and completes the pair needed to animate the property. Click Enter or Return to accept.

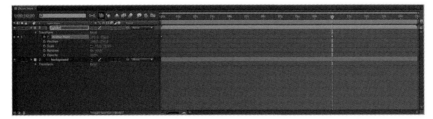

Two is the minimum number of keyframes required to create animation.

13   Click on the playhead and drag it to the beginning of the Timeline. Press the spacebar on your keyboard to preview the animation. The globe layer slides to the right, while the background layer is static.

14   Save your file by choosing File > Save or by pressing Ctrl+S (Windows) or Command+S (Mac OS) on the keyboard.

Animating rotation

Animating rotation allows you to spin a layer around its central z-axis. You can use it to simulate a swinging pendulum, the hands of a clock, or a flipping coin. In this exercise, you will animate the layers in the Archaic Wheels composition to spin a series of decorative circles around a common center point.

In this exercise, you will work with one of the imported Illustrator compositions that were added to the project earlier in the lesson.

1   If it is not already open, open your Lesson4-working.aep project that you saved at the beginning of this lesson. This project has the Photoshop and Illustrator compositions that were imported previously, along with the folders that were automatically created to organize each file's individual layers.

2   In the Project panel, double-click on the Archaic Wheels comp to preview it in the Composition panel and Timeline. If necessary, change the magnification of the Composition window so that you can see the comp area. In the figure below, it is set to Fit up to 100% percent, but the exact setting you need will depend on your monitor size and resolution.

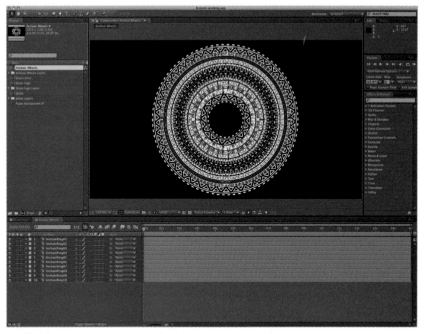

Double-clicking on any composition immediately causes it to preview in the Composition panel.

3   In the Timeline, click on the first layer, ArchaicRing01, to highlight it. To reveal the Rotation property, press the **R** key on your keyboard.

There are keyboard shortcuts for revealing each layer property: P is for Position, A is for Anchor Point, R is for Rotation, T is for Opacity, and S is for Scale. A good mnemonic device for remembering them is the acronym PARTS. Using these keyboard commands will hide any other layer properties that are visible. To reveal multiple properties at once, hold down the Shift key while using the shortcut.

4   Make sure your playhead is at the beginning of the Timeline (0;00;00;00) and click the Time-Vary Stopwatch (⬤) to the left of Rotation to enable animation for this property and create the first keyframe.

5   Drag the playhead to the end of the Timeline (15 seconds). For this animation you will make the ring rotate five times. Click the first number in the rotation value, change it to **5**, and press the Enter (Windows) or Return (Mac OS) key on your keyboard. This causes the ring to rotate once every three seconds in order to complete five rotations.

The first field in the rotation value is the number of times to make a complete rotation, and the second field is the finishing angle.

A quick way to jump to the beginning or end of your Timeline is to use the home and end keys found on your keyboard's extended keypad. If using a laptop, you may need to access these keys by using the FN key.

6   Move the playhead back to the beginning of the Timeline and press the spacebar on the keyboard to preview the animation. The ring rotates clockwise five times between the start of the time line and the end, or approximately one rotation every 3 seconds. Press the spacebar again to stop the rotation.

7   In the Timeline, click on the second layer, ArchaicRing02, to highlight it and reveal the Rotation property by pressing the **R** key on your keyboard.

8   Again, make sure your playhead is at the origin of the Timeline and click the Time-Vary Stopwatch (●) to the left of Rotation to enable animation for this property and create a keyframe.

A keyframe is automatically created when the stopwatch icon that enables animation for the property is turned on.

9   Again, drag the playhead to the end of the Timeline (15 seconds), and type -5 in the first numerical text field for the number of rotations and press Enter (Windows) or Return (Mac OS) to create the new keyframe. This creates an animation that rotates counter-clockwise.

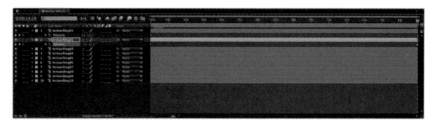

Once animation has been enabled for a property, any change to the value of that property creates a keyframe at the playhead's current position.

10   Save your file by choosing File > Save or by pressing Ctrl+S (Windows) or Command+S (Mac OS) on the keyboard.

Using layer parenting to ease repetition

The wheel graphic used in this exercise actually consists of a series of concentric circles, each with its own design and each on its own layer. You have just animated the first two layers moving in opposing directions, but what about the others? If you want to continue the pattern and have each circle rotating in the opposite direction as its predecessor, you could add keyframes to all them manually, but this would be a bit tedious. All these individual keyframes would also create a nightmare if you decided to change the timing of the animation later. A situation like this is where parenting becomes important.

Parenting is a tool for eliminating the repetition that is often inherent in complex animations. With it you can link layers together so that one layer will follow another. Child layers inherit Position, Rotation, Anchor Point, and Scale properties from their parent layer, but not Opacity. A real advantage of parenting is that while a layer follows the movement of its parent, this movement is relative, so each property can still have its own independent keyframes.

In this exercise, all the odd-numbered layers will be the children of layer 1, while all the even-numbered layers will be the children of layer 2.

1 In the Timeline, click on layer 3 to highlight it. Hold down the Ctrl (Windows) or Command (Mac OS) key on your keyboard and click on layers 5, 7, and 9 to highlight them as well.

Hold down the Ctrl (Windows) or Command (Mac OS) key to highlight non-sequential layers.

2 In the Parent pane to the right of the Layer Switches pane, click the drop-down menu for layer 3 and choose 1.ArchaicRing01 as the parent for all the odd-numbered layers.

When multiple layers are highlighted, any change made to the properties of one of them is made to all them.

3 Click on layer 4 to highlight it. Hold down the Ctrl (Windows) or Command (Mac OS) key on your keyboard and click on layers 6, 8, and 10 to highlight them as well.

4 In the Parent pane, click the drop-down menu for layer 4 and choose 2.ArchicRing02 as the parent for all the even-numbered layers.

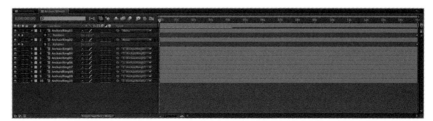

Because parenting creates movement that is relative to the original layer's movement, you can adjust each layer's properties as needed.

5 Move the playhead to 0, then press the spacebar on your keyboard to preview the animation. Press the spacebar again to stop animation. then save your file by choosing File > Save.

Animating position

Perhaps the most common type of layer animation is positional animation. When working with two-dimensional layers, you animate both the X and Y position values, which appear in the Timeline panel in the form of 500, 300. Remember that when working in the Timeline, the X position (horizontal) value comes first, followed by the Y position (vertical) value. In this section you will animate the Dison logo to make it begin off screen and then fly into view.

1 If it is not already open, open your Lesson4–working.aep project that you saved at the beginning of this lesson. This project has the Photoshop and Illustrator compositions that were imported previously, along with the folders that were automatically created to organize each file's individual layers.

2   In the Project panel, double-click on the dison logo comp to load it into the Composition and Timeline panels. The problem that you have here is that the comp's background color is black and so is the logo, so much of the logo is currently not visible.

In After Effects, the traditional background color is black.

3   Choose Composition > Composition Settings to open the Composition Settings dialog box.

You can also use the keyboard shortcut Ctrl+K (Windows) or Command+K (Mac OS).

4   In the dialog box, click on the Background color swatch to open the Background Color dialog box. Type **165** for the R (Red), G (Green), and B (Blue) color values. This sets the background color to a neutral gray.

5   Click OK to close the Background Color dialog box and click OK again in the Composition Settings dialog box.

6 Notice that the comp is composed of three visible layers: globe, DISON, and worldwide. The fourth layer, dot on I, is not visible at the moment. For this animation, the two parts of the logo are going to fly in from opposite sides of the screen. So the first thing you will do is parent the globe layer to the DISON layer.

In the Timeline, click on the globe layer's Parent drop-down menu and select 3. DISON as its parent layer. Repeat this action to parent the dot on I layer to the 3. DISON layer as well.

Even though the dot on I layer is currently hidden, it will be helpful to parent it to the DISON layer to preserve its relative position.

The dot on I layer is invisible because when the Illustrator files were imported, that layer's visibility had been turned off. When importing comps from Photoshop and Illustrator, you have a situation where what you see is what you get.

7 Click on the layer named DISON to highlight it, and press the **P** key on your keyboard to reveal the Position property.

8 Confirm that your playhead is at the beginning of the Timeline, and click the Time-Vary Stopwatch (●) to the left of the Position property to enable animation of this property and create the first keyframe.

9 Move your playhead to the 3 second (0;00;03;00) mark on the Timeline.

Remember that you can move the playhead by either dragging it directly, or clicking on the Current Time field in the upper-left corner of the Timeline panel, typing in 300, and pressing the Enter (Windows) or Return (Mac OS) key on your keyboard.

10 Click the Add or Remove Keyframe at Current Time button; it is a diamond icon (◆) to the far left of the Position property. This creates another keyframe at the playhead's current position on the Timeline. The new keyframe is created with the same values as the one before it. This acts as the keyframe for the final position of the layer.

The Add or Remove Keyframe at Current Time button is very helpful in a situation like this where you already have your artwork on screen in what you intend to be its final location. It is also a very good way to create static or placeholder keyframes when you simply want to continue to hold a property at a previous value.

Click on the arrow (◄) to the left of the Add or Remove Keyframe at Current Time button. This is the Go to Previous Keyframe button, and causes the playhead to jump to the previous keyframe of this property.

Click the Go to Previous Keyframe button.

11 Change the magnification of the Composition window so that you can see the comp area and the background area outside of it. In the figure below, it is set to 25 percent, but the exact setting you need will depend on your monitor size and resolution.

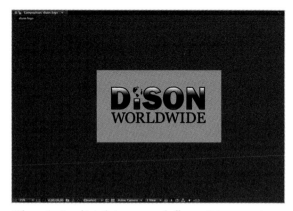

When animating objects that move on and off screen, it is necessary to zoom out to see the area around the comp border.

12 Back at the beginning of your Timeline, place your cursor over the DISON layer's X position property. The cursor changes from the familiar black arrow to a finger icon with two horizontal arrows. This icon indicates that you are hovering over a dynamic text slider.

In one motion, click and drag to the left with your mouse while hovering over the X position field. As you do so, the value changes and the layer slides to the left. Change the X position until it reads -725. This operation will stop once you reach the edge of your screen, so you may have to repeat it several times. If you have a hard time making the text slider stop at -725, you can just click on the numerical field and type the value.

The text sliders are very helpful because they can show you the changes you are making as real-time previews.

13 If necessary, move the playhead back to the beginning (0;00;00;00) of the Timeline. Then click on the layer named worldwide, press the **P** key on your keyboard to reveal its Position property, and click on the Time-Vary Stopwatch (⏱) to enable animation for this property and create the first keyframe.

14 Press the **K** key on your keyboard. This causes the playhead to jump to the next visible keyframe. Click the Add or Remove Keyframe at Current Time button (◆) to insert a second keyframe.

You can jump between keyframes on the Timeline by pressing the J and K keys on the keyboard. J jumps to the previous keyframe while K jumps to the next keyframe. If there are no further keyframes, the shortcuts jump to the beginning or end of the Timeline. You can also navigate from keyframe to keyframe using the Go To Next and Go To Previous arrows to the side of the property name display as you did before, but they are limited to the specific property they are attached to.

15 Move the playhead back to the beginning of the Timeline and change the layer's X position value to **2700**. This pushes it to the right outside of the composition border.

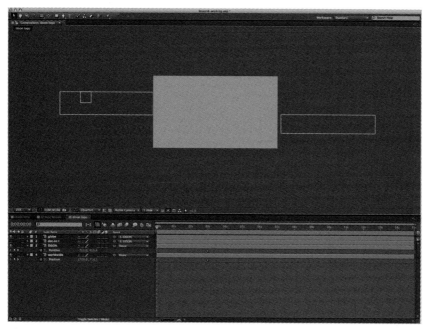

The text layers begin off screen and fly in to form the logo.

16 Preview the animation by pressing the spacebar on your keyboard. You now have an animation in which the words fly in from opposite sides of the screen and come together to form the logo.

17 Save your file by choosing File > Save.

Understanding motion paths

A motion path is the visual representation of the movement of a layer. Motion paths are shown when you animate special properties such as Anchor Point and Position. The motion path appears as a series of small dots along a line. Each dot represents the position of that layer at each frame of the animation. The property keyframes are represented by small squares along the motion path. Motion paths appear as straight lines but on closer examination, they can be seen to have control points that allow them to be bent and warped. In this exercise, you will warp the motion path of the DISON layer so that instead of moving in a straight line it appears to make a short hop to appear on screen.

1   Move your cursor to the beginning of the Timeline and click on the DISON layer to highlight it. You should see the motion path in the Composition panel.

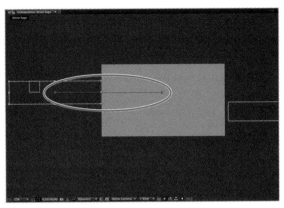

When a layer is highlighted, its motion path is visible.

2   Click on the small square icon at the beginning of the motion path that represents the keyframe so it is highlighted. You may need to change your zoom magnification to do this. This reveals its direction lines, which will allow you to edit the shape of the path. Motion paths can be warped only at keyframes by manipulating these lines.

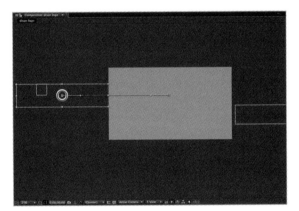

Directional handles are only visible when the keyframes they correspond to are selected.

In order to see directional handles, you can select the keyframe in either the Composition or Timeline panel; the results will be the same.

3 The small circle at the end of a direction line is the direction handle. Click and drag the direction handle up, which causes the motion path to curve upwards. Move the direction handle until the path matches the figure below.

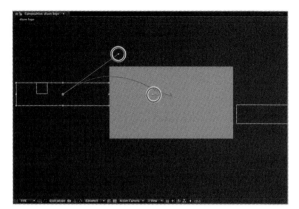

The height and curvature of the path are determined by the length and angle of the direction line.

The direction lines and handles can sometimes be a little hard to see and you may have to increase the magnification of the Composition panel to make them visible.

4 Move your playhead to the beginning of the Timeline and press the spacebar to preview your animation. The DISON layer now travels along an arcing path instead of a straight line.

5 Save your file by choosing File > Save.

Using layer motion blur

There is an optical trick that appears in video and photography in which objects in motion can be made to appear blurry. This effect, called motion blur, is something that people have become accustomed to over time. Computer graphics typically don't include this motion blur effect automatically and as a result their movement can seem unnatural and unrealistic. Any layer can have its motion blur enabled to create more visually appealing animations. In this exercise you will add motion blur to the animated logo to enhance the illusion of motion.

1 If it is not already open, open your Lesson4-working.aep project that you saved at the beginning of this lesson. Double-click on the dison logo composition to make it active in the Composition and Timeline panels.

2 Move your playhead to the 2 second mark (0;00;02;00) and adjust the magnification of the Composition panel so that you are zoomed in enough to see the details of the logo. You will notice that the two parts of the logo appear perfectly clear and this seems a little unrealistic and static. Adding blur to them will improve the sense of movement.

By default, computer animations don't normally have motion blur, which can make the animations seem unrealistic.

3 Click the Motion Blur layer switch (⬤) for the *DISON* and *worldwide* layers. Notice that nothing happens; the layers are still not blurry. This is because the Motion Blur effects don't automatically preview in the Composition panel, but you can change this.

4 Click the Motion Blur Comp button (⬤) located at the top of the Timeline panel to enable motion blur for all layers that have their layer switches set at the top of the Timeline panel. The stock Motion Blur effect is very subtle and may hardly even appear noticeable at its current settings. In the next part of this lesson, you will adjust the motion blur effect to produce a stronger effect.

5 Save your file by choosing File > Save.

Adjusting Motion Blur settings

If you are lucky, just applying motion blur produces the effect you want, but if not, you can adjust the composition's Motion Blur settings. Keep in mind that any change to these settings will affect all layers with the motion blur switch enabled. The two most important settings to control the effect are Shutter Angle and Shutter Phase. Increase the Shutter Angle to strengthen the effect; higher values equate to a stronger blur. When applying motion blur to a moving object, its position on screen changes, and may appear offset from when the effect wasn't applied. You can use the Shutter Phase effect to adjust this offset, which is helpful when precise position or timing is required.

1 With the dison logo comp active in the Composition and Timeline panels, move the playhead to the beginning of the Timeline and preview the animation. Notice that the moving layers do have a motion blur applied to them but it is a little weak. You will edit this effect now.

2   Choose Composition > Composition Settings to open the Composition Settings dialog box. You can also press Ctrl+K (Windows) or Command+K (Mac OS) on your keyboard to open the dialog box.

The Composition Settings dialog box allows you to make changes to the properties of the composition.

If the menu item is grayed out, it is probably because the comp is inactive; simply click anywhere in the Timeline or Composition panel to activate it and try again.

3   In the Composition Settings dialog box, click on the Advanced tab at the top.

4   Click on the Shutter Angle value and change it to **720**. Click OK to exit the dialog box.

The Shutter Angle value controls the amount of blur for the Motion Blur effect.

5 Move the playhead to the beginning of the Timeline and preview your animation. The Motion Blur effect is much stronger that it was at the beginning of the exercise.

6 Save your file by choosing File > Save.

Using blending modes

For users of Adobe Photoshop, blending modes should be very familiar. Blending modes allow you to control how the content of two or more layers mix or blend together. By default, layers interact in a very straightforward fashion: opaque areas of layers simply cover and hide anything below them. But you can change this to create more interesting compositions. In this exercise, you will add a new shape layer to the comp and use blending modes to make it tint the layers below it.

1 If it is not already open, open the Lesson4-working.aep project that you saved at the beginning of this lesson. In the Project panel, double-click on the Dison Intro comp to make it active in the Composition and Timeline panels.

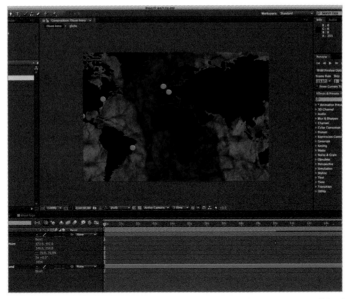

Double clicking on a composition in the Project panel opens it in the Composition and Timeline Panels.

2 Deselect all the layers in the Timeline by choosing Edit > Deselect All.

You can also use a keyboard shortcut, Ctrl+Shift+A (Windows) or Command+Shift+A (Mac OS), to deselect all layers. The reason you have to deselect all your layers is that if you try to use any of the shape tools with a layer still highlighted, the tools do not create a shape layer; they instead create a mask on the active layer. You will learn all about masks in Lesson 5.

3 From the Tools panel at the top of the After Effects interface, click on the Rectangle tool (▦) to select it as your active tool. This activates the Fill and Stroke options to the right.

Activating the shape tools automatically enables the properties for Fill and Stroke.

4 Click on the word Fill in the Tool panel to open the Fill Options dialog box, and choose the second button to fill the new shape with a Solid Color. Confirm that the drop–down menu is set to Normal, the Opacity is 100 percent, and the Preview checkbox is enabled, and click OK to close the dialog box. The Fill is the interior color of a vector shape and you can set it to a solid color, a linear or radial gradient, or none.

Shapes can be assigned fill and/or stroke colors before or after they are created.

5 Click on the color swatch to the side of the word Fill to open the Shape Fill Color dialog box. Choose a dark blue color as the Fill by setting the RGB values to R: **5**, G: **16**, B: **103**. Click OK to close the dialog box.

Instead of typing in the color values you could choose the colors visually using the slider and color box on the left side of the dialog.

6   Click on the word Stroke in the Tool panel to open the Stroke Options dialog box, and choose the first button to set the new shape's Stroke to None. Confirm that the Preview checkbox is enabled and click OK to close the dialog box.

The stroke is the outline of a vector shape, and by choosing None, you disable it so that this shape only has a Fill color.

7   Double-click on the Rectangle tool in the Tools panel to create a rectangle that is the same size as the composition. Because the new layer is placed above the two previous layers, the entire Composition panel is filled with blue.

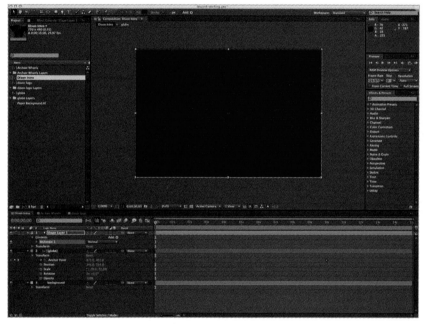

Double-clicking on any shape tool will automatically create a shape that conforms to the size of the composition.

You can also create a new rectangle shape by clicking and dragging with your cursor in the Composition panel. This allows you to create a shape of any size.

8   Click on the new Shape layer to highlight it. Press the Enter (Windows) or Return (Mac OS) key on your keyboard to make the layer name editable and change it to **Overlay**. Press Enter/Return again.

9   Click on the Expand Transfer Controls Pane button (🔲) in the lower-left corner of the Timeline panel to reveal the (Blending) Mode controls, and change the Overlay layers mode from Normal to Soft Light. This gives the composition a soft purple tint.

10 In the Timeline, drag the Overlay layer below the globe layer so that the color tinting only affects the Background layer.

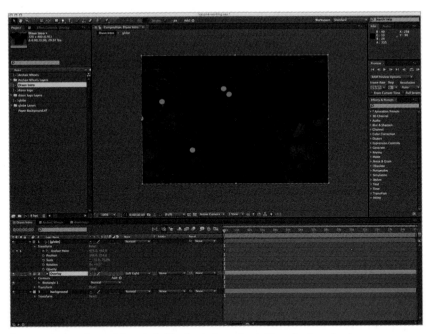

Layers can be dragged up and down in the Timeline to change the stacking order at any time.

11 Save your file by choosing File > Save.

Applying layer styles

Layer styles are sets of pre-built effects, such as drop shadow and outer glow, that map almost exactly to their Photoshop counterparts. They are intended to extend the usefulness of Photoshop imports and provide you with a set of easily editable effects. In this exercise, you will add a drop shadow layer style to the map graphic layer in the Dison Intro composition.

1 If it is not already active, double-click on the Dison Intro comp to make it active in the Composition and Timeline panels.

2 Click on the globe layer to make it active and choose Layer > Layer Styles > Drop Shadow. A new property group named Layer Styles is added to the Timeline and a Drop Shadow is now visible in the Composition panel.

3 Click on the reveal triangle for the Drop Shadow style and set the following options:

- Blend Mode: Multiply
- Color: Black (R: 0, G: 0, B: 0). You must click on the color swatch to see RGB values.
- Opacity: 50%
- Use Global Light: Off
- Angle: 0 x + 116.0
- Distance: 11.0
- Spread: 0.0 %
- Size: 5.0
- Noise: 0.0%
- Layer Knocks Out Drop Shadow: On

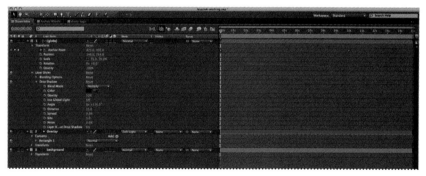

Clicking on the reveal triangle for a layer style will show or hide all the style's options.

The best way to learn what the different properties of the layer styles do is to experiment with them. If you are a Photoshop user, you will find that they compare almost exactly to the layer styles in that program.

As you are setting the values for the drop shadow's properties you will notice that they all have Time-Vary stopwatches. Nearly every property in After Effects, whether it belongs to a layer style, transform property or effect, can be animated. In fact, the entire process of creating and animating properties with keyframes is the same, regardless of what you are animating.

4 Save your file by choosing File > Save.

Understanding nested compositions and precomposing

Complex projects are rarely created as a single composition; instead, they are the result of multiple comps that are animated individually. This process of placing one comp inside of another is called nesting. Nesting allows you to create sequential or consecutive animations because each comp has its own independent Timeline. Precomposing is a technique that allows you to create a comp from layers already on your Timeline and replace those layers with the new comp. It can be a very helpful technique when you want to combine multiple layers into a new comp, so that you can apply effects or transformations to all them simultaneously, or as a tool for keeping the Timeline panel orderly.

Adding nested styles

In this exercise you will add the Archaic Wheels and dison logo comps that you animated at the beginning of the lesson to the Dison Intro composition.

1   If it is not already open, open the Lesson4-working.aep project that you saved earlier in this lesson, and double-click on the Dison Intro comp to make it active in the Composition and Timeline panels.

2   In the Project panel, click on the Archaic Wheels comp and drag it into the Timeline. Place it at the top of the layer stack so that it becomes the top-most layer.

When you drag footage into the Timeline, a black line appears to indicate where the new layer will be added.

3   The new layer's size and position need to be adjusted to better fit this comp. With the Archaic Wheel layer highlighted, press the **P** key on your keyboard to reveal the Position property. Next, hold down the Shift key and press the **S** key, to reveal the Scale property as well.

If you want to remove a visible property, you can hold down the Shift key and press the keyboard shortcut that corresponds to the property.

4 The chain link icon to the right of the Scale values constrains the proportions, ensuring that if you change the horizontal scale, the vertical scale will change by a relative amount, maintaining the appearance of the layer. Confirm that constrain proportions is turned on by confirming the chain link icon is visible and change either of the Scale values to **75** percent. While still large, this will make it a more manageable size.

5 Click on the X position property and change it to **0** (zero). Change the Y position property to **480**. This moves the layer's anchor point to the lower-left corner of the comp. Your work should now look like the figure below.

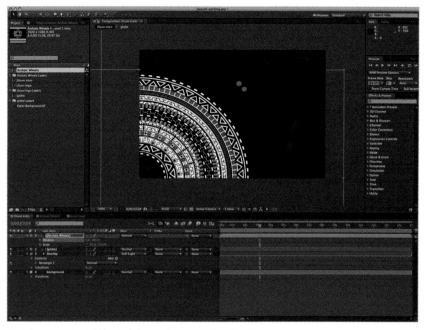

Nested comps are treated like single layers whenever you transform them.

6 If it is not already open, click the Expand Transfer Controls Pane button ( ) in the lower-left corner of the Timeline panel to reveal the Blending Mode menus. Choose Soft Light as the blending mode of the Archaic Wheels layer. This allows the colors from the lower two layers, globe and background, to mix with the colors of the wheel, producing a more subtle design.

7 Drag the dison logo comp from the Projects panel and place it at the top of the layer stack in the Timeline. Then, with the Dison logo layer highlighted, press the **S** key to reveal the Scale property. Next, hold down the Shift key and press the **P** key on your keyboard to reveal the Position property as well.

8 With the Constrain Proportions option enabled, change the Dison logo's Scale to **44**, change the X position to **365**, and the Y position to **240**. Preview your animation by dragging the playhead back and forth along the Timeline, a process called scrubbing.

Notice that the darkest parts of the logo are very difficult to see; the globe above the letter I, for example, is completely lost. You will correct this in the next step by adding a stroke to it.

9 With the dison logo layer highlighted, choose Layer > Layer Styles > Stroke. This adds the default red, 3-pixel stroke to the entire layer.

10 Click the reveal triangle next to the Stroke layer style in the Timeline panel to reveal its properties. Click on the Color swatch to open the Color dialog box and set the RGB values to R: **255**, G: **255**, B: **255** to give you a white stroke. Click OK to close the Color dialog box.

11 Click on the size value and change it to **2**. Leave all other values unchanged so that they match the example below.

The Stroke properties contain additional settings for opacity and position that were left unchanged in this exercise, though you may want to experiment with them.

12 Preview your animation by scrubbing the playhead. Notice that while the playhead is moving, the preview seems rough and blocky. Remember to pause at various points along the Timeline to allow the program to preview individual frames for you at high quality.

If you prefer, you can press the spacebar to preview the animation, but you will have to wait for the green bar at the top of the Timeline before the application can build a real-time preview. This may take some time, depending on the power of the computer you are using.

The white stroke makes the logo much easier to view.

13 Save your file by choosing File > Save.

Pre-composing layers

The overlay and background layers are intended to be used together, so if one moves they should both move together. In a situation like this, combining them into a single composition is beneficial. In this exercise, you will pre-compose the overlay and background layers into a new comp, to make them easier to work with as a set.

1 Click on any area of the Timeline panel to make it active. You can tell the active panel by the orange border surrounding it. Over the last several exercises you have revealed several layer properties, and because of this it may be a little hard to find the lower layers in the Timeline without scrolling.

2 Choose Edit > Select All or use the keyboard shortcut Ctrl+A (Windows) or Command+A (Mac OS) to highlight all layers, and press Ctrl+~ (both Mac OS and Windows). This hides all the visible layer properties for the currently selected layers.

You can also use the Ctrl+~ keyboard command if you want to reveal all the properties of a selected layer.

3 Choose Edit > Deselect All or use the keyboard shortcut Ctrl+Shift+A (Windows) or Command+Shift+A (Mac OS) to deselect all the highlighted layers. Then click on the layer named Overlay, press and hold the Shift key on your keyboard, and click on the background. If you have followed along with every step up to this point in the lesson, these should be the two bottom-most layers in the composition.

Holding down the Shift key while clicking on layers allows you to select a sequential range of layers while holding down the Command (Mac OS) or Control (Windows) allows you to select layer out of sequence.

4 Choose Layer > Pre-compose or use the keyboard shortcut Ctrl+Shift+C (Windows) or Command+Shift+C (Mac OS) to open the Pre-compose dialog box.

Only the highlighted layers are included in the pre-compose operation.

5 Name the new composition **background comp**. The only other available choice would be to open the new comp as a tab in the Timeline. This is helpful if you want to edit it right away but is not required here.

Pre-composing can be a very helpful tool for keeping the Timeline panel neat and organized.

In the dialog box, there are two options for how the Pre-compose operation treats animation on the selected layers. Because this comp is made from a group of layers, the only available choice is to keep each layer's attributes intact and move them into the new comp. This is called creating an intermediate composition. Another alternative that you have when pre-composing individual layers is to leave all attributes in the comp. Effectively, this option would take the keyframes and effects on the layer and transfer them to the new comp. Click OK to close the dialog box and create the new comp. Your Timeline should now look like the figure below.

6 Save your file by choosing File > Save.

Creating a fade-in by animating Opacity and Scale

The final two properties built into all visible layers are Opacity and Scale. Opacity animations allow you to control the transparency of layers, while you can use Scale to manipulate the size of layers horizontally and vertically. In this exercise, you will animate the Archaic Wheel layer so that it fades in and scales down simultaneously to appear on screen.

1   If it is not already open, open the Lesson4-working.aep project that you saved earlier in this lesson.

2   Highlight the Archaic Wheel layer in the Timeline panel and press Ctrl+~ on your keyboard to reveal all this layer's Transform properties.

Technically, the Ctrl+~ command actually reveals all the attributes of a layer, not just the Transform properties.

3   Move the playhead to the 2 second (0;00;02;00) mark on the Timeline and click the stopwatch icons for the Opacity and Scale properties to enable animation of these attributes.

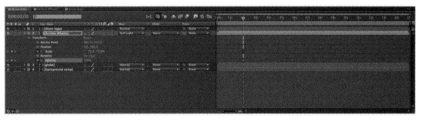

Because the layer is already at its final position in the comp, the ending keyframes of the animation are created first.

4   Move the playhead to the beginning (0;00;00;00) of the Timeline and change the layer's Opacity value to **0** (zero) percent. Make sure that the icon for Constrain Proportions is enabled and change its scale to **760** percent.

5   Preview the animation to see the ring appear on screen in time with the logo, creating a more synchronous and visually appealing animation. Depending upon the speed of your computer, this may take a moment to complete.

6   Save your file by choosing File > Save.

Congratulations! You have completed the lesson.

Self study

Use the elements provided in this lesson, or your own, to create an animation that uses nested compositions to create multiple levels of animation.

Review

Questions

1 When creating new compositions, how do you determine the size and frame rate to create them at?

2 What are the five transform properties that are inherent in all visual layers?

3 What is the point of using the Motion Blur effect and how do you apply it?

Answers

1 New comps should always be set to match your output media.

2 Position, Anchor Point, Rotation, Opacity, and Scale.

3 You use motion blur to give layers a stronger sense of movement, slightly blurring them to mimic the look of moving objects on film. Each layer has to have its Motion Blur switch enabled, and the Composition Motion Blur switch must be enabled, to preview the effect.

What you'll learn in this lesson:

- Creating vector based masks to show and hide areas of a layer.
- Importing animated Photoshop layers and use them as track mattes.
- Keying-out background colors for use with a blue or green screen.

Working with Masks, Track Mattes, and Keys

Masks, track mattes, and keys offer three ways of creating transparency on a layer. You can use these tools together or separately for both motion graphics and compositing projects. In this lesson, you will work with a series of video files to both create standalone effects and prepare files for later compositing.

Starting up

You will work with several files from the ae05lessons folder in this lesson. Make sure that you have loaded the aelessons folder onto your hard drive from the supplied DVD. See "Loading lesson files" on page 4.

See Lesson 5 in action!

Use the accompanying video to gain a better understanding of how to use some of the features shown in this lesson. The video tutorial for this lesson can be found on the included DVD.

Setting up

As you work in After Effects, you will inevitably open and close many panels, depending on the type of project you are creating. However, when working through the projects in this book, it is important to have an interface that matches the lessons. To this end, you should always reset your workspace to the preset standard configuration.

1   Choose Window > Workspace > Standard to set your current workspace configuration.

2   Choose Window > Workspace > Reset "Standard" to reset the standard workspace in case you have modified it at some point.

Working with masks

In After Effects, masks are vector-based paths used to hide or reveal parts of a layer. If you use applications such as Adobe Photoshop and Illustrator, you will find masks in After Effects to be similar to clipping masks in those applications, with the exception that masks in After Effects can be added to video as well as still images. You can create masks from simple primitive objects such as rectangles and circles, import them from vector-based drawing programs, such as Adobe Illustrator, or create them from scratch in After Effects using the Pen and shape tools. As with other vector objects, masks are composed of a series of vertices connected by line segments. These vertices represent single points in space and are used to anchor each line segment so that you can create lines and shapes. You can animate these vertices to create masks that change their shape and size to match the content of your video. For example, you can animate the Mask Path frame by frame to create a mask that moves to follow the path of a cloud traveling across the sky or a car traveling along the road.

Like vector paths in other applications, masks in After Effects can have both corner and Bézier vertices. It is the vertices that determine the length and shape of the line segments between them. Corner points always create straight lines, while Bézier points are used to create curved line segments. The curvature of these Bézier curves is determined by the direction handles attached to each vertex, as shown in the illustration below.

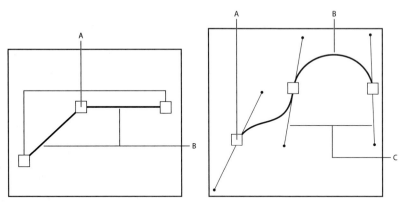

A. Vertex. B. Line segment. C. Direction handle.

In After Effects, you can have multiple masks on a single layer. When this is the case, the order of masks in the Timeline panel, called the stacking order, and the properties of each individual mask will determine the cumulative effect of all the masks.

Design programs such as Photoshop and Illustrator use the term anchor point to refer to vertices. Even though the terminology is different, they are the same object.

Understanding mask properties

You use masks to control the transparency of layers. The first mask you create affects the alpha channel of the layer, and any additional masks that you create interact with all masks above the first. All masks have four properties that you can modify and animate:

Mask Path: This property specifies the position of the points that make up the mask. This property is animated whether you want to move all the points of a mask or only some of them, to create the effect of a mask moving around a layer or changing shape.

Mask Feather: This property specifies the softness of the edge of a mask. As a result of feathering, a mask's edge becomes more transparent, creating the effect of a layer with edges that fade into its background.

Mask Opacity: This property sets the amount of influence that a mask has over the visibility of the layer it is on. When you set this property at its default value of 100 percent, the layer the mask encloses will be at full opacity.

Mask Expansion: You can use this property to expand or contract the edges of a mask.

In addition to these properties, each mask also has a mode setting that controls how it interacts with the mask above it in the stacking order:

None: When you set the mode to None, the mask does not affect the alpha channel of the layer. This setting is helpful when you are using the mask as the target of an effect or as a motion path for text.

Add: The effect of the mask is added to the masks above it in the stacking order. The Add setting makes the content of a layer visible.

Subtract: The effect of the mask is subtracted from the masks above it, creating a hole. If it is the only mask on a layer, this setting hides anything inside the mask.

Intersect: The effect of this mask adds to the ones above it. In areas where the mask does not overlap with the masks above it, the result is complete opacity. However, when all masks on a layer are set to Intersect, only the areas formed by overlapping these masks are visible.

Lighten: The effect of this mask is added to the masks above it. When multiple masks intersect, the highest Mask Opacity value is used for all overlapping areas.

Darken: The effect of this mask is added to the masks above it. When multiple masks intersect, the lowest Mask Opacity value is used for all overlapping areas.

Difference: The effect of this mask adds to the ones above it. When using multiple masks on a layer, masks with this setting behave as if they are set to Add when not overlapping. When overlapping with another mask, this setting allows the mask to behave as if it is set to Subtract mode.

The cumulative effects of these modes vary, depending on the number of masks on a layer, their position in the mask stacking order, and the mode of each. The best way to get a feel for how different mask modes will interact is to experiment with them.

Creating masks with the shape tools

You can use the shape tools in After Effects to create masks or shape layers. They create both simple shapes such as rectangles and circles, and more complex ones such as polygons and stars. Once created, these masks can be transformed, modified, and animated. In this exercise you will create a new project, import a video file, and create a rectangular mask for it.

1 Choose File > New > New Project. If you have another project open and haven't saved it, you are prompted to do so now.

2 In the new project, choose File > Import > File. In the Import dialog box, navigate to the ae05lessons folder and then to the video subfolder.

Double-click on the Creating Shape Masks.mov file to import it. This footage is composed of a montage of video and still images of Washington, D.C.

3 In the Project panel, drag the Creating Shape Masks.mov footage item to the New Composition button (▣) at the bottom of the panel. This creates a new comp that matches the properties of the video file.

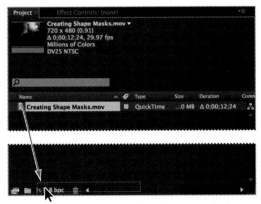

Dragging any piece of footage to the New Composition button creates a new comp that matches the dimensions and length of that footage.

4 In the Timeline panel, click on the Creating Shape Masks.mov layer to highlight it, and press the Enter (Windows) or Return (Mac OS) key on the keyboard to make the name field editable. Rename this layer **video 1**.

5   With the video 1 layer highlighted, click on the Rectangle tool (■) to make it active, then click and drag in the Composition panel to create a mask on this layer.

In order to create a mask, you must have a layer selected before using the shape tools.

As you are working in the Composition panel, a new mask is being created and added to the Timeline panel. You should now see Mask 1 below the layer name along with its mask path property. Don't worry about the size and shape of the mask for now, as you will adjust it in the next exercise.

6   Choose File > Save As. Navigate to the ae05lessons folder on your hard drive. In the Save As field, name the file **Creating Shape Masks-working.aep** and click Save.

Selecting and manipulating masks

If you can always draw your masks perfectly the first time, you must be one really lucky individual. It is more likely that once you have created a mask you will have to edit its size or position at least once. Editing a mask can seem a little confusing to the novice, but with a little practice you will master it. If you are used to other programs that work with vector graphics such as Adobe Illustrator and Photoshop, then you will be used to having two cursors, one to manipulate the entire path and the other to edit individual vertices. After Effects is a little different in that both the mask's position on screen and the position of each vertex are adjusted using the Selection tool. In this exercise, you will use the proportional grid as a guide to refine the shape and size of the mask that you created previously.

1   With the Creating Shape Masks-working project open, choose Proportional Grid from the Grid and Guide Options drop-down menu at the bottom of the Composition panel.

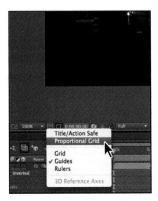

The proportional grid is very helpful in creating shapes that are a relative size to the composition.

2   Click on the video 1 layer in the Timeline panel to highlight it. This reveals the edge of Mask 1 along with its vertices.

3   In the Composition panel, double-click on any one of the mask's vertices. This causes a bounding box to appear around the mask. A bounding box defines the boundary area of a mask and is used to move, rotate, or scale it.

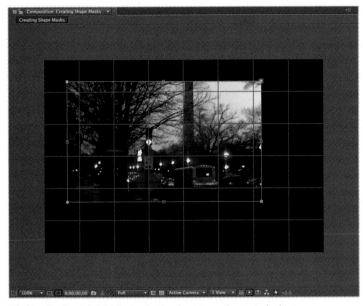

The bounding box is helpful for transforming the entire mask as a single object.

The vertices located at the corners and sides of a bounding box are used to scale it. However, if you position the Selection tool (↖) outside the box, it becomes a curved cursor allowing you to rotate the mask. Clicking and dragging on a corner point scales the mask horizontally and vertically, while the points on the top, bottom, and sides constrain the scaling to that axis.

4 Using the Selection tool, adjust the points of the bounding box to match the example below. The mask's new shape and position make it the height of the first two rows of the proportional grid, while its width should extend slightly outside the comp to each side.

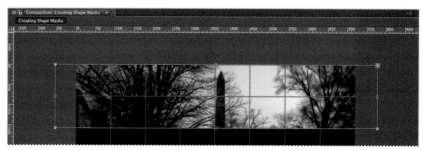

Clicking and dragging on a corner point of a bounding box lets you scale it both horizontally and vertically simultaneously while the middle points constrain the scale to a specific direction.

5 With the video 1 layer still selected, click on the Rectangle tool (▪) to make it active. Click and drag with your cursor in the Composition panel to create a new mask on the left side of the panel that is the width of the first two columns of the grid, and whose height extends slightly beyond the boundary of the comp.

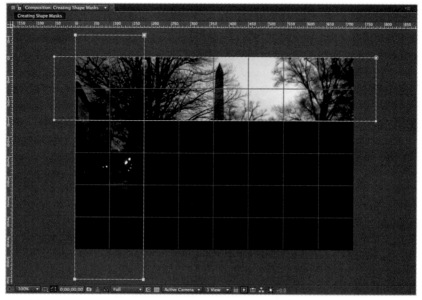

A single layer can have multiple masks applied to it, this can be used to create interesting visual effects as the different masks interact with one another.

6 Save your file by choosing File > Save.

In the next exercise, you will animate the position of these masks to create an effect where the masks slowly reveal the entire image.

If you use Adobe Illustrator, then you will be happy to know that you can bring vector paths from Illustrator into After Effects using a simple copy-and-paste command.

Animating the position of masks

Of the four mask properties described previously, not one of them is named Mask Position. Because they are part of a layer, masks do not have the same type of position property that layers do. Instead, the Mask Path property is used to animate all a mask's transform properties. It does this by storing a keyframe for the position of each individual vertex along a mask's path. So when vertices are moved either separately (such as when you change the shape of a path) or as a group (such as when you scale, rotate, or move it), the Mask Path property is the one that is affected. In this exercise, you will animate the position and shape of the two masks that you created previously to reveal the video.

1 With the Creating Shape Masks-working project open, highlight the video 1 layer and press the **M** key on the keyboard twice in rapid succession to reveal all the properties of Mask 1 and Mask 2.

*Pressing the **M** key only once shows only the Mask Path property.*

2 Click on Mask 1 to highlight it and press the Enter (Windows) or Return (Mac OS) key on your keyboard to make the name field editable. Rename it **horizontal mask**. Click on Mask 2 to highlight it and press Enter/Return again, and rename it **vertical mask**.

3 Move the playhead to the beginning of the Timeline and click the Time-Vary stopwatch (⏱) next to the Mask Path property of both masks to enable animation for this property and create the first keyframes.

Even though it may seem counter intuitive, animating the Mask Path property will affect its position.

4   Move the playhead to the 1 second (0;00;01;00) mark on the Timeline. In the Timeline, click on the mask named horizontal mask; this highlights the mask in the Composition panel and selects all its keyframes. In the Composition panel, place your Selection tool (k) on the lower-right vertex of the mask.

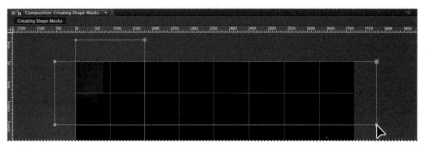

In After Effects, the cursor changes to indicate a new function of the currently active tool.

The Selection tool becomes an arrowhead without a stem. This icon indicates that the tool will move the selected vertex.

Click on the vertex and drag the mask to the bottom of the composition. Stop when the mask occupies the lower two rows of the proportional grid.

After you begin dragging the mask, you can press and hold the Shift key on your keyboard to constrain the movement of the mask to a straight line.

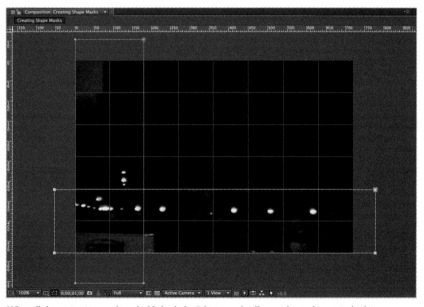

When all the vertices in a mask are highlighted, the Selection tool will move the mask as a single object.

5 In the Timeline, click on the mask named vertical mask. Just as before, this highlights the mask in the Composition panel and selects all its keyframes.

In the Composition panel, place your Selection tool on the lower-right vertex of the mask.

Click on the vertex and drag the mask to the right of the composition. Stop when the mask occupies the right two columns of the proportional grid.

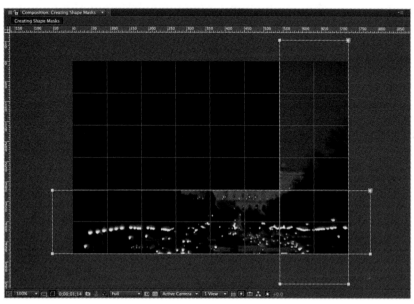

It is important to make sure that all the vertexs in a mask are highlighted when you try to move it in the Composition panel.

6 Move the playhead to the 1 second 14 frame (0;00;01;14) mark on the Timeline and click on the Add/Remove Keyframe switch (◆) to the left of the Mask Path property for both masks. This creates a new keyframe that has the same value as the ones at 1 second. They act as placeholders to keep the masks in their current position for 15 frames.

The Add/Remove keyframe switch adds keyframes at the current position of the playhead.

7 Move the playhead to the 3 second (0;00;03;00) mark on the Timeline and move the masks as you did in steps 4 and 5, so that they match the figure below.

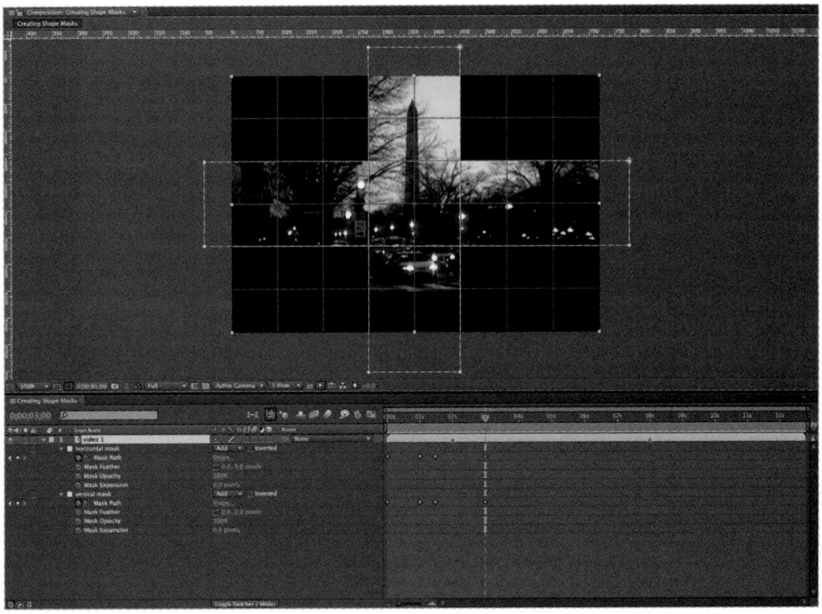

The mask should now be positioned towards the middle of the composition.

8 Move the playhead to the 3 second 14 frame (0;00;03;14) mark on the Timeline and again click the Add/Remove Keyframe switch to the left of the Mask Path property for both masks to create another pair of placeholder keyframes.

9 Move the playhead to the 5 second (0;00;05;00) mark on the Timeline.

Now that you have moved the masks to the middle of the composition, you will animate their paths to scale them up so that they reveal the entire video.

In the Timeline, click on the mask named horizontal mask to highlight it and show the mask's vertices.

10 With the mask selected, double-click on the lower-right vertex in the Composition panel to activate the mask's bounding box.

Place your Selection tool (↖) on the middle top control point of the bounding box, and click and drag upwards until the mask has reached the composition border.

Repeat this process with the lower middle control point to reveal the entire video.

11 In the Timeline, click on the mask named vertical mask to highlight it and show the mask's vertices. With this mask selected, double-click on its lower-right vertex in the Composition panel to activate the mask's bounding box.

Place your Selection tool on the middle-right control point of the bounding box, then click and drag right until the mask has reached the composition border.

Repeat this process with the middle-left control point until the mask extends to the composition border on both sides.

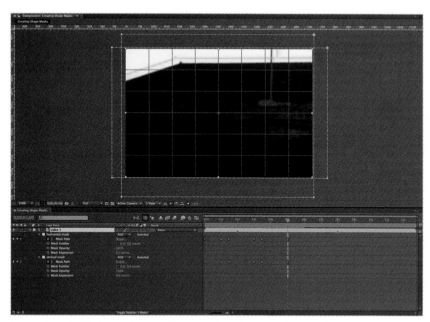

Because the mode of both masks is set to Add, any area that either one overlaps is visible.

 It is okay if the masks extend past the borders of the composition.

12 Preview the Timeline to see your animation, and then save your file by choosing File > Save or by pressing Ctrl+S (Windows) or Command+S (Mac OS) on the keyboard.

Creating freeform masks

Geometric masks can be very useful design tools, especially when creating title sequences or other onscreen graphics. However, the weakness of only being able to create masks in uniform shapes becomes obvious the moment you need a mask to follow a specific contour. In situations like this, the Pen tool is one of the most powerful and helpful tools you have. Similar to the Pen tool in applications such as Photoshop and Illustrator, the Pen tool in After Effects creates vector paths that when closed, form masks that hide or reveal areas of a layer. The Pen tool creates vertices that can be either corner points to form straight lines or Bézier points to form curves.

In this exercise, you will create a path composed of both curves and straight lines that follows the contour of an object in a video source, and you will then animate the mask's vertices as the object's position on screen changes.

Setting up the project

1   Choose File > New > New Project. If you haven't already saved your current project, you are prompted to do so now. This creates a new Untitled project for you to work in.

2   Once you have created the new project, choose File > Import > File. In the Import dialog box, navigate to the ae05lessons folder, and then to the video subfolder.

Double-click on the Creating Freeform Masks.mov file to import it. This footage is composed of a montage of automobiles driving towards the camera.

3   In the Project panel, drag the Creating Freeform Masks.mov footage item to the New Composition button (⬛) at the bottom of the panel. This creates a new comp that matches the properties of the video file.

4   Again choose File > Import > File and navigate to the images subfolder of the ae05lessons folder. Locate the file named Tony Black Presents.tif and double-click to import it.

In the Interpret Footage dialog box, choose Straight–Unmatted as the Alpha channel type and click OK.

Drag the file into the Creating Freeform Masks composition above the video layer.

Alpha channels allow layers to have transparent areas.

5   Click on the first layer, the one named Tony Black Presents.tif. Press the Enter (Windows) or Return (Mac OS) key on your keyboard and rename it to 3D logo.

Rename the Creating Freeform Masks.mov layer to **car video**.

6 Move the playhead to the 5 second (0;00;05;00) mark on the Timeline and click on the 3D logo layer to highlight it.

The beginning of a layer is called the In Point, while the end is called the Out Point. When added to the Timeline, image layers are assigned a duration that matches the length of the composition. You can trim them (that is, you can adjust their In and Out points) so that you can specify their duration. Place the Selection tool (⬏) at the beginning of the layer duration bar. When a double-headed arrow appears, press and hold the Shift key on your keyboard and click and drag the layer's In Point to the playhead.

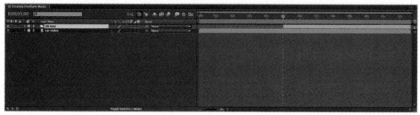

If you prefer keyboard commands, then pressing Alt+[(Windows) or Option+[(Mac OS) trims the In Point of the layer to the playhead.

Holding down the Shift key makes the layer In Point snap to the playhead.

7 With the 3D logo layer still highlighted, move the playhead to the 7 second (0;00;07;00) mark on the Timeline.

Place the Selection tool at the end of the layer duration bar. When a double-headed arrow appears, again press and hold the Shift key on your keyboard and click and drag the layer's Out Point to the playhead.

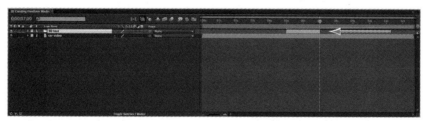

If you prefer keyboard commands, pressing the Alt+] (Windows) key or Option+] (Mac OS) trims the Out Point of the layer to the playhead.

8 With the 3D text layer highlighted, press the **I** key on your keyboard to jump to the In Point of the layer. Choose File > Save As. Navigate to the ae05lessons folder on your hard drive. In the Save As field, name the file **Creating Freeform Masks-working.aep** and click Save.

In the next exercise, you will use the Pen tool (◊) to create a mask that conforms to the contour of the car.

Drawing the mask

For this exercise, you will create a mask that follows the right-side contour of the car and then extends outside the composition boundaries to enclose the content of the 3D logo layer.

1 With the Creating Freeform Masks-working project open, choose Proportional Grid from the Grid and Guide Options drop-down menu at the bottom of the Composition panel.

2 Set the Magnification ratio to 200% from the drop-down menu on the left side of the Composition panel.

You may have to pan the Composition panel using the Hand tool (☜) so that you see the top of the proportional grid. Depending on your screen resolution, you may have to do this several times while creating the mask.

While hovering over the Composition panel, you can press and hold the spacebar on the keyboard to toggle the active tool to the Hand tool.

3 Click on the 3D logo layer in the Timeline to highlight it, and click on the Pen tool in the Tools panel at the top of the After Effects interface.

Click with the Pen tool at the topmost point of the second vertical grid line from the left to create the first vertex of your path.

Masks are always applied to the layer that you want them to affect.

4 Place the Pen tool where the grid line intersects the top of the car and click to create a second vertex.

Use the Pen tool to create vertices, the line segments are created between them automatically.

5 Place the Pen tool at the top of the windshield just below the T in Tony. Click and drag with the mouse to create a curved line segment that matches the shape of the car's roof.

To create curved line segments, you must always remember to click and drag with your mouse.

As long as you don't release the mouse button, the program allows you to reposition the curve you are currently creating, but the moment you release the button, the line segment is created.

There are two problems that you must now address. The first is that the default mask color is yellow, which is very hard to see against the video's white sky background. The second problem is that the graphic that you want to mask is currently obstructing your view of the car's shape.

6 Press the **M** key twice in rapid succession to reveal the mask's properties in the Timeline.

To the left of the mask name is a small yellow box that represents the mask's color; click on this box to open the Mask Color dialog box.

The default color of the mask's outline can be changed to make it easier to view.

Change the color to R: **0**, G: **78**, B: **255** and click OK. This results in a light-blue mask color that is much easier to see.

Fixing the visibility issue is even easier; just click off the Video switch for the 3D logo layer. A layer doesn't have to be visible for you to create a mask on it.

7 Returning to the Composition panel, if you were to try and create the next vertex, it wouldn't fit the curve of the windshield exactly. This is because of the position of the third vertex's point's directional handle, which must be adjusted so that it matches the beginning angle of the windshield's arc.

Place the Pen tool on the downward-pointing directional handle. When you do this, the pen changes to a karat symbol (∧). This is the Convert vertex tool and you can use it to refine directional handles. Click and drag with the tool to move the handle so that it matches the images below. The length and angle of a directional handle control the height and angle of the curve it creates.

As you become more skilled with using the Pen tool, you will have to make fewer adjustments to your initial Mask Paths.

The best color to use when creating a mask makes depends on several factors, including the colors used in the video footage, the color settings of your monitor and personal preference. You can change the mask color at any time until you find a color that makes it easy for you to work with the mask.

8   Place the Pen tool at the top of the side mirror, then click and drag to form the curve of the windshield.

Adjust the directional handle as in the previous step to match the length and angle of the mirror's curve.

Continue to create the vertices and adjust the direction handles until you reach the top of the bumper.

As you practice and use the pen tool more often you will be able to better estimate where to place your vertices.

9   Now at the top of the bumper you want to create a straight line, but that smooth point will always try to create a curve, and so it has to go. Place the Pen tool over the direction handle until it becomes the Convert vertex tool, then click and drag the direction handle into the vertex. This collapses it, creating a corner point and now allows you to create a straight line.

Smooth points have two directional handles while corner points tend to have only one or zero direction handles.

10   Click at the outside edge of the bumper, and then again outside of the composition border to the right. Create another vertex outside the top right of the composition as shown in the image below.

When creating masks it is often helpful to extend them just beyond the composition border as it is easier than trying to create a mask that conforms to the border edge.

11   Place the Pen tool on top of the first vertex that you created at the beginning of this exercise until it becomes a pen head icon (![pen icon]) with a circle next to it. This indicates that you will close the path and complete the mask.

12   Click the 3D logo layer's Video switch back on to see the effect of the mask. Any part of the layer that is outside of the Mask Path is hidden.

13   Save your file by choosing File > Save.

Animating the shape of masks

The Mask Path property stores the position of all the individual vertices in a mask. When the position of these vertices is changed over time, After Effects automatically interpolates the change to create a smooth blending of the different Mask Paths. In this section, you will animate the vertices of the path that you previously created so that it will adjust as the car moves in the video.

1   With the Creating Freeform Masks-working project still open, set the Magnification ratio of the Creating Freeform Masks composition to Fit Up To 100% in the drop-down menu on the left side of the Composition panel.

2   In the Timeline, click on the 3D logo layer to highlight it; this also highlights all the vertices of the mask.

With the playhead at the In Point of the layer, activate the Time-Vary Stopwatch (🔘) for the Mask Path property to enable animation and create the first keyframe. When animating the Mask Path property, any change made to the position of the mask's vertices creates a new keyframe.

3   Press the **O** key on the keyboard to jump to the Out Point of the layer. Now that the car is in a different position, you must adjust the mask. Click on the layer name to deselect the mask.

It is very important that you deselect the mask before attempting to move the vertices. When the mask is selected, the Selection tool moves all its points simultaneously, which isn't what you want to do here.

Using the Selection tool, click on the vertex that used to be at the top of the car's roof, and drag it up so that it matches the new position of the car.

Repeat this with the rest of the vertices until they all match the figure below. For some of the vertices, moving them won't be enough, and you will also have to adjust their direction handles to match the curvature of the car.

Once you begin to animate the Mask's path some of the vertices may seem unnecessary. What ever you do, do not delete any of them. Deleting a vertex will remove that same vertex across all your keyframes, changing the shape of the mask so that it may no longer match the contour of the car.

This adds a second keyframe to set the ending position of the mask

4 Move the playhead to the 6 second (0;00;06;00) mark on the Timeline. This places it right in the middle of the two keyframes you just created.

Adjust the mask vertices to match the contour of the car, as shown below.

You now have a third Mask Path keyframe in between the first two.

5 Move the playhead to the 5 second 15 frame (0;00;05;15) mark on the Timeline. This places it right in the middle of the first two keyframes. Again adjust the mask vertices to match the contour of the car.

6 Move the playhead to the 6 second 15 frame (0;00;06;15) mark on the Timeline. This places it in the middle of the last two keyframes. Adjust the vertices again so that they follow the shape of the car.

7 In the Timeline, change the Mask Feather property to 2.0. With the Constrain Proportions switch enabled, you only have to change one of the values.

8 Move the playhead to the 4 second (0;00;04;00) mark on the Timeline and preview the animation. The mask is now animated so that it hides the 3D logo as the car moves across the screen.

This example needed very few keyframes to work well; the more movement there is in the video, the more keyframes are usually required. This technique of adding keyframes in between keyframes is more efficient than adding a new keyframe to every frame sequentially.

9 Save your file by choosing File > Save or by pressing Ctrl+S (Windows) or Command+S (Mac OS) on the keyboard.

Understanding track mattes

Track mattes, also called traveling mattes, are a technique used to hide or reveal areas of a video layer. They are similar to masks in this way but very different in how they create the effect. While masks use vector-based line shapes to isolate areas of a layer, track mattes can use either alpha or luminance. Alpha is the technical name for what most people call transparency, while luminance is a measure of brightness.

A very common source for track mattes is a text layer. This technique, often called clipping masks in programs such as Photoshop and Illustrator, allows the text layer to mask out the layer below it so that you can see an image or video inside the text shapes. Because track mattes are layers, you can animate them by adding keyframes for the layers' properties such as scale, position, and vertices, or by animating effects that change their appearance.

Creating track mattes

You can create track mattes from the alpha or luminance channels of video or still-image layers. Layers with an alpha channel are usually the easiest to work with, though using luminance can be just as successful if you have a high-contrast image to use as your matte. There are two things to keep in mind when working with the track matte feature in After Effects: the first is that the track matte must be the layer right above the one to be masked out and the second is that you can only have one track matte per masked layer. If you need to have multiple layers acting as a track matte, then you must first combine those layers into a new composition.

In this part of the lesson, you will use an animation that has been built in After Effects to construct a track matte effect to reveal a hidden video layer.

1   Choose File > Open Project and navigate to the ae05lessons folder. Locate the file named Creating a Track Matte.aep and double-click to open it. If you haven't already saved your current project, you are prompted to do so now.

Preview the animation by scrubbing the playhead, and you see that the project contains an animation where text is flying in from off screen and then disappears by flying forward towards the viewer.

2   Choose File > Import > File and navigate to the video subfolder of the ae05lessons folder. Locate the file named Creating Track Mattes.mov and double-click to import it.

3   Drag the Creating Track Mattes video file from the Project panel to the Timeline. Place it below the [Comp-in 1 Minute] layer. This covers the layer with the Washington, D.C. title on it, but that will be automatically corrected once you turn the top layer into a track matte.

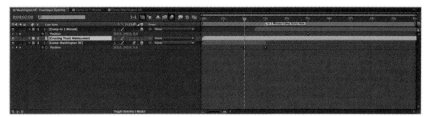

Track mattes must either be layers with very high contrast (usually black and white) or layers that have transparent areas.

4   Click the Expand or Collapse Transfer Controls Pane switch located at the bottom left of the Timeline to expand the pane and reveal the Track Matte option.

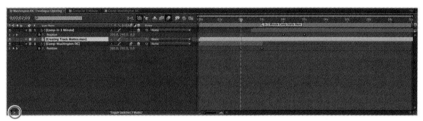

The different panes in the timeline panel can be expanded or contracted at will.

5   Choose Alpha Matte "[Comp-in 1 Minute]" from the TrkMat drop-down menu in the pane. The video layer is completely hidden. Preview the animation, and you can see that the video is now only visible when the content of the [Comp-in 1 Minute] layer is onscreen.

The video layer now uses the alpha channel of the layer above it to control what areas are visible. Wherever the layer is opaque, you can now see the video layer, so as the animation progresses you can see more and more of the video until it is fully revealed.

6   Choose File > Save As. Navigate to the ae05lessons folder on your hard drive. In the Save As field, name the file **Creating a Track Matte-complete.aep** and click Save.

Creating mattes from animated Photoshop files

While there are some people who only work in After Effects, the majority of users also work with other graphics programs such as Photoshop and Illustrator to create artwork either as standalone graphics to animate or to build support graphics such as masks and track mattes. Most people are familiar with Photoshop as an image editing and painting program, but what many do not realize is that Photoshop also has a Timeline very similar to After Effects. The Photoshop animation that is used in this section was created by animating a brush to fill the screen over time, until the entire screen is black. When this document is imported into After Effects, it will be treated as a video file. In this section, you will create a new project and use an animated Photoshop file to create a track matte for a video file.

1   Choose File > New > New Project. If you haven't saved your current project, you are prompted to do so now.

2   In the new project, choose File > Import > Multiple Files and navigate to the video subfolder of the ae05lessons folder. Locate the file named Creating Track Mattes.mov and double-click to import it. When the Import dialog box opens, again navigate to the images subfolder of the ae05lessons folder and double-click on ani track matte.psd to import it as well. Importing a Photoshop file will open a secondary options dialog, in this Import options dialog box, choose Footage as the Import Kind and confirm that the Merged Layers radio button is active.

   Click OK to import this file.

Photoshop files have extra options that can be set in a secondary dialog box when they are imported into After Effects.

   When the Import dialog box appears again, click the Cancel button to close it.

3 Click on the Creating Track Mattes.mov footage item in the project panel and drag it into the empty Timeline panel. This automatically creates a new composition with the same properties and name as the video file, and is the most efficient way to create a composition that matches the settings of a specific piece of footage.

Creating a composition in this manner set the background color to the color that was used the last time a comp was created. Choose Composition > Composition Settings and at the bottom of the dialog box click on the background color swatch and change it to black.

4 Drag the ani track matte.psd footage item into the Timeline and place it above the video layer. You should now see a large, black ink spot on a white background covering the composition.

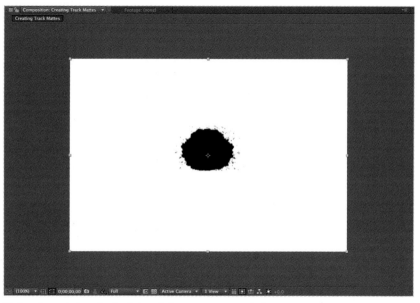

Track mattes must always be placed above the layer you want to apply them to.

5 Scrub the playhead to preview the Photoshop animation. The ink spot multiplies until it completely overtakes the white background. The high-contrast image will make a good luminosity-based track matte.

If it is not already visible, expand the Transfer Controls pane by clicking the switch (⊙) on the lower-left corner of the Timeline panel.

6   Choose Luma Inverted Matte "ani Track Matte.psd" from the video layer's TrkMat drop-down menu. The video layer is now visible in the shape of the ink spot, and surrounding it you see the composition's background color.

Track Mattes are often used to create custom transitions in video like the one you are creating in this exercise.

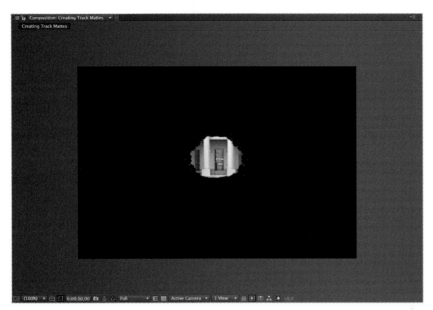

Animated Photoshop files can be a very good way of creating a custom transition and they are a lot of fun to make.

7   Choose File > Import > File and navigate to the video subfolder of the ae05lessons folder. Locate the file named Creating Shape Masks.mov and double-click to import it.

Drag the Creating Shape Masks.mov footage item from the Project panel to the Timeline and place it below the video layer so that it become the new lowest layer.

8   Preview the animation and then save the file by choosing File > Save As. Navigate to the ae05lessons folder on your hard drive. In the Save As field, name the file **Photoshop Track Mattes_final.aep** and click Save.

Creating a chroma key

Masks and track mattes can be very good tools for isolating and revealing areas of a video image. However, when dealing with subjects that move a lot or where you need a great deal of detail, trying to use either technique would be extremely time-consuming. This is where chroma keying comes in. Chroma keying allows you to composite two images together by removing a specific color from one of them. Most often, chroma keying is used when you shoot video of your subject in front of a blue or green screen and then replace it with a different background. This technique is often referred to as color keying, blue screening, or green screening and is often used on television in weather reporting and in films that make extensive use of virtual backgrounds and set extensions.

In this part of the lesson, you will create a new project, import the video you will use, and set up the Timeline.

1 Choose File > New > New Project. If you haven't saved your current project, you are prompted to do so now. If you have just opened After Effects it will not prompt you to save the default project if you haven't added anything to it.

2 Choose File > Import > File and navigate to the video subfolder of the ae05lessons folder. Locate the file named greenscreen footage.mov, then press and hold the Control key (Windows) or command key (Mac OS) on your keyboard, and click on Creating Track Mattes.mov to add it to your selection. Click the Open button to import both files.

Once the files have been imported you can preview them in the footage panel by double clicking on either footage item in the Project panel. You have worked with the Creating Track Mattes file earlier in this lesson, here it will be used as the background of the composition. The Greenscreen-BusinessMan video file is footage of an actor in a suit shot in front of a greenscreen.

3 Choose Composition > New Composition to open the Composition Settings dialog box.

- Change the Composition Name to **Secret Agent Man**.

- Set the Preset drop-down menu to NTSC DV.

- Set the Resolution drop-down menu to Full.

- Set the Duration to 8 seconds (**0;00;08;00**) and the background color to black (R: **0**, B: **0**, G: **0**).

The NTSC preset is used for creating footage that conforms to the standard definition broadcast standard used in the United States.

Click OK to close the Composition Settings dialog box and create the new comp.

4 Drag the Creating Track Mattes.mov footage item from the Project panel to the Timeline, and then add the greenscreen footage.mov item above it.

5 The greenscreen footage was shot in a high definition widescreen format and then converted to the standard definition file you see here. Because of this there are black bars at the top and bottom of the video frame that place the actor's body above the base of the composition frame.

If necessary, move the playhead to the beginning (0;00;00;00) of the Timeline and then click on the greenscreen footage.mov layer and press the **P** key on your keyboard to reveal its position property. Change the Y position to 300. This makes the new position value 360.0, 300.0. Move the actor to the base of the composition so that he won't appear to be cut off at the waist once the layer's background is removed.

When combining video shot at different aspect ratios of sizes it is often necessary to adjust positioning manually.

6   Choose File > Save As. Navigate to the ae05lessons folder on your hard drive. In the Save As field, name the file **Creating a Chroma Key-working.aep** and click Save.

Creating a garbage matte

The first step in the chroma keying process is to create a garbage matte to isolate the subject and the area immediately around it. A garbage matte is a quickly drawn mask; it doesn't have to be that precise, just a rough shape that removes any extraneous areas of the video frame. When using a green screen, technically the only area that matters is the area around your subject, especially if it is moving. Often you will see parts of the set, such as a light stand or the frame holding the screen at the edges of the video frame; the garbage matte blocks all those elements out.

An important point to remember about using a garbage matte is that it has to completely enclose the subject. If the subject is moving, the vertices of the mask may need to be animated as well. When used properly, garbage mattes also allow the keying effect to be focused on a smaller area, which allows it to be applied more quickly. This footage is an example of a situation where the greenscreen is only used behind the actor. If you look at the right and left sides of the video you can clearly see the black border and part of the frame that was used to hold up the screen for the video shoot. A garbage matte will be used to hide these areas, as well as the black letter boxing bars at the top and bottom.

1   With the Creating a Chroma Key-working project still open, click on the green screen footage layer in the Timeline to highlight it.

Move the playhead to the 6 second and 24 frame (0;00;06;24) mark on the timeline. The actor moves a bit and this point on the timeline show the point at which he is furthest to the right of the screen. When you have greenscreen footage where your subjects are moving, it is important to make sure your garbage matte is large enough to accommodate it.

2   With the greenscreen footage layer still selected click on the Rectangle tool in the Tool panel to activate it.

Click and drag with the Rectangle tool from the upper left of the green screen footage to the lower right to create a mask like the one seen in the figure below. You want to create the mask so that the figure ends up with only the green screen background around him. Make sure that the mask crops out the stand that was used to hold up the greenscreen, you should be able to see it on the far right and left of the video frame.

The mask doesn't have to be exact, which is why it's called a garbage matte.

When creating a garbage matte, you want to use enough vertices that you will be able to animate it if necessary to fit the movements of your subject.

3   Preview the video file by dragging the playhead slowly back and forth. The subject moves a little left and right in this video, so make sure the mask doesn't cut off any part of him. The most likely areas to cause a problem are the top of his head, and his left and right arms.

As you are doing this, you may notice that you have misjudged the space you will need around the figure; at this point you can adjust the vertices of the mask with the Selection tool, as you learned how to do earlier in this lesson.

In this lesson, you only have to create a garbage matte that is large enough to not cut out any of the figure's action. To do this, you create a rather large mask, an alternative approach would be to create a smaller mask that matches the contours of the figure and then animate the position of the points on the path using the Mask Path property so that it adjusts to the actual movement of the figure and stays as tight as possible in all frames.

4   Save your file by choosing File > Save, you can also use a keyboard command, by pressing Ctrl+S (Windows) or Command+S (Mac OS) to save the file..

Creating a chroma key

There are actually several different chroma keys that you can use in After Effects. On this footage, you will apply a color range key that allows you to select multiple colors to remove instead of only one. This is very helpful in situations such as this, where the background screen may not be evenly lit, producing a range of green or blue tones. In this part of the lesson, you will add a Color Range key to remove the green screen background.

1   With the Creating a Chroma Key-working project still open, click on the green screen footage layer in the Timeline to highlight it.

     If necessary, move the playhead to the 6 second and 24 frame (0;00;06;24) mark on the Timeline.

2   With the green screen footage layer highlighted, choose Effect > Keying > Color Range. This opens the Effect Controls panel if it is not already open so that you can edit the properties of the effect you have just applied.

The default setting of the Color Range effect will sometimes be enough to remove parts of the footage.

A side effect of applying the key is that a part of the figure's body will automatically be removed; you will correct this when you set the actual key color in the next step.

3   The Color Range effect uses three eyedroppers: one to set the key color and the other two to add or remove colors from the color range to key out. Click on the top Eyedropper tool (🖋) in the Effect Controls panel next to the black-and-white thumbnail of the layer, and then click on the green background near the man's left shoulder; this begins keying out the background.

Use the three Eyedropper tools to set the color range to key out.

4   Click on the second eyedropper (🖋), the one with the plus sign next to it, this eyedropper is used to add colors to the color range that the effect removes. With this eyedropper active, click on the area that is still green near the man's head. Since the green screen consists of a wide range of colors, depending on which area of green you click on your results will vary.

Use the second eyedropper to add areas to the color range to key out.

5   Again click on the eyedropper with the plus sign next to it and continue to use it to add green areas to the selection until there is only a slight green border surrounding the man.

Look at the Black and White thumbnail in the Effect Controls panel; it represents the alpha channel of the layer. The white area represents the opaque parts of the layer while the black areas represent the parts that are transparent. Your goal is to have the contour of the figure entirely white, while the rest of the layer is entirely black.

You have to click on the plus eyedropper tool every time you want to add a new color to the color range that you want to make transparent.

The Color Range effect tends to leave a fringe around your subjects, which you can remove by adding additional effects to the layer.

6 In the Effect Controls panel, change the Fuzziness to **30**. Fuzziness is the tolerance of the effect; increasing the value for tolerance widens the range of colors being selected. In this case, it removes some of the green fringe around the figure.

You often need to complement a chroma key with additional effects before it can be considered acceptable.

If you increase the fuzziness too much, it begins to remove the figure as well; when using a chroma key, it is usually better to err on the side of caution, leaving a fringe around the subject and using other tools to remove it later. This is what you will do in the next part of this lesson.

7 Save your file by choosing File > Save or by pressing Ctrl+S (Windows) or Command+S (Mac OS) on the keyboard.

Refining the matte

After the chroma key is created, it is often necessary to refine the mask that it creates in order to remove additional background area. Instead of trying to overdo any one effect, it is usually best to combine different effects until you have removed the color background. Now that you have used the Color Range Key effect to create a matte, you will enhance it with a Matte Choker effect and then the Spill Suppressor effect. When using the Matte Choker effect, there are three properties you must be aware of:

Geometric Softness: This property is used to specify the largest possible spread or choke for the effect.

Choke: This property sets the amount of the choke or spread. You use positive values to choke the matte, and negative values to spread it.

Gray Level Softness: This property specifies how feathered (soft) the edges of the matte are. A setting of 100 percent produces the softest edge and can sometimes appear blurry.

Each property has both a primary (labeled with the number 1) and secondary (labeled with the number 2) effect. The reason for the repeat settings is so that the effect can be used to both spread and choke a matte simultaneously. In general, the secondary settings are used to inverse the effect of the primary ones.

1   With the Creating a Chroma Key-working project still open, click on the green screen footage layer in the Timeline to highlight it.

2   Choose Effect > Matte > Matte Choker to apply the Matte Choker effect to the footage.

The Matte Choker is an effect that you use to both choke (tighten) and spread (loosen) a matte. You can use it to fill in transparent holes that can be created as a result of using a keying effect or to modify the edge of a keyed area while preserving its shape. The effect can perform both a choke and spread because it duplicates the effect using a primary and secondary set of properties.

The default settings of the effect will choke the matte and cut off the outside edge of the figure, removing much of the green fringe.

The default settings of matte choker can be helpful but you will usually want to adjust them to fit the specifics of your footage.

3   Move the playhead to the beginning (0;00;00;00) of the timeline and then press the spacebar to preview the animation; the edge of the matte looks a little rough and jagged. You can also still see areas of the greenscreen in the space between the figure's arms and body. This is especially noticeable when his arms are moving. Move the playhead back to the 6 second and 24 frame (0;00;06;24) mark on the timeline. In the Effect Controls panel make the following adjustments to the properties of the Matte Choker effect.

- Change the value for Geometric Softness 1 to **3.0**.

- Change the value for Choke 1 to **50**.

- Change the value for Gray Level Softness 1 to **20%**.

This softens the matte edge for this footage so that is no longer appear so jagged and trims away less of the figure himself.

Finding the right settings for chroma-keying effects usually requires a lot of trial and error.

Keep in mind that the settings listed here are the result of trial and error. To achieve them, different settings were tested and previewed to find the ones that produced the best results. The settings that you use will vary, depending on the footage and your needs. Even in this exercise, depending on how tight you were able to make the initial color range key you may want to use different values on the Matte Choker effect to achieve a better result on your own footage.

4   Move the playhead to the beginning (0;00;00;00) of the timeline and then press the spacebar to preview the animation. You can still see those small areas of the greenscreen in the space between the figure's arms and body. To remove these you will go back to the Color Range effect and add these areas to the color range that is being keyed out.

Move the playhead to the 2 second and 15 frame (0;00;02;15) mark on the timeline. At this point you should be able to see semi-transparent area of the greenscreen between his arms.

In the Effect Controls panel change the Fuzziness property to 40. This will refine the key and help remove additional green areas.

5   There is still a slight green fringe around the figure; you can remove this using an effect named Spill Suppressor.

With the green screen footage layer highlighted, choose Effect > Keying > Spill Suppressor to add the effect. The default setting suppresses blue and must be adjusted to work on the green fringe, but it's very difficult to select the green background with the Color Range effect enabled.

6   In the Effect Controls panel, disable the Color Range effect by clicking the *fx* switch to the left of the effect name.

With the effect now disabled, click on the eyedropper switch (↦) for the Color to Suppress property. With the eyedropper active, click on the green background to suppress it.

The ability to toggle effects on and off can be very helpful for preview purposes.

Re-enable the Color Range effect by clicking the *fx* switch back on.

If you find it difficult to see the results of the Spill Suppressor effect, you can disable and re-enable it to see how it neutralizes the green tint both around the edge and inside the figure.

When you click on the green background with the Color Suppression selector, the background turns gray. This effect only appears this way because the Color Range Keying effect has been disabled. Once all the layer's effects are active, again they are applied in the order they are listed in the Effect Controls panel.

7   Save your file by choosing File > Save or by pressing Ctrl+S (Windows) or Command+S (Mac OS) on the keyboard.

Self study

Reopen the Creating Shape Mask-working project that you created earlier in this lesson and experiment with changing mask modes on both masks to see what types of effects you can create using the exact same animation.

Review

Questions

1 What are the four properties of masks and what does each one do?

2 What are the two properties that a track matte can be based on in After Effects?

3 What is the reason for creating a garbage matte?

Answers

1 The Mask Path property specifies the position of the points that make up the mask. This property is animated whether you want to move all the points of a mask or only some of them, to create the effect of a mask moving around a layer or changing shape.

The Mask Feather property specifies the softness of the edge of a mask. As a result of feathering, a mask's edge becomes more transparent, creating the effect of a layer with edges that fade into its background.

The Mask Opacity property sets the amount of influence that a mask has over the visibility of the layer that it is on. Set at its default value of 100 percent, the layer the mask encloses will be at full opacity.

The Mask Expansion property expands or contracts the edges of a mask.

2 Alpha and luminance. Alpha is the transparency information of a layer, while luminance is the brightness information of a layer. Track mattes can be created by applying either the straight alpha or luminance information or by inverting it.

3 A garbage matte is used to remove extraneous areas of the background that aren't necessary for the chroma key effect.

What you'll learn in this lesson:

- Create and edit text
- Create and save text animators
- Apply animation presets
- Create and animate text that follows a path

Working with Text

Even in the days of film and video, text remains a very powerful tool for communicating ideas. The animation features in After Effects make it an extremely powerful application for working with text. In this lesson, you will learn about the different types of text and how to work with them.

Starting up

You will work with several files from the ae06lessons folder in this lesson. Make sure that you have loaded the aelessons folder onto your hard drive from the supplied DVD. See "Loading lesson files" on page 4.

See Lesson 6 in action!

Use the accompanying video to gain a better understanding of how to use some of the features shown in this lesson. The video tutorial for this lesson can be found on the included DVD.

Setting up

As you work in After Effects, you will inevitably open and close many panels depending on the type of project you are creating. However, when working through the projects in this book, it is important to have an interface that matches the lessons. To this end, you should always reset your workspace to the preset Standard configuration.

1 Choose Window > Workspace > Standard to set your current workspace configuration.

2 Choose Window > Workspace > Reset "Standard" to reset the standard workspace in case you have modified it at some point.

Creating text

Creating and editing text in After Effects is very similar to creating text in design applications such as Adobe Photoshop or Illustrator, and once you create it, the way you edit it is almost identical to how you would edit it in a word processing program. You can adjust most of the common text properties that you may be familiar with, such as font family and style, size, leading, tracking, and kerning. There are two kinds of text that you can create in After Effects: point text and paragraph text. In this exercise, you will create a new document and then add text to it. You will then be guided through how to format and animate that text. The text you will be working with in this lesson is from the poem "Jabberwocky" by Lewis Carroll.

Point Text: You create point text when you click with the Text tool and just start typing. This text lacks a frame, and a new line is only created when you press the Return (Mac OS) or Enter (Windows) key on your keyboard. Point text is good for stand–alone areas of text and offers a very intuitive way of working. It also works well when you want to create a headline or other small area of text, but it lacks the ease of use of paragraph text for longer text blocks.

Paragraph Text: This text behaves similarly to text in a word processing program. You create it by clicking and dragging with the Text tool to create a text frame of a set width and height. You can then type or paste text into this frame, and the text automatically wraps to form new lines as needed. When using Paragraph text, it is possible to place more text than the frame allows, causing the text to be hidden; this is called overset text. Paragraph text works when you have to fit text into a specific area of your composition or when working with large amounts of text.

1 Choose File > New > New Project to create a new project. Once the new project has been created, choose Composition > New Composition and in the New Composition dialog box, change the default name to **Jabberwocky**.

Choose NTSC DV from the preset menu and set the duration to ten seconds (00;00;10;00). Set the background color to black (R:**0**, G:**0**, B:**0**) and leave all other fields at their defaults and click OK.

2   From the Grid and Guide Options button at the bottom of the Composition panel, choose Title/Action Safe to display the Title-Safe and Action-Safe margins.

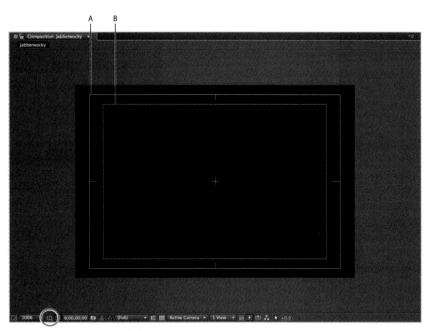

A. Action-Safe margin. B. Title-Safe margin.

The Title-Safe and Action-Safe margins are used in video to compensate for the fact that most televisions do not display the full image area of a video frame. The Action-Safe margin is the outer rectangle and represents approximately 90 percent of the available screen space, while the Title-Safe area represented by the inner rectangle is approximately 80 percent of the full frame size. If you want to be sure that your graphics, titles, and animations display on all television screens, you should keep them inside the Title-Safe boundary. These boundaries vary by television format and you should ignore them if creating graphics solely for display on computer monitors and projectors, as these devices display the entire video frame.

3   Click on the Horizontal Type tool (T) in the Tools panel to make it active. When you activate the Type tool for the first time, the Character and Paragraph panels automatically open.

4 The Character and Paragraph panels retain the last settings that you used to create or edit text. These values remain even when you shut the application down. It is usually best to set the initial text properties before you create the text, and then adjust them to fit each composition's needs. In the Character panel, set the font family drop-down menu to Georgia and the font style to Regular, and then set the font size to **40**. In the Paragraph panel, make sure the alignment is set to left. All other values should match those in the image below.

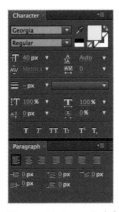

You can set text properties before or after you create the text.

5 In the Composition panel, click and drag from the upper-left corner to the lower-right corner of the Title-Safe margin to create a text frame.

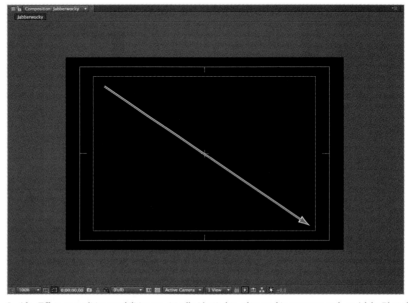

In After Effects, text-editing capabilities are virtually identical to other graphics programs such as Adobe Photoshop and Illustrator.

When you release the mouse, the text cursor becomes active. Type the following text:

Beware the Jabberwock, my son!

The jaws that bite, the claws that catch!

Lewis Carroll (1832–1898)

When displayed in the text box, it looks a little different than it does above. This is due to the way that paragraph text breaks to form new lines so that it doesn't exceed the width of the text frame. You will adjust the text in the next exercise.

Please note that you should press Enter (Windows) or Return (Mac OS) at the ends of the first and second lines of text, the way you see them above.

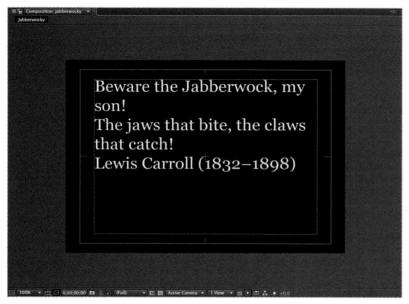

An advantage of paragraph text is that new lines are formed automatically, based on the width of the text frame and the amount of text.

6 Choose File > Save As. In the Save As dialog box, navigate to the ae06lessons folder, rename the file **Jabberwocky.aep**, and click the Save button.

Setting text properties globally

The text that you create in the Composition panel is called the source text, and it is placed on a layer in the Timeline. It has properties that you can adjust to create text that conforms to the needs of your project. You edit text properties using the Character or Paragraph panels. You can use the commands in the Character panel to control the appearance of individual characters of text (such as font family, size, and color), while you can use the Paragraph panel to change the formatting of each paragraph (such as margin alignment and the space between paragraphs). In this section, you will learn how to format the entire text area at once, and later you will format individual characters.

Character and Paragraph panel options

Character panel options

Font family: More technically called a typeface, this is a collection of letters, numbers, and symbols that all share a same overall design; examples include Georgia, Times New Roman, and Arial.

Font style: A variant of a typeface that usually modifies one property such as character thickness or rotation as in the case of bold and italic styles.

Font size: Specifies the size of the text in pixels.

Leading: Sets the space between the different lines of text. The term is taken from the days of printing when type was set by hand and strips of lead were used to separate the lines of text.

Kerning: Sets the space between any specific pair of letters. When you place the text cursor between a pair of letters, you can specify a numerical value, but when you select multiple letters or the entire text field, the only choices are Metrics, Optical, and Zero.

Tracking: Sets the letter spacing (the amount of space between groups of letters).

Stroke width: Specifies the thickness of the outline around the text.

Vertical scale: Sets the amount of vertical scaling on text characters. This setting does not affect the font size.

Horizontal scale: Sets the amount of horizontal scaling on text characters. This setting does not affect the font size.

Baseline shift: The baseline is the invisible line that the bottom of each line of text sits on. This setting specifies an offset to move text either above or below the baseline.

Tsume: Reduces the space to the left and right of a selected character by a specified percentage. While this setting is intended for use with Asian font families, you can apply it to western typefaces as well.

Note that in addition to the text properties listed above, there are six switches located at the bottom for Faux bold, Faux italic, All caps, Small caps, Super script, and Sub script.

Paragraph Panel options

Paragraph alignment: Similar to a word processing program, this property sets the alignment of all lines in the paragraph.

Left margin: Sets the amount of space that the paragraph is indented from the left side of the text box.

Right margin: Sets the amount of space that the paragraph is indented from the right side of the text box.

Space before paragraph: Sets the distance between the paragraph this setting is applied to and the paragraph before it.

Space after paragraph: Sets the distance between the paragraph this setting is applied to and the paragraph that comes after it.

First line indent: Sets the amount of indentation on only the first line of a paragraph. This is a similar effect to those seen in word processing programs when you place a tab at the beginning of a line.

1 With the Jabberwocky.aep file still open, activate the Selection tool (⬉) by clicking on it in the Tools panel. Then click once on the text box in the Composition panel to highlight it.

If the Character and Paragraph panels are not visible, you can reveal them by using the Window menu at the top of the application interface. Choose Window > Character or choose Window > Paragraph. Each panel also has a keyboard command to allow you to quickly toggle it open or closed. To reveal or hide the Character panel, press Ctrl+6 (Windows) or Command+6 (Mac OS), and to toggle the Paragraph panel, press Ctrl+7 (Windows) or Command+7 (Mac OS).

2 In the Character panel, adjust the font size, leading, and tracking properties as follows:

- Font size: **30**
- Leading: **50**
- Tracking: **2**

It is usually helpful to establish a general base setting that makes all your text visible.

These settings will provide a base to work from when you begin formatting the text to create a more visually appealing typographic design that makes all your text visible. These settings changed the formatting of all the text on this text layer because it had been highlighted with the selection tool. Later in this lesson you will modify the appearance of individual words and letters.

In this exercise, you are given the values that will work for this text, but when working on your own, you will have to decide what works best for you. Typing in values and then waiting to see the results is a slow and tedious process; it is usually better to use the text slider function of the cursor to try different values. Simply hold your cursor over the value you want to adjust until it becomes a hand icon (🖑), and then click and drag left or right to adjust the value. Your Composition panel's display adjusts in real time.

3 Choose File > Save to save your After Effects file with the new text settings. Do not close the file, as you will need it in the next exercise.

Formatting individual characters

As you have seen, text can be edited globally, but to achieve more interesting type effects, you need to make changes to the individual characters in a text field. When you select individual characters, you can edit them to create more visually appealing designs. When active inside a text frame, the cursor allows you to select any number of characters, words, or lines. Once selected, changes made in the Character and Paragraph panels affect only the highlighted text. This way of working with text is actually very similar to using a word processing program or editing the text when you send an e-mail, so most people find it an easy adjustment to make. In this section, you will edit individual characters and an individual word in the text to create a more interesting composition.

1   With the Jabberwocky.aep file still open and the Selection tool active, double-click on the text layer's name field in the Timeline panel to select it. Two things happen: the Type tool (T) activates and all the text on the layer becomes highlighted.

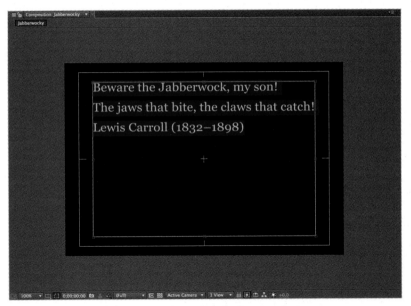

Double-clicking on a text layer is a very quick way of selecting the text on that layer.

2 Now that the text is selected and the Type tool is active, double-click on the word *Jabberwock* in the first line to select it. In the Character panel, change the font size, tracking, and vertical scale properties as follows. To display these options, you may need to undock the panel by clicking and dragging it by its name to the center of the work area.

- Font size: **50**

- Tracking: **–20**

- Vertical scale: **110%**

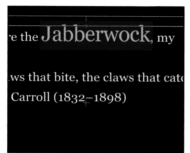

Changes that you make to text are visible in real-time.

This changes the word so that it appears narrower and taller compared to the other letters, allowing it to tower over them the way the Jabberwocky towers over the boy in the poem.

Double-clicking on any word with the Type tool automatically selects that word.

3 Tracking affects the amount of space between all words and letters equally, and the result of making it a negative value is that the letters in the word *Jabberwock* are now closer together. However, some of the letters may become too close and overlap each other, as the *r* and *w* do now. To fix this, you will change the kerning between this letter pair.

Kerning is the term used to refer to the space between any two letters. In this example, you will loosen the kerning between the r and the w to move them further apart.

With the Type tool still active, click on the space between the letters *r* and *w* in *Jabberwock*. Click on the Kerning value and type in **70**. This moves the letters farther apart and prevents them from touching one another.

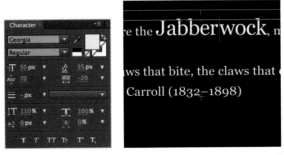

The kerning property only accepts numerical values when the text cursor is between a pair of letters. At any other time, it only accepts Metrics, Optical, and Zero as values.

4 Click and drag the Type tool over the *B* in *Beware* to highlight it, and change its font size property to **80**. As the letter becomes larger, it creates a strange appearance, because the rest of the words on the line don't line up with it any longer. To fix this, you will baseline shift the *B* so that its center lines up with the rest of the text.

The baseline is an imaginary line that all type sits on. This is why the bottoms of letters line up with one another. When you baseline shift text you can move it above or below this line.

In the Character panel, change the baseline shift value to **–28**. If the baseline shift option is not visible in the character panel, undock it by dragging the panel to the center of the work area. There now seems to be a little too much space between the letters *B* and *e*, and an adjustment to kerning will correct this. Click once in the space between these two letters and change the kerning value to **–40**.

 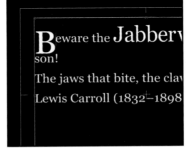

The baseline shift property works best when only applied to a portion of the text on a line.

5   One more adjustment—this time to the word *son!*—and this line should be done. Click once to place the text cursor in front of the *s* in *son!*. Then press the Tab key on the keyboard twice to insert two tabs and move the text over so that it is no longer directly underneath the *B*. The word is still a little close to the *B*, so press the spacebar on your keyboard twice to shift it over a bit more.

Change the kerning value to **–80**; this moves the word to the left and helps it line up better with the rest of the word *Beware*. Click three times on the word son to highlight the entire line, and change its leading value to **40**.

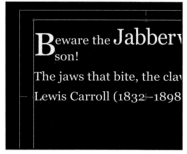

You can only edit leading when you select an entire line of text or the entire text box.

The great thing about betting creative with typography is that you have a great deal of freedom and control over how the composition will turn out. Each typeface is a little different in appearance, size, and formatting so my making subtle changes to individual characters of words you can produce widely varied results. When working on this exercise, you can achieve different results by adding extra spaces or changing the size of the text.

6   Select the word *jaws* and change its font size to **70**, and then adjust the value of baseline shift to **–10**. Select the word *claws* and sets its font size and baseline shift to the same values that you just used for *jaws*. The enlarged size places greater emphasis on these two words and gives them more impact in the composition.

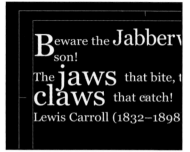

After Effects makes it very easy to try out different text formatting in your composition. You can easily adjust text properties to fit your needs.

7 Highlight the word *bite* and change its font size property to **50**, and then do the same for the word *catch*. Then select the exclamation point at the end of the poem and change its font size to **150**.

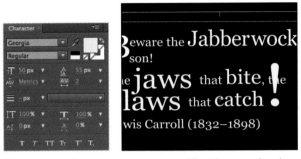

Changes made to character size can cause text on different lines to overlap when you have set a leading value.

8 Because of the size change in the last step, the text on the line above the exclamation point is now concealed. You can fix this by making an adjustment to kerning. Click in the space just before the exclamation point and change the kerning value to **600**. This reveals the text that was hidden underneath it.

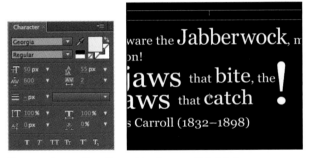

If you experiment with tracking and kerning, you will find that you can use them to create many interesting visual effects.

9 Click four times in succession on the word *jaws* to select the entire second paragraph the word resides in, and change the value of the tracking property to **60**. This creates additional space between the lines and ensures that the enlarged words are not touching one another.

Clicking four times on any word in a paragraph selects that entire paragraph.

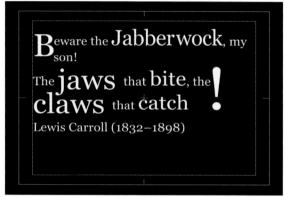

When editing text, remember that changing one value such as font size may require that you change another value such as leading, tracking, or kerning to maintain the legibility of the text.

If you deviated from any of the steps listed above your text will look different from the example here. This is perfectly alright and is one of the great things about being creative with type. You have the ability and freedom to create a typographical treatment that is completely unique from anything else you have seen before.

10 Click three times on the name *Lewis* in the last paragraph; this highlights the entire line of text. In the Character panel, change the font size property for all the text in this line to **20**.

In the Paragraph panel, change this line's alignment to Right align and change the value for Space Before Paragraph to **10**.

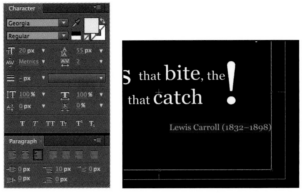

Working with the Character and Paragraph panels is very similar to working with a word processing program and is one of the easiest features of After Effects to adjust to.

11 Choose File > Save to save your After Effects file with the new text settings. Do not close the file, as you will need it in the next exercise.

Animating text properties

Text layers have two sets of properties that you can animate. The first set of properties are the standard transform properties that belong to every layer—Anchor Point, Position, Rotation, Scale, and Opacity—while the second set of properties, often called text animators, are only applicable to text layers. There are 15 text animators: Anchor Point, Position, Scale, Skew, Rotation, Opacity, Fill Color, Stroke Color, Stroke Width, Tracking, Line Anchor, Line Spacing, Character Offset, Character Value, and Blur. Keyframes are often not added directly to the animators; instead, text selectors are used to control the range and effect of the animators.

Text animator properties function much like other layer properties; the main difference is that for text animators, the properties only affect the text that lies between the range selectors. Any text outside of these selectors will have the appearance and properties that were in effect before the animator was applied. The pairing of animators and selectors is called an animator group, and these groups can contain multiple text animators and selectors.

In this part of the lesson, you will use animators on the text you created previously in this lesson to animate the text entering onto the screen. This effect is sometimes called an Animate In, or an Animated Intro.

1   With the Jabberwocky.aep file still open, click on the text layer in the Timeline panel to select it. Then click on the reveal triangle to the left of the layer name to show the layer's Text and Transform properties. This also reveals the Animate menu located in the layer switches/modes column for this layer.

2   Click the triangle button to the right of the Animate label, and from the list that appears, choose Position to add a new animator group to this text layer.

Text Animators have greater functionality than simply animating a layers transform properties.

3   Notice that the Position property only has two values. To enable three-dimensional positional changes, you must enable per-character 3D for this text layer.

Again, click on the Animate menu, and this time choose Enable per-character 3D from the top of the list. The animator group's Position property now has three values: the first value represents the X position, the second value the Y position, and the third value the Z position.

4   Change the Z position value to **–800**. This moves the text towards the viewer, making it appear larger and moving most of it off screen.

When animating along the z-axis negative numbers are closer to the viewer.

5   If you leave it like this, the text will be useless, so you must animate the range selector that is part of the animator group. You may ask yourself, "Why can't I just animate the Position property?" The reason lies with what happens when you add more properties to the group. It is far less work and easier to synchronize the different properties if the range selector is handling all the animation.

Click the reveal triangle to the left of Range Selector 1 to show the range selector's properties. Notice that the Start property is set to 0 percent and the End property is set to 100 percent, meaning that the range selector encompasses all the text on the layer.

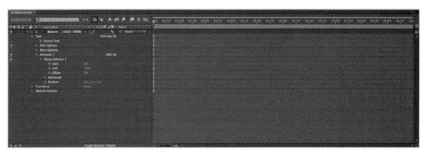

By default, the range selectors encompass the entire text layer.

6   Move the playhead to the beginning of the Timeline (0;00;00;00) and click the Time-Vary Stopwatch (●) to the left of the Start property of Range Selector 1 to enable animation and create your first keyframe.

7   Move the playhead to the 4 second (0;00;04;00) mark of the Timeline and change the value of the Start property to 100%. The effect of this change moves the start range selector to the end of the text layer, leaving all the text on the layer outside of the selectors and unaffected by the animator.

8   Move the playhead to the beginning of the Timeline and preview the animation. While the text does indeed fly in, some of the text that should be hidden instead remains visible at the beginning of the animation. You can easily adjust this by adding the Opacity property to the animator group.

Click on the triangle button to the right of the Add menu and choose Property > Opacity from the list that appears.

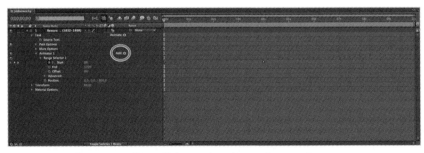

Animator groups allow you to combine multiple properties and range selectors together.

9   Change the Opacity value to zero and preview the animation to see the effect. Not only does this remove the text that is in the way at the beginning, but it also adds another animated feature to the text.

10 One additional property might make this animation even more visually appealing. You can easily add the Scale property to the group using the Add menu.

Click on the Add menu and choose Property > Scale; then change any of the three scale values to 1000. Because they are all linked together, this causes all three scale values to change simultaneously.

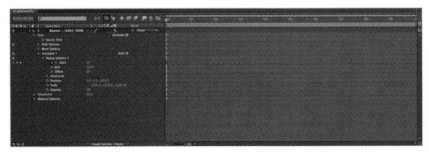

When multiple properties are added to an animator groups they are all controlled by the same range selector.

11 Preview your animation and then choose File > Save to save your After Effects file with the animation you have just created. Do not close the file, as you will need it in the next exercise.

Understanding Text Animators: Text Properties

Text Animators are composed of Text properties and Range Selector properties, both of which have their own properties that you can animate.

Text Properties

Anchor Point: Sets the anchor point for the characters; this is the point at which all transformations are centered.

Position: Specifies the X and Y position of the text in relation to the comp size. The Z position value is enabled only when you activate per-character 3D.

Scale: Specifies the horizontal (X) and vertical (Y) scale of the characters.

Skew: distorts the text by rotating individual characters.

Rotation, X Rotation, Y Rotation, Z Rotation: Sets character rotation. This is not the rotation of the text frame; instead, each character on a text layer receives its own individual rotation. If you enable per-character 3D, you can set a separate rotation value for each axis.

All Transform Properties: Used to add all transform properties to the animator group simultaneously.

Line Anchor: Specifies the point of alignment for the tracking in a line of text. A value of 0 percent is left alignment, 50 percent is center alignment, and 100 percent is right alignment.

Line Spacing: Sets the leading value (the space between lines).

Character Offset: Specifies the amount of offset of characters in your text layer. You can use this property to shift characters in a text layer to form random words.

Character Value: Replaces all the characters in a word by the selected value amount. You can use this property to shift characters in a text layer to form groups of the same letter.

Character Range: This property appears whenever you add the Character Offset or Character Value property to a layer. This specifies limits on the character changes made by the properties.

Blur: Sets the amount of Gaussian blur to be added to the characters.

Understanding Text Animators: Range Selector Properties

Text Animators are composed of Text properties and Range Selector properties, both of which have their own properties that you can animate.

Range Selector Properties

Start and End: The beginning and end of the selection. The animator only affects text between the selectors.

Offset: The amount to offset from the current position of the Start and End points of the range selector.

Shape: Sets how characters are selected between the Start and End points of the range selector.

Mode: Creates a similar effect to how multiple masks combine when you apply a mask mode property. Sets how each selector combines with the text and with the selector above it.

Amount: Controls the strength of an animator's effect, and sets how much the range of characters is affected by the animator's properties.

Units and Based On: The units of measure for Start, End, and Offset. You can base the selection of the range selector on the characters, characters excluding spaces, words, or lines.

Smoothness: Sets the amount of time the animation takes to transition from one character to another; higher numbers produce softer transitions.

Ease High and Ease Low: Used to create a sense of acceleration or deceleration when animating with text animators. The values set the speed of change as selection values change from fully included (high) to fully excluded (low).

Randomize Order: Randomizes the order in which the property is applied to the characters specified by the range selector.

Random Seed: This option is only available when you enable Randomize Order. You use it to set the randomized order of a range selector when the Randomize Order option is set to On, and it is useful when combining multiple range selectors in one animator group.

Saving an animator as a preset

Now that you have spent so much time creating a custom text animation, you don't want it to go to waste. By creating a preset for this text animator, you will be able to reapply it to text in this and future projects.

1   With the Jabberwocky.aep file still open, click on the text layer in the Timeline panel to select it. Then click on the reveal triangle to the left of the layer name to show the layer's Text and Transform properties.

Click on the reveal triangle next to the Text property and click on Animator 1 to select it.

2   With Animator 1 selected, press the Enter (Windows) or Return (Mac OS) key on your keyboard to make the name editable. Change the animator's name to Fade-Fly In. Press Enter/Return to complete editing the text.

3   With the Fade-Fly In animator selected, choose Animation > Save Animation Preset to open the Save Animation Preset as dialog box. Change the name of the preset to Fade-Fly In. By default, the preset is saved in the User Presets folder on your hard drive, but if you find it more convenient, you can choose another location. Click the Save button to finish saving the file.

4   You can now access the preset through the Effects & Presets panel under Animation Presets > User Presets.

If you know the name of the effect or preset you want to use you can type it into the search field at the top of the panel.

5   Choose File > Save to save your After Effects file with the animation you have just created. You may now close the file by choosing File > Close Project.

Working with text animation presets

In order to speed animation and make it easier for new users to become accustomed to working with text animators, After Effects ships with a wide variety of prebuilt animations for text. You can find these text animation presets in the Effects & Presets panel or browse for them in Adobe Bridge. Unlike other applications that use pre-rendered effects, every preset here is fully editable, created and animated using live effects. This allows you to apply as well as modify these effects to fit the needs of your specific project.

Browsing and applying text animation presets

Installed as part of the Creative Suite, Adobe Bridge is used as a file browser and metadata editor. Some users consider it the hub for the Creative Suite applications. While in After Effects, the use of Bridge may not be as integral as it is in other applications; one very important use is as a tool to preview and apply the application's built-in animation presets. While the Effects & Presets panel is a simple text list of preset names, Bridge offers full animated preview of all the built in presets as a well as a quick way to apply them to layers in After Effects.

In this exercise, you will work with a prebuilt After Effects project. The project contains four text layers describing the life of Albert Einstein. The text layers are arranged on the Timeline so that each text block is visible on stage for a total of only six seconds. You will add a preset animation to enhance the effect of this project.

1   Choose File > Open Project. In the Open Project dialog box, navigate to the Lesson 6 folder and double-click on Albert Einstein.aep to open it.

2   In the Timeline panel, position the playhead at the beginning (0;00;00;00) of the Timeline, and then highlight the layer numbered 1 (the layer is named *in school, HE was considered a below average student......................*).

The layer name may be truncated; you can reveal the entire layer name by lengthening the Layer name column using the dividers that separate each column's name.

3   In the Effects & Presets panel, choose Browse Presets from the panel menu (·≡). This launches Bridge and automatically takes you to the Presets folder.

When working with After Effects, Bridge is used to browse and preview presets and media files.

If Bridge is not already open, it may take a few moments to open the application. Don't panic—this is normal. If you are not familiar with Bridge, it is an application that can preview and browse files, as well as performing other tasks. In this exercise, you will use it to preview the preset text animators that are available to you in After Effects. If this is the first time you have opened Bridge you will be prompted to choose whether or not you would like it to automatically start at logon and may also be prompted to approve the installation of one or more extensions that allow it to communicate with the other application of the Creative Suite.

4   In Bridge, from the Presets folder, double-click on the Text folder, and then on the Animate In folder.

In the Animate In folder, double-click on Random Word Shuffle In.ffx. A few things happen at once: first, the Bridge interface disappears and is replaced by the After Effects interface; second, the effect that you double-clicked on is automatically applied to layer 1, the layer you had previously selected.

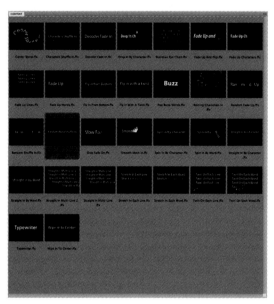

If you plan to use Bridge to apply effects you must have your target layer selected in After Effects before you go to Bridge.

5   You can tell that the effects were applied because the text is now partially off screen. The effect is built for a standard-definition project and you must adjust the values of the position change to fit the HD project you are working in now. You will adjust this setting in the next exercise. Make certain the layer is selected, otherwise the effect is not applied.

6   Choose File > Save As. In the Save As dialog box, navigate to the ae06lessons folder, rename the file **Albert Einstein-working.aep**, and click Save. Do not close this file, as you will use it in the next section.

Modifying animation presets

What good would animation presets be if you couldn't modify them to fit the needs of your specific project? This is a major advantage that After Effects has over some other motion graphics programs. While in some programs, the coolest parts of their built-in preset effects are pre-rendered and not editable, every After Effects text animation preset is fully editable.

In this exercise, you will edit properties of the Random Word Shuffle In.ffx effect that you previously applied.

1 With the Albert Einstein_working.aep file that you created in the previous exercise open, hold down Ctrl (Windows) or Command (Mac OS) and click on the reveal triangle for this layer to reveal all the layer's properties at once.

Locate Animator 1 underneath the Text property; it is composed of a range selector and a Position property.

You may have to scroll the Timeline panel vertically in order to see both the range selector and Position property.

2 Change the X value of the Position property to **1900**; this places the text completely off screen. Underneath the Advanced properties of Range Selector 1, change the Based On property to lines. This changes the entire animation so that now, instead having each word fly in individually, each line of text flies in from the left.

The Based On property of range selectors controls which parts of a text layer are actually being animated. The choices are Characters, Characters Excluding Spaces, Words, and Lines. A simple adjustment to this property can completely change the nature and appearance of a text animator.

3 Move the playhead to the 2 second (0;00;02;00) mark of the Timeline. Click on the second keyframe of Range Selector 1's Offset property to select it.

Hold down the Shift key on your keyboard and drag the keyframe toward the playhead until it snaps into position at the 2 second mark.

When dragging keyframes or In and Out points the shift key lets them snap to the playhead.

4 Now that you have amended the timing of the preset, you can add to it to create a new animation where the text enters the screen, holds for two seconds, and then leaves the screen.

Move the playhead to the 4 second (0;00;04;00) mark on the Timeline and click the Add or Remove Keyframe at Current Time button to the left of the Offset property to insert a keyframe at 4 seconds. When using this button, it always sets a keyframe at the property's current value, so it is a great way to create a placeholder keyframe.

When the Add or Remove Keyframe at Current Time button is gray, it means the playhead is not currently on a keyframe and it will add one to the property; when it is yellow, it means that it will remove the keyframe that is at the current time of the playhead.

5   With the layer still selected, press the letter **O** key on the keyboard to move the playhead to the out point of the layer.

Click on the first keyframe of the Offset property and choose Edit > Copy. This is very similar to the way you can copy text in a word processing program so that you can move it to another section of your document. Choose Edit > Paste to create a copy of the keyframe at the current position of the playhead.

*The keyboard command for moving the playhead to the in point of the current layer is **I**, and the command for moving to the out point of the layer is **o**.*

6   The animation is not bad, but it might be more visually appealing if the text were to leave the screen in the opposite direction from which it appears. You can easily achieve this effect by creating keyframes for the animator's Position property.

Move the playhead to the beginning (0;00;00;00) of the Timeline and click on the Time-Vary Stopwatch (●) of the Position property of Animator 1 to create a keyframe.

7   Move the playhead to the 2 second (0;00;02;00) mark on the Timeline and click the Add or Remove Keyframe at Current Time button (◆) to the left of the Position property to create a placeholder.

8   Move the playhead to the 4 second (0;00;04;00) mark of the Timeline and change the X value of the Position property to **–1900**.

When working with the X position property, negative values move a layer to the left.

Preview the animation. The lines of text now enter the screen from the left and exit it to the right.

9   With Animator 1 selected, press the Enter (Windows) or Return (Mac OS) key on your keyboard to make the name editable. Change the animator's name to Enter **Left-Exit Right**. Press Enter/Return to complete editing the text.

10 With the Enter Left-Exit Right animator selected, choose Animation > Save Animation Preset to open the Save Animation Preset As dialog box. Change the name of the preset to Enter **Left-Exit Right** to match the name that you assigned to the animator in the previous step. Click Save to save the file in the default location in the User Presets folder. In the dialog box, navigate to the After Effects Text Presets folder. If you are using a Mac OS computer, the folder is located here: Applications > Adobe After Effects CS5 > Presets > Text, and Windows users can find the folder here: Windows: Program Files > Adobe After Effects CS5 > Presets > Text.

11 If it does not already exist, create a new folder inside the Presets folder and name it Favorites. Click on this new folder to select it and press the Save button. From this point forward you can access your custom preset through the Effect & Presets panel under Animation Presets > Text > Favorites.

12 Choose File > Save to save your After Effects file with the animation you have just created. You may now close the file by choosing File > Close Project.

Finding additional presets

Animation Presets were previously called favorite effects; this is the reason the file extension for them is .ffx. In addition to the presets that are included with the application and the presets that you create, there are other places you can find presets to optimize your workflow.

To provide a single, unified location for sharing presets, plug-ins, and other content between users of the Creative Suite, Adobe created the Marketplace & Exchange site at *www.adobe.com/cfusion/exchange/*. At Adobe Marketplace & Exchange, you can find a source for free animation and text animation presets for After Effects as well as free and for-pay plug-ins, project templates, and scripts. If you use other Adobe applications, you can find additional supporting content for them as well.

Creating custom text animators

Once you are comfortable with applying presets from the library, you may want to venture out and create your own. The entire point of creating and saving a text animation preset is that it allows you to reuse animations and tweak them instead of creating everything from scratch.

Creating a typewriter effect

A classic and often-used effect is the typewriter. In this effect, text appears on screen one letter at a time, as if it is being typed in front of you.

1   Choose File > Open Project. In the Open Project dialog box, navigate to the ae06lessons folder and double-click on Creating a Typewriter Effect.aep to open it.

2   Click on the text layer in the Timeline panel to select it. Then click on the reveal triangle to the left of the layer name to show the layer's Text and Transform properties.

Then click the triangle button to the right of the Animate label and from the list that appears, choose Opacity to add a new animator group to the layer.

3   Set the Opacity property to **0%**, and then click on the reveal triangle to the left of Range Selector 1 to view its properties.

4   Move the playhead to the beginning (0;00;00;00) of the Timeline and click on the Time-Vary Stopwatch (⏱) of the range selector's Start property to enable animation and create a keyframe for the property's default value of 0 percent.

5   Move the playhead to the 5 second (0;00;05;00) mark on the Timeline and change the value of the Start property to **100%**.

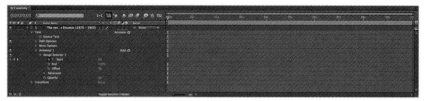

By default, the start property of a range selector is 0% and the end property is 100% so that the selector encloses all the text on the layer.

Preview the animation. You should notice that while the text does indeed appear letter by letter, the letters each seem to fade in as opposed to the harsh, invisible/visible effect that would occur if they were actually being typed by a typewriter. Fortunately, this is easy to fix by adjusting the range selector's Advanced properties.

6   Click on the reveal triangle to the left of the Advanced property group for Range Selector 1. Change the Smoothness value to **0%**. This eliminates the fading effect that you saw in the previous preview. Preview the animation.

7   With Animator 1 selected, press the Enter (Windows) or Return (Mac OS) key on your keyboard to make the name editable. Change the animator's name to Typewriter. Press Enter/Return to complete editing the text.

8   With the Typewriter animator selected, choose Animation > Save Animation Preset to open the Save Animation Preset As dialog box. Change the name of the preset to **Typewriter** to match the name that you gave to the animator in the previous step. In the dialog box, navigate to the After Effects Text Presets folder. Locate the Favorites folder that you created earlier in this lesson. Double-click on this folder to select it and press the Save button.

9   Choose File > Save to save your After Effects file with the animation you have just created. You may now close the file by choosing File > Close Project.

Creating a blur-in effect

Animating the appearance of text on screen can make otherwise dull presentation graphics more visually appealing and fun. A blur-in effect begins with text that is invisible and gradually reveals the text by animating an increase in its opacity and a decrease in blurriness.

1 Choose File > Open Project. In the Open Project dialog box, navigate to the ae06lessons folder and double-click to open Creating a Blur in Effect.aep.

2 Click on the text layer in the Timeline panel to select it. Then click on the reveal triangle to the left of the layer name to show the layer's Text and Transform properties.

Then click the triangle button to the right of the Animate label and from the list that appears, choose Blur to add a new animator group to the layer.

3 Click on the chain link icon to disable the Blur property's Constrain Proportions option and set the horizontal blur value (the first number) to 100. Then click on the reveal triangle to the left of Range Selector 1 to view its properties.

The blur property is used to create per character blurs on text.

4 Move the playhead to the beginning (0;00;00;00) of the Timeline and click on the Time-Vary Stopwatch (●) of the range selector's Start property to enable animation and create a keyframe for the property's default value of 0 percent.

5 Move the playhead to the 5 second (0;00;05;00) mark on the Timeline and change the value of the Start property to **100%**.

6 Click on the reveal triangle to the left of the Advanced property group for Range Selector 1. Change the Randomize Order value to On by clicking on the current value which is set to Off. This causes the range selector to un-blur the text seemingly at random and creates a more frenetic effect. Preview your animation to see what you have created.

7 With Animator 1 selected, press the Enter (Windows) or Return (Mac OS) key on your keyboard to make the name editable. Change the animator's name to **Blur In.** Press Enter/Return to complete editing the text.

8   With the Blur In animator selected, choose Animation > Save Animation Preset to open the Save Animation Preset As dialog box. Change the name of the preset to **Blur In**.

Just as you did in the previous part of the lesson, navigate to the After Effects Text Presets folder. In the dialog box, double-click on your Favorites folder to select it and press the Save button.

9   Choose File > Save to save your After Effects file with the animation you have just created. You may now close the file by choosing File > Close Project.

Creating text on a path

Text can be combined with mask paths and animated to create text that follows a specific course. When combined with a mask path in this way, text can escape its normal box and instead be fit to a wide variety of possible shapes. There are five properties available once you have created text on a path:

Reverse Path: You use this property to reverse the direction of a path. This property is useful when a path is drawn in the wrong direction, causing text to appear backwards.

Perpendicular To Path: You use this property to rotate each character so that it is perpendicular to the path instead of horizontal to it.

Force Alignment: You use this property to justify the text, forcing the first character to be positioned at the beginning of the path, and the last character at the end of the path, and then evenly spacing the remainder of the text along the path.

First Margin: This property sets the position of the first character relative to the start of the path.

Last Margin: This property sets the position of the last character relative to the end of the path.

In this exercise, you will work with a prebuilt After Effects project. The project consists of two layers, and each is made up of point text. Each layer also has a mask path on it that was created with the Pen tool.

1   Choose File > Open Project. In the Open Project dialog box, navigate to the ae06lessons folder and double-click to open Creating Text on a Path.aep.

2   In the Timeline panel, click on the first layer, the one named LIFE is like a ROLLER COASTER, to select it. When you select a layer, any masks on that layer immediately become visible.

Click on the reveal triangle to the left of the layer name to show the layer's Text and Transform properties, and then click on the reveal triangle to the left of Text to reveal the Path Options. Click on the reveal triangle to the left of Path Options to reveal the Path property. Text can be attached to any mask shape on the text layer. The paths you will use here were created by drawing Bézier curves with the Pen tool.

The path options property group attaches a mask path on a text layer as a motion guide for the text.

3   From the Path property's drop-down menu, select the path named Guide Path 01. Once you have selected a path, the additional path properties appear.

4   Move the playhead to the beginning (0;00;00;00) of the Timeline and change the value of the First Margin property to **–210**. Then click on the property's time-vary stopwatch icon to create a keyframe and enable animation for this property. Once you type in the value, it automatically creates a new keyframe.

Remember that when you are animating properties, new keyframes are always created at the current position of the playhead. When the Time-Vary stopwatch is first enabled, a keyframe is automatically created. Once animation has been enabled for a property any change in the value of that property; either by adjusting a numerical value in the Timeline or Effect Controls panel or by directly transforming the layer in the Composition panel creates a new keyframe.

5   Move the playhead to the 5 second (0;00;05;00) mark on the Timeline and change the First Margin's property value to **470**.

6   Click on the second layer, named Full of Downs and Ups, to select it and use the reveal triangles to view the Path property.

7   From the Path property's drop-down menu, select the path named Guide Path 02. This time, there is a little problem: this path was drawn from right to left and as a result, the text is reversed.

Enable the Reverse Path property by clicking on the current value, which is set to Off. This corrects the text, leaving it right side up. The starting and ending vertices of a path control where the text placed on it begins and ends. Properties such as Reverse Path allow you to override the default positioning of path text.

8   Again move the playhead to the beginning (0;00;00;00) of the Timeline and change the value of the First Margin property to **780**. Then click on the property's time-vary stopwatch icon to create a keyframe and enable animation. Once you type in the value, it automatically creates a new keyframe.

Move the playhead to the 5 second (0;00;05;00) mark on the Timeline and change the property's value to **210**.

Preview your animation; each text layer moves along its path from off to onscreen simultaneously.

10   Choose File > Save to save your After Effects file with the animation you have just created. You may now close the file by choosing File > Close Project.

Self study

Now that you have learned how to create and animate text in After Effect you can create your own custom type treatment and animate it appearing on the screen. Remember that you should try to create a visually appealing design so that you can engage your audience in the animation.

Review

Questions

1   What are the two types of text you can create in After Effects and how are they each created?

2   What is the advantage of using Bridge to preview animation?

3   What is the advantage of saving a custom text animator as a preset?

Answers

1   The two types of text that you can create in After Effects are Point and Paragraph text. Point text is created when you click with the Type tool and just start typing, while Paragraph text is created by clicking and dragging with the Type tool to create a text frame of a set width and height.

2   Animation presets have video preview when viewed in Bridge as opposed to the simple text list that you see in the Effects & Presets panel.

3   By creating a preset for a text animator, you will be able to reapply it to text in any project that you create in After Effects.

What you'll learn in this lesson:

- Loop audio files
- Animate audio levels
- Use Timeline markers to set sync points
- Add audio effects

Working with Audio

When working in After Effects, audio can be an often-overlooked but integral part of your compositions. You can use audio either as a support for animation or as a motivator for it.

Starting up

You will work with several files from the ae07lessons folder in this lesson. Make sure that you have loaded the aelessons folder onto your hard drive from the supplied DVD. See "Loading lesson files" on page 4.

See Lesson 7 in action!

Use the accompanying video to gain a better understanding of how to use some of the features shown in this lesson. The video tutorial for this lesson can be found on the included DVD.

Setting up

As you work in After Effects, you will inevitably open and close many panels, depending on the type of project you are creating. However, when working through the projects in this book, it is important to have an interface that matches the lessons. To this end, you should always reset your workspace to the preset Standard configuration.

1 Choose Window > Workspace > Standard to set your current workspace configuration.

2 Choose Window > Workspace > Reset "Standard" to reset the standard workspace in case you have modified it at some point.

Audio in After Effects

There are many different types of audio files that you will come into contact with. After Effects can import the following formats:

FILE FORMATS	FILE TYPE EXTENSIONS
Adobe Sound Document	ASND
Advanced Audio Coding	AAC, M4A
Audio Interchange File Format	AIF, AIFF
MPEG-1 Audio Layer 3 (MP3)	MP3, MPEG, MPG, MPA, MPE

Although there are several different audio formats that you can import, most experienced users prefer to use one of the uncompressed formats that are intended for editing, such as WAV or AIFF. Uncompressed audio formats tend to preview better in After Effects. Also, because they are uncompressed, they usually produce a higher-quality sound when exported than files that have already been compressed and are again re-compressed when you output them. If you are using Adobe SoundBooth to create your audio files, the native multi-track document format ASND makes an excellent lossless format to use in After Effects.

Unfortunately, many people overlook audio when working with After Effects projects. In fact, except at the highest levels, the audio aspect of motion graphics design is something that many designers don't think about until nearly the end of the project, at which point they often try to find music to match the visuals they have already created. This often results in a project where the audio, whether it is music or a voice-over track, seems tacked on. A better method is to take a holistic approach to the process, where the visual and audio elements of your design are given equal weight. Sometimes you may want to create your audio to follow the visual animation, and other times create the motion graphics to reflect the audio, such as when graphics are created to match music.

Unfortunately, with today's short deadlines, a holistic design approach is not always practical or possible. Luckily, After Effects gives you several ways of working with audio in your project that will help you streamline the process of integrating it with your animations.

All the audio used in this lesson was recorded, edited, or created in Adobe SoundBooth. If you are not familiar with it, SoundBooth is a part of the Creative Suite and is basically a scaled-down version of Adobe Audition. It is intended to put a set of very powerful audio-editing tools into the hands of users who are not audio professionals, and offers an interface and workflow that is very friendly to video editors and designers.

Previewing audio

Very often when you want to preview your animation, you can simply press the spacebar, and this generates a preview from the current position of the playhead. However, audio does not preview on the Timeline when you press the spacebar to preview animation. To preview the audio portion of the Timeline, either as part of the overall animation or alone, you can do one of the following:

PREVIEW TYPE	FUNCTION	HOW TO PERFORM
RAM Preview	Uses your computer's RAM to render and play back video and audio in the composition, footage, or layer panels in real time.	1 Choose Composition > Preview > RAM Preview. 2 Click the RAM Preview button on the Preview panel. 3 Press the zero key on the number pad.
Scrubbing through audio on the Timeline	Plays sound on the Timeline as you drag the playhead forward or backward. The speed of the playback is based on how fast you move the playhead.	1 Hold down the Ctrl (Windows) or Command (Mac OS) key while dragging the playhead on the Timeline.
Previewing audio only	Renders and plays back only the audio portion of the Timeline.	1 Choose Composition > Preview > Audio Preview (Here Forward). 2 Choose Composition > Preview > Audio Preview (Work Area). 3 Press the period key on the number pad.

Adding audio files to the Timeline

In After Effects, audio files are imported into the project and added to a composition just like any other footage item. However, the differences become apparent once you begin working with audio files on the Timeline. Because they are not visual, audio footage layers lack the transform properties that you have become used to working with, and instead have only a levels property that allows you to control the volume of the track.

In this exercise, you will open an After Effects project with a prebuilt text animation and add a background audio track and sound effects to match the animation.

1   Choose File > Open Project and in the Open dialog box, navigate to the ae07lessons folder. Locate the file named Working With Audio Files.aep and either double-click on it or click the Open button in the dialog box.

This project consists of two compositions. The main composition is called From word to deed and contains a text layer containing a French proverb, "from word to deed is a great space," and another composition named Background. The Background composition contains several layers that create the textured cloud effect you see.

2   In the Timeline panel, click the text layer to select it and press the letter **U** key on the keyboard. This keyboard command reveals only the layer properties that have animation enabled.

The animation in this file is pretty simple; the text layer has an animated range selector with keyframes at 2, 4, 6, and 8 seconds. Scrub the playhead to see that the text blurs in vertically one line at a time. The two-second delay before the first keyframe prevents the animation from starting right away, while the space at the end of the animation allows for the text to remain on screen so the viewer has time to read the message after it appears.

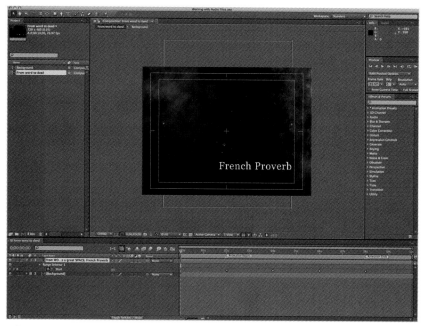

When animating text on screen it is important to give the viewer time at the end of an animation to read the text.

3 You will start by creating a folder in the Project panel to keep it organized. These folders function similarly to the folders on your hard drive, and are an excellent organizational tool. Click on the Create new Folder icon at the bottom of the Project panel.

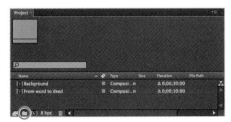

Project panel folders are an excellent method of organizing your footage items.

Name the new folder **audio** and press the Enter (Windows) or Return (Mac OS) key on your keyboard to finalize the name change. Because the default sorting method of the panel is alphabetical, the folder jumps to the top of the list.

Click on the audio folder's icon to highlight it and choose File > Import > File. In the Import dialog box, navigate to the ae07lessons folder.

The keyboard commands to open the Import dialog box are Ctrl+I (Windows) or Command+I (Mac OS).

Click on the file named Outer Space Zero.asnd, an Adobe Soundbooth audio file, press and hold the Ctrl (Windows) or Command (Mac OS) key on your keyboard, and then click on Loop-Metallic Clang.wav to highlight them both.

Click the Open button to import both files. Because the audio folder was highlighted when you used the import command, the two audio files are placed directly into this folder.

The import command will place files into whatever folder is highlighted in the Project panel. If there are no folders or none of them are highlighted then the footage items are placed into the main Project panel.

4   Click on any empty area of the Project panel to deselect the two imported audio files. Click on the Outer Space Zero.ansd file, drag it into the Timeline, and place it below the background layer.

Whenever you import a file, it is automatically highlighted in the Project panel, and when multiple files are imported simultaneously, you must deselect them all before you can reselect the file or files you want to work with.

5   RAM Preview the composition to hear and see how the audio works with the animation.

A RAM Preview is necessary to view Timeline animations with audio because audio doesn't preview when you use a standard Timeline preview by pressing the spacebar.

6   Choose File > Save As and in the dialog box that appears, navigate to the ae07lessons folder and change the name of the file to **Working with Audio Files-working.aep**.

Click the Save button to close the dialog box. Don't close the file, as you will need it in the next part of the lesson.

Viewing audio file metadata

What is metadata? Meta comes from a Greek word meaning *above* or *beyond*, so metadata is data that is above the data of an image. It is sometimes referred to as *data about data*, because it contains information about the actual file. When metadata is used with video, audio, and images, this data usually describes information such as the formatting, file structure, creator, and keywords. Metadata has long been a part of the digital imaging fields, and digital photo cameras and software such as Adobe Photoshop add it to files to aid in identification, indexing, and cataloging. However, the use of metadata is still fairly new to motion graphic design. As the video and film industries shift from tape-based to tapeless recording formats, metadata is becoming more important for archiving, searching, and retrieving files.

When working with the Adobe Creative Suite, you can add metadata to files, or edit it using Bridge or by using the Metadata panel in After Effects.

1   With the Working With Audio Files-working.aep file open, choose Window > Metadata to view the Metadata panel.

2   Click on the reveal triangle for Dublin Core in the Project section to see the editable fields. In the Description field, type **Text based animation with background audio and sound fx**.

The word effects is often abbreviated as fx by visual effects and graphic artists, as it is here.

This data is added to the After Effects project file and viewable and searchable in metadata editors such as Bridge.

Metadata is quickly becoming an integral part of video editing, visual effects and motion graphics workflows.

3   Hide the project's metadata fields by clicking the triangle to the left of the words Dublin Core at the top of the panel. In the Project panel, click on the Loop-Metallic Clang.wav file to highlight it, and then click the reveal triangle next to Dublin Core in the Files section of the Metadata panel. This file is an edited version of one of the sound effects found on Adobe Resource Central named Module Production Title Imaging Electronic Whoosh Digital Beeps Screech.

4   In the Description field, type **2 second looping digital sound effect**. Just like the file's metadata, when you exit the text field, the data is automatically added to the file.

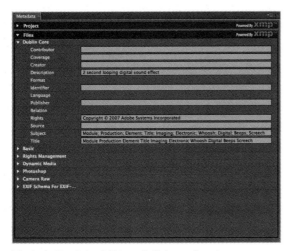

Text in the Description field is searchable in metadata viewers.

If you are not familiar with Resource Central, it is a feature built into some applications that allows you to access a central location to download sound effects, SoundBooth scores, Encore DVD templates, and other assets for use in video and motion graphics production.

5   Close the Metadata panel, as you have finished working with it. There is no need to save the project because editing metadata does not directly affect it, but you will need it open to complete the next segment of the lesson.

Looping audio files

Like a video file, audio has a set duration, plays once, and then stops. But you can change this by setting a loop value in the Interpret Footage dialog box. If the audio file has been created so that it seamlessly loops, this can be a great way to create a background musical track for animations. In this section, you will loop a background sound that corresponds with the blur in animation of the text of this project. The Loop-Metallic Clang.wav file was created in SoundBooth to match the timing of this project's animation. However, there is a problem: the audio file is approximately two seconds in length, while the animation takes a full six seconds to complete and needs the sound effect to repeat three times in succession. Fortunately, with the Interpret Footage dialog box, you can easily rectify this situation by looping the file.

1   With the Working with Audio Files-working.aep file open, click on the Loop-Metallic Clang.wav file to highlight it. This also makes the Project panel active (notice the orange outline around it), press the tilde (~) key on your keyboard to maximize this panel and make it easier to see all the columns.

Notice that the duration is currently listed as 2 seconds and three frames (0:00:02:03).

The properties of a footage item are visible in the Project panel when you highlight it.

2   With the project panel still active press the tilde (~) key again to return to the Standard workspace configuration. Right-click on the Loop-Metallic Clang.wav file in the audio folder in the Project panel. From the menu that appears, choose Interpret Footage > Main to open the Interpret Footage dialog box.

3   In the Other Options section of the dialog box, type **3** into the Loop field.

Looping the file 3 times like this changes its duration to 6 seconds and 7 frames (0;00;06;07).

Click the OK button to close the dialog box.

Both audio and video footage items can be set to loop a specified number of times.

4   Drag the Loop-Metallic Clang.wav file into the Timeline and place it above the Outer Space Zero.asnd layer.

The stacking order of audio layers is irrelevant; because they are not visible, they can't hide other layers and so all layers play at once.

5   Move the playhead to the first animation keyframe at the 2 second mark (0;00;02;00) and click on the Loop-Metallic Clang.wav layer to highlight it.

Press the left bracket ([) key on the keyboard to move the beginning of the layer to the current position of the playhead.

By pressing the left bracket key, you cause the In point of the layer you have selected to jump to the current position of the playhead. The right bracket key causes the Out point of the layer to jump to the playhead's current position. Be aware that this does not change the duration of the layer; the entire layer slides over as a whole.

6   RAM Preview the animation. Notice that the metallic clang corresponds with the middle of the blur-in effect of the text animation.

7   Choose File > Save to save these changes to your After Effects project. Do not close the file, as you will need it again in the next part of the lesson.

Animating audio levels

While visual layers such as images, video, and text have several transform properties that you can animate, audio layers have only the Audio Levels property to work with. The simplest definition for this property is that audio levels control the volume of the audio layer, and you can add keyframes to produce an effect where the sound gently fades in or out, or perhaps starts or stops abruptly.

In the previous section, the metallic sound effect was added to the Timeline. This creates a bit of a problem because when it plays during the animation, the background audio track's volume makes it hard to distinguish the two sounds. A solution is to lower the volume of the track so that you can better hear the sound effects, but because you want the background audio louder before the animation starts and after it ends, the best solution is to animate the layer's Audio Levels property to allow the music to fade out as the animation starts and fade in once it ends.

1   With the Working with Audio Files-working.aep file open, move the playhead to the beginning (0;00;00;00) of the Timeline panel.

2   Click the reveal triangle to the left of the Outer Space Zero.ansd layer to show the Audio property; then click the reveal triangle for this property to show the Audio Levels, and then finally reveal the Waveform as well.

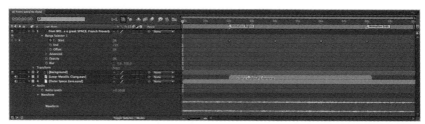

Audio layers only have a single property that you can animate: Audio Levels.

The waveform of an audio layer isn't editable; however, it is a good tool for figuring out the relative volume of the audio file at specific points in time.

3   Move the playhead to the 1 second (0;00;01;00) mark on the Timeline; this is where you will place the first keyframe.

Click the Time-Vary Stopwatch for the Audio Levels property to create the first keyframe with the default value of 0.00 dB.

The units of measure for audio files are decibels (abbreviated dB). The value 0.00 dB does not mean that there is no sound; it is simply the baseline at which the sound value starts. Positive numbers (the maximum value is +12.00 dB) raise the volume, while negative numbers (the minimum value is -48.00 dB) decrease it. You can watch the waveform to see a visual representation of the effects that level changes make to the audio file.

4   Move the playhead to the 2 second (0;00;02;00) mark on the Timeline and change the Audio Levels value to -10.00 dB.

5   Move the playhead to the 8 second (0;00;08;00) mark on the Timeline and click on the Add or Remove Keyframe button to the left of the property name to create a new keyframe with the exact same value as the previous one.

This will hold the value of the property at -10.00 dB for the duration of the animation.

6   Move the playhead to the 9 second (0;00;09;00) mark of the Timeline and change the Audio Levels value back to 0.00 dB.

The Timeline now has four keyframes, as shown in the following figure.

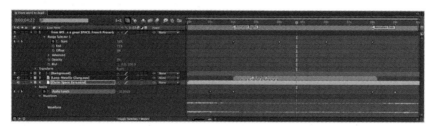

The first two keyframes are used to fade the volume down, while the second two are used to fade it back up. Because the middle two keyframes have the exact same value, there can be no change in volume between them.

7   RAM Preview the animation to hear the fade-down and fade-up effects you just created. Choose File > Save to save these changes to your After Effects project. Do not close the file, as you will need it again in the next part of the lesson.

Working with audio effects

You can apply effects to audio layers in the same way that you apply them to visual layers, and while your choice of effects is much more limited, they can still be useful for quick corrections or modifications. In this exercise, you will add an audio effect to the Loop-Metallic Clang.wav layer to make the sound a bit more ethereal and otherworldly.

1   With the Working with Audio Files-working.aep file open, click on the Timeline panel to highlight it, and then choose Edit > Select All to highlight all the layers in the composition.

With all the layers selected, press Ctrl+~ (Windows and Mac OS) on your keyboard to collapse the visible properties of all the highlighted layers. This makes it easier to navigate the Timeline, as you no longer have to scroll up and down.

If you are not familiar with the tilde (~) key, it is located above the Tab key on the left side of your keyboard. The keyboard command to select all unlocked and visible layers is Command+A (Mac OS) or Ctrl+A (Windows).

2 Choose Edit > Deselect All and then click on the Loop-Metallic Clang.wav layer to highlight it alone.

3 Choose Effect > Audio > Modulator to apply the modulator effect to the audio layer. As a result of your applying the effect, the Effect Controls panel opens.

The Modulator effect causes sound to pulsate and tremble by manipulating the frequency and amplitude of the file. It has only four settings:

Modulation Type: This setting specifies the type of waveform to use for the effects distortion. A sine wave produces smoother modulation, but using the triangular setting results in more abrupt or sharp changes.

Modulation Rate: This setting specifies the rate at which the effect varies the audio file. This value is measured in hertz (Hz) and is equivalent to setting the strength of other effects.

Modulation Depth: This setting specifies the amount by which the effect modulates or varies the frequency.

Amplitude Modulation: This setting specifies the amount by which the effect modulates or varies the amplitude.

4 Move the playhead to the beginning (0;00;00;00) of the Timeline and press the period key on your computer's numerical keypad. If you do not have a numerical keypad, you can use the menu command to preview only the audio portions of a composition by choosing Composition > Preview > Audio Preview (Here Forward).

This causes After Effects to render and preview only the audio of the composition. This allows you to quickly assess how the Modulator is affecting the sound effect. Stop the playback by pressing the period key again.

5 In the Effect Controls panel, leave Modulation Type as Sine, and then make the following changes to the other properties of Modulator:

• Modulation Rate: **30.00**

• Modulation Depth: **10.00%**

• Amplitude Modulation: **10.00%**

RAM Preview the animation. The Modulator effect produces a sound that seems to tremble and sounds hollow.

6 To add a second audio effect, choose Effect > Audio > Backwards. The Backwards effect reverses the audio of a layer by playing it from the last frame to the first instead of in the normal order. Aside from a switch that allows you to swap the left and right channels of a stereo file, this effect doesn't offer any customization.

7 RAM Preview the composition to see how the audio and animation interact with one another. Choose File > Save to save these changes to your After Effects project. You may now close this project, as you're done with it.

Using composition markers to set the beat

In animations that must be synced to audio, you can use composition markers to set or mark the beat. Like the markers found in video and audio editing programs such as Premiere Pro and SoundBooth, you can add After Effects markers to any point on the Timeline or any individual layer. Each marker can have a duration assigned to it and be given a unique, descriptive set of comments that display in the Timeline panel. An additional feature of markers, which only applies when you are outputting the file to certain file types, is the ability to create chapter and Web links or Flash cue points.

In this section, you will add an audio file that contains a voice-over to a project that contains a prebuilt animation. You will then use the features for previewing audio that are built into After Effects to help add Timeline markers that you can use to synchronize the animation to the spoken word.

1 Choose File > Open Project and navigate to the ae07lessons folder. Locate the Syncing Animation to Audio.aep file and double-click on it to open the project.

Scrub the playhead to quickly preview the animation. It consists of a series of animated typographic treatments of part of a poem by William Blake named "The Tiger" that was originally published as "The Tyger" in 1794. Notice that the second stanza of the poem overlaps the first; you will correct this overlap as part of this lesson.

2 Choose File > Import > File, navigate to the ae07lessons folder, and double-click on the file named Tiger Tiger.wav to add it to the Project panel.

Drag the Tiger Tiger.wav file into the Timeline and place it above the layer named TIGER, so that it becomes the new first layer.

While an audio file can be placed anywhere in the layer stacking order, in this lesson it is kept above the other layers so that it is easy to see with out having to scroll vertically.

3   This section of the exercise is going to focus on the first stanza and so it may be more convenient to hide the layers that you are not going to be working with. To free up space in the Timeline panel, you will use the shy switch.

Click on the layer named what (layer number 12) to select it. Then hold down the Shift key and click on the bottom layer (layer number 21) to select every layer between them.

Place your cursor over any of the selected layers and right-click. Choose Switches > Shy to enable the shy switch for every highlighted layer.

In this step, an alternative to right-clicking in this step is to click on the Shy switch for any one of the selected layers to shy them all.

4   Click the Hide Shy Layers Compositions switch (⊕) at the top of the Timeline panel to hide all layers that have the shy layer switch enabled.

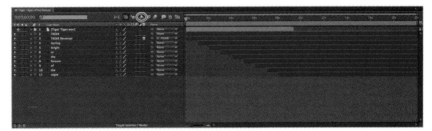

Layers that have the Shy switch enabled still preview and render in the Composition panel.

The Shy switch hides layers from the Timeline display, but these layers are still visible when you preview the animation in the Composition panel. This command is almost the exact opposite of the layer visibility switch, which hides a layer in the Composition panel but still displays it in the Timeline.

Shy switch enabled. Shy switch disabled.

5   Now that you have some free space in the Timeline panel, click on the reveal triangle of the audio layer so that you can view its properties. Continue to reveal layer properties until you can see the layer's waveform.

Creating composition markers isn't hard, but to create them while previewing the audio file is a little tricky and requires a bit of practice, good hearing, and a familiarity with the audio. It also requires that you use a keyboard command to create the markers. The spoken text is as follows:

Tiger, tiger, burning bright

In the forests of the night,

What immortal hand or eye

Dare frame thy fearful symmetry?

When creating the markers, you are going to place them at the beginning of every word.

6 Choose Edit > Deselect All to make sure none of the layers are selected.

Start the audio playback by pressing the period key on your keyboard's numerical keypad or by choosing Composition > Preview > Audio Preview (Work Area). As the audio plays back, press the asterisk key on the number pad to set a Timeline marker at the beginning of every word. This technique takes come practice to get right and rarely works perfectly the first time through. If you make a mistake in where you place the markers don't worry, you can always adjust them later. You will do this later in this lesson to name and refine their position.

While performing this technique, if you pause the audio playback and use the undo command; Command+Z (Mac OS) or Ctrl+Z (Windows), you will remove all the markers that have been added to the timeline.

If you do not have a number pad on your keyboard, you can use the keyboard command Ctrl+8 to add markers to the Timeline.

You should end up with 20 markers in all. If you have more than 20 markers, then you should preview the audio again, right-click on any extraneous markers, and choose Remove Marker from the menu that appears. When using this technique, some people tend to place markers at every syllable instead of every word.

The position of the markers must usually be refined, but this technique is a good start.

The markers will not be exactly at the right point on the Timeline for a couple of reasons: first, there is a delay in your reaction time to hearing the word and pressing the asterisk key, and second, there is also a short delay while After Effects processes the keyboard command and creates a marker. However, this technique usually produces better and quicker results than just trying to play through the Timeline. In the next section, you will use the layer's waveform to help refine the position of each marker.

This technique may take a couple of tries to perfect. You can always remove the markers by right-clicking on any marker along the time ruler at the top of the Timeline and choosing Delete All Markers from the menu that appears.

7 Choose File > Save As, and in the dialog box that appears, navigate to the ae07lessons folder and change the file name to **Syncing Animation to Audio-working.aep**.

Click the Save button to close the dialog box. Don't close the file, as you will need it in the next part of the lesson.

Naming composition markers

Technically, composition markers don't have names, but they do allow you to add comments that will display on the Timeline. You can often use this comment field to stand in for a name, and it makes identifying individual markers much easier. In this section, you will name the 20 markers you created in the previous exercise.

1 With the Syncing Animation to Audio-working.aep file open, double-click on the first composition marker to display the Composition Marker dialog box.

2 In the Comment field, type **Tiger 1st** and click OK to close the dialog box. A label with the comment is now displayed next to the marker.

Comments assigned to labels will display in the Timeline.

3 Double-click on the second marker and in the Comment field in the dialog box, type **Tiger 2nd**.

4 Press the plus (+) key on your keyboard to zoom in on the Timeline and make the markers larger. Use the horizontal scroll bar at the bottom of the Timeline to reveal more keyframes. Follow the table below to label the rest of the markers:

MARKER NUMBER	COMMENT	MARKER NUMBER	COMMENT
1	Tiger 1st	11	What
2	Tiger 2nd	12	Immortal
3	Burning	13	Hand
4	Bright	14	Or
5	In	15	Eye
6	The	16	Dare
7	Forests	17	Claim
8	Of	18	Thy
9	The	19	Fearful
10	Night	20	Symmetry

The marker labels have a tendency to overlap when the markers are close to one another, so zoom in on the Timeline to see them individually.

5 Choose File > Save to save these changes to your After Effects project. Do not close the file, as you will need it again in the next part of the lesson.

Refining the position of composition markers

Once added to the Timeline, markers are easy to work with, as you learned in the previous exercises. In this section, you will refine the position of the markers by using the layer's waveform as a guide.

1 With the Syncing Animation to Audio-working.aep file open, click on the playhead and move it to the 1 second (0;00;01;00) mark on the Timeline; this is where the first major peaks in the waveform are located.

Waveforms represent the volume of an audio file over time, so the peaks represent when the speaker is talking and the relatively level areas represent periods of silence.

The first two sets of peaks are where the speaker says the word *Tiger*.

You can make the waveform clearer by zooming in on the Timeline.

 You may have to zoom in on the Timeline to make the peaks visible.

2 Hold down the Ctrl (Windows) or Command (Mac OS) key on your keyboard and scrub the playhead over these first few peaks in the waveform to confirm that you are in the right place on the Timeline.

 Normally when scrubbing the playhead, the audio portion of the composition does not preview, but by holding down the Command (Mac OS) or Ctrl (Windows) key, you can enable it.

Through a little trial and error, you will find that the word *Tiger* begins at approximately 29 frames into the Timeline.

3 Move the playhead to the 29 frame (0;00;00;29) mark on the Timeline.

Drag the first marker, the one labeled Tiger 1st, toward the playhead until it snaps into position.

4 The second time the speaker says the word *Tiger* is at the 1 second 7 frames (0;00;01;07) mark on the Timeline.

Move the playhead to this position and drag the second marker to the playhead.

5 Continue to position the markers so that they correspond with the actual position of the words as they are spoken. You will find that some markers are closer than others. Follow the matrix below to synchronize the markers with the words.

MARKER NAME	POSITION	MARKER NAME	POSITION
Tiger 1st	0;00;00;29	What	0;00;04;26
Tiger 2nd	0;00;01;07	Immortal	0;00;04;29
Burning	0;00;01;25	Hand	0;00;05;15
Bright	0;00;02;04	Or	0;00;05;24
In	0;00;02;23	Eye	0;00;05;27
The	0;00;02;26	Dare	0;00;06;11
Forests	0;00;03;05	Claim	0;00;06;22
Of	0;00;03;20	Thy	0;00;06;27
The	0;00;03;24	Fearful	0;00;07;06
Night	0;00;03;26	Symmetry	0;00;07;21

6 Choose File > Save to save these changes to your After Effects project. Do not close the file, as you will need it again in the next part of the lesson.

Syncing animation to composition markers

Now that you have completed the most complex part of this process, actually syncing the animation keyframes to the markers will be much easier. In this section, you will sync the animation for the first stanza with the composition markers you have just created and synced to the text.

The syncing process can be tedious, so you'll want to start this lesson when you have some time to concentrate, and when your patience level is high. Syncing is an important skill for animating in After Effects, so keep going even when it gets to be a bit repetitious..

1 With the Syncing Animation to Audio-working.aep file open, click on the reveal triangle for the Tiger Tiger.wav file to hide its properties.

2 Click on the layer named TIGER (layer number 2), hold down the Shift key, and click on the layer named night (layer number 11) to select all these layers simultaneously. Press the **U** key on your keyboard to reveal only the properties that have animation enabled for each layer.

Once the properties are revealed, click in any empty area of the Timeline to deselect all the layers.

3 Move the playhead to the first composition marker, the one named Tiger 1st. Click on the layer named *TIGER* to select it and press the left bracket ([) key on your keyboard. This moves the In point of the layer to the current position of the playhead.

This causes the first keyframe of the layer's animation to also become aligned with the first marker.

The left bracket ([ ) key aligns the In point of a layer with the current position of the playhead and the right bracket ( ]) aligns the Out Point of a layer with the playhead. Neither command trims or shortens the layer.

4 Click on the second keyframe of the animation, hold down the Shift key on your keyboard, and drag it to the left until it snaps to the position of the second marker, the one named *Tiger 2nd*.

You can tell a keyframe is selected because it changes color from gray to bright yellow.

Holding down the Shift key on your keyboard forces the keyframes to snap to the composition markers when you move them.

5   Move the playhead to the second composition marker, the one named *Tiger 2nd*. Hold down the Shift key on the keyboard and drag the first keyframe for the layer named *TIGER Reversal* to the current position of the playhead.

Hold down the Alt key on your keyboard and press the left bracket key. This trims the In point of the TIGER Reversal layer to the position of the playhead.

Remember that layers are only visible in the composition for the duration specified by their In and Out points.

 Trimming a layer actually shortens the layer's duration. Holding down the Alt (Windows) or Option (Mac OS) key on your keyboard and pressing the left bracket ([) key trims the In point of the layer, while pressing the right bracket (]) key trims the layer's Out point.

6   Click on the second keyframe of the TIGER Reversal layer, hold down the Shift key, and drag it to the marker named *Burning*.

7   Move the playhead to the marker named *Burning*, click on the layer named *burning* to select it, and press the left bracket key on your keyboard to move the In point of the layer to the playhead.

Click on the second keyframe of this layer, hold down the Shift key, and move it to the marker named *Bright*. Be sure the layer is selected before holding down shift and moving it.

The Shift key is used to insure that the playhead snaps to markers on the timeline. It also forces it to snap to layer In and Out points and keyframes as well.

8 Move the playhead to the marker named *Bright*, click on the layer named *bright* to select it, and press the left bracket key on your keyboard to move the In point of the layer to the playhead.

Click on the second keyframe of this layer, hold down the Shift key, and move it to the marker named *In*.

9 Move the playhead to the marker named *In*, click on the layer named *in* to select it, and press the left bracket key on your keyboard to move the In point of the layer to the playhead.

Click on the second keyframe of this layer, hold down the Shift key, and move it to the marker named *The*.

10 Move the playhead to the marker named *The*, click on the layer named *the* to select it, and press the left bracket key on your keyboard to move the In point of the layer to the playhead.

Click on the second keyframe of this layer, hold down the Shift key, and move it to the marker named *Forests*.

11 Move the playhead to the marker named *Forests*, click on the layer named *forests* to select it, and press the left bracket key on your keyboard to move the In point of the layer to the playhead.

Click on the second keyframe of this layer, hold down the Shift key, and move it to the marker named *of*.

12 Move the playhead to the marker named *Of*, click on the layer named *of* to select it, and press the left bracket key on your keyboard to move the In point of the layer to the playhead.

Click on the second keyframe of this layer, hold down the Shift key, and move it to the marker named *The*.

13 Move the playhead to the marker named *The*, click on the layer named *the* to select it, and press the left bracket key on your keyboard to move the In point of the layer to the playhead.

Click on the second keyframe of this layer, hold down the Shift key, and move it to the marker named *Night*.

14 Move the playhead to the marker named *Night*, click on the layer named *night* to select it, and press the left bracket key on your keyboard to move the In point of the layer to the playhead.

Move the playhead to the 4 second 5 frame (0;00;04;05) mark on the Timeline, hold down the Shift key, and drag the second keyframe to the playhead. Remember to click before pressing shift as you discovered in step 7 of this exercise.

Keyframes can be moved on the timeline similar to the way layers can be dragged in the composition.

15 The last thing to do is to trim the Out points of all the layers so that you will have room for the second stanza to display.

Move the playhead to the marker named *What*. Click on the layer named *TIGER* (layer number 2), hold down the Shift key, and click on the layer named *night* (layer number 11) to again select all these layers simultaneously.

Hold down the Alt (Windows) or Option (Mac OS) key on the keyboard and press the right bracket key to trim all the Out points of the selected layers to the playhead's current position.

16 Disable the shy switch at the top of the Composition panel to reveal the hidden layers. RAM Preview the animation to see what you have accomplished. The second half of the poem is still visible when you preview the animation. This is because the shy command only hides layers in the Timeline panel but leaves these same layers visible in the Composition. While you will not work with them as part of this lesson, these layers are available to you should you wish to continue to practice this technique of syncing audio with animation.

Choose File > Save to save these changes to your After Effects project. You may now close the file, as you are finished with it.

Creating keyframes from audio files

Audio isn't always used on its own or to support animation; sometimes it's actually used to run or trigger the animation of other layers. The audio information in a file can be converted into keyframes and then linked to properties on another layer using expressions, the scripting language built into After Effects. While you will learn more about expressions in Lesson 9, "Advanced Animation," you are going to use a very simple feature of expressions here.

In this exercise, you will add an audio file to a prebuilt project and then use it to control the scaling of a series of objects in a composition.

1   Choose File > Open Project and navigate to the ae07lessons folder. Locate the Creating keyframes from audio files.aep file and double-click on it to open this project.
The Main Composition consists of a background layer and a series of semi-transparent circles above it. The circles are themselves each individual comps, duplicates of the Scaling Circle composition.

2   At the top of the Composition panel, click on the arrow in the flowchart selector to the right of the main composition to open the Mini-Flowchart view.

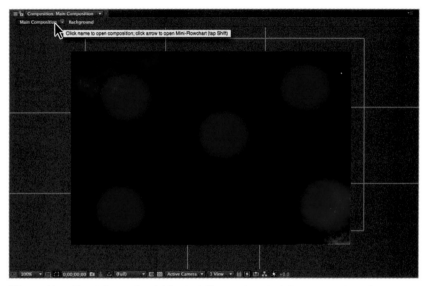

When working with nested comps the mini-flowchart allows you to navigate from one comp to another.

3   As you can see in the Mini-Flowchart view, this composition is made up of the background comp and five iterations of the Scaling Circle comp.

Click on the Scaling Circle (5) label in the Mini-Flowchart view to open this composition.

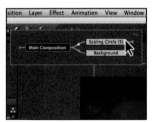

The mini-flowchart view makes it easy to navigate between your compositions without leaving the Timeline or Composition panels.

4 Once the Scaling Circle comp opens, you can see that it is composed of one layer, a shape layer named *circle*.

In the Project panel, click on the audio folder to highlight it and choose File > Import > File.

In the Import File dialog box, navigate to the ae07lessons folder, locate the file named Captain Zero 16seconds.wav, and double-click to import it. It is automatically placed inside the audio folder.

5 Drag the Captain Zero 16 seconds.wav file to the Timeline and place it below the circle layer.

The audio file is a bit low, so you will adjust its audio levels to make it louder and produce a better effect.

6 Click on the reveal triangle for the audio layer to show the Audio property group. Then click on the reveal triangle for the property group to show the Audio Levels property. Change the value of the Audio Levels property to +12.00 dB.

7 With the Captain Zero 16seconds.wav layer selected, choose Animation > Keyframe Assistant > Convert Audio to Keyframes. This creates a new layer named Audio Amplitude.

The Convert Audio to Keyframes command converts the volume information in the audio file into keyframes and stores that information in this new layer.

8 With the Audio Amplitude layer selected, press the Return (Mac OS) or Enter (Windows) key on your keyboard to make the layer name editable, and change it to audio-volume keyframes. Then click on the reveal triangle to show the Effects and Transform property groups.

Click on the reveal triangle for the Effects group to reveal the Left, Right, and Both Channels properties.

Finally, click the reveal triangle for the Both Channels property to reveal the slider control of this property. You will use expressions to attach the Scale property of the circle to this slider.

The keyframes for the layer are deeply nested inside the property group.

9 Click on the circle layer to select it and press the **S** key on the keyboard to reveal its Scale property. Click on the Scale property and choose Animation > Add Expression.

Adding an expression to a layer adds a series of controls and a text field to the layer where you can input the expression code. You can learn more about expressions in Lesson 9, "Advanced Animation." For now, you are simply going to use the Expression Pick whip (⊚) to connect the Scale property to the Both Channels slider.

10 Click on the Expression Pick whip and drag it to the Both Channels slider above. When the slider property becomes highlighted, this is your cue that the Pick whip has found its target.

The Expression pick whip can be used to connect any layer property to any other layer property.

When you release the Pick whip, it automatically adds the code that links the two properties to the text files in the Timeline.

11 Click on the Main Composition tab in the Timeline panel to return to that comp.

RAM Preview the animation to see the effect of your work. Notice that the circles now oscillate in time to the music's beat. Be sure to adjust your computer's volume to suit your needs so that the playback is neither too loud nor too soft.

Choose File > Save As. In the dialog box that appears, navigate to the ae07lessons folder and change the file name to **Creating keyframes from audio files-working.aep**.

Click Save to close the dialog box. You can now close the project, as you are done with it. Congratulations! You have completed the lesson.

Self study

1   Complete the animation for the Syncing Animation to Audio-working.aep project; there is still an entire stanza left to animate.

2   Create a new Composition and import your own audio files, convert them into keyframes, and use the Expressions Pick whip to experiment with linking them to different transform properties of visual layers such as Opacity and Position. You can also link them to the properties of effects.

Review

Questions

1   What is the advantage of using uncompressed audio files in After Effects?

2   What are the three ways to preview audio on the Timeline?

3   Why is it helpful to name composition markers?

Answers

1   Uncompressed audio files tend to preview better in After Effects. Also, because they are uncompressed, they usually produce a higher-quality sound when exported than files that have already been compressed and are again re-compressed when you output them.

2   You can preview audio on the Timeline using a RAM Preview, or by scrubbing the playhead while holding the Ctrl (Windows) or Command (Mac OS) key. You can also preview it separately by choosing Composition > Preview > Audio Preview(Here Forward) or choosing Composition > Preview > Audio Preview(Work Area).

3   Naming composition markers is helpful because it makes identifying and locating them more convenient.

Lesson 8

What you'll learn in this lesson:

- Creating and animating 3D layers
- Understanding 3D Transformations
- Using lights and cameras
- Working with Photoshop 3D objects

Working with 3D in After Effects

The real world has more than two dimensions, and so do your After Effects projects. Even experienced After Effects users can find working in three dimensions a little daunting, but after an initial learning curve you will come to see how much more visually compelling your work can be when using all three dimensions.

Starting up

You will work with several files from the ae08lessons folder in this lesson. Make sure that you have loaded the aelessons folder onto your hard drive from the supplied DVD. See "Loading lesson files" on page 4.

See Lesson 8 in action!

Use the accompanying video to gain a better understanding of how to use some of the features shown in this lesson. The video tutorial for this lesson can be found on the included DVD.

Setting up

As you work in After Effects you will inevitably open and close many panels, depending on the type of project you are creating. However, when working through the projects in this book, it is important to have an interface that matches the lessons. To this end, you should always reset your workspace to the preset Standard configuration.

1   Choose Window > Workspace > Standard to set your current workspace configuration.

2   Choose Window > Workspace > Reset "Standard" to reset the standard workspace in case you have modified it at some point.

Previewing animation with RAM preview

Animations that you preview by pressing the spacebar or just scrubbing the playhead are not in real time, nor can you use them to preview audio in your composition. Instead, you can have After Effects render a video preview by using your system's RAM. The length of the preview depends on both the amount of RAM allocated to the program and the current settings of the Preview panel. There are two sets of RAM preview options available: RAM preview (the standard) and Shift-RAM preview. These options are simply a way of saving two different render settings. For example, you may set the RAM preview options to render at full frame rate and resolution and set the Shift-RAM options for lower resolution and to mute audio. Lower-quality settings require less RAM, and therefore you can render longer previews more quickly.

*A. Go To First Frame. **B**. Go To Previous Frame. **C**. Play/Pause Timeline. **D**: Go To Next Frame. **E**. Go To Last Frame. **F**. Mute Audio. **G**. Loop Options. **H**. RAM Preview.*

The options available when setting up a RAM preview are:

Mute Audio: By default, RAM preview, unlike the spacebar preview, includes audio on the Timeline. The Mute button allows you to exclude it to create a quicker preview.

Frame Rate: This option specifies the frame rate for the rendered preview. If you choose the Auto setting, it uses the previewed composition's frame rate.

Skip: This option specifies the number of frames to skip between a rendered frame and the next rendered frame. Choose zero to render all frames. This setting is helpful for building previews more quickly.

Resolution: This option specifies the resolution of the rendered preview. For example, setting this option to half renders every other pixel in the composition, resulting in a lower quality but faster preview. You should choose Auto to use the composition's current resolution setting as specified in the Resolution/Down Sample Factor popup menu.

From Current Time: By default, a RAM preview plays from the beginning of the work area bar to the end. Select From Current Time to play from the current position of the playhead instead.

Full Screen: Normally the RAM preview plays in the workspace. Choose this option to isolate the preview on screen against a flat background.

1   Click and drag to position the work area bar's start and end points over the area you want to preview.

*You can press the **B** key on the keyboard to move the beginning of the work area bar to the playhead and the **N** key to move the end of the bar to the current position of the playhead.*

2   Click the RAM Preview button ( ) in the Preview panel to begin rendering the Timeline.

Working the 3D capabilities of After Effects

You can set any layer or composition in After Effects as a 3D layer by enabling the 3D features from the Switches pane of the Timeline. Three things happen when you turn this switch on: the layer can now be affected by lights and camera movement, a new properties group called Material Options is added to the layer, and the existing Transform properties (with the exception of Opacity) are appended to include a z-axis value. In the case of Rotation, a new property is added called Orientation and the Rotation property is split into three different properties: X Rotation, Y Rotation, and Z Rotation.

Creating 3D layers

Unlike other motion graphics programs, After Effects allows you to combine both 2D and 3D layers together in the same composition. By default, all layers, including layers made from nested compositions, start off as 2D and can be easily converted to 3D by turning on a switch. In this set of exercises you will work with a pre-built composition to animate layers so that they appear to rotate towards the viewer in 3D space. But first you must convert them to 3D layers.

1   Open the SecretOfSuccess.aep file found in your ae08lessons folder. This After Effects project is composed of a single composition with seven layers, one layer for each of the words in the phrase, "THE SECRET OF SUCCESS IS Sincerity," and one for the background. Move the playhead to any time after the 00;00;03;15 mark. The layers in the composition already have an opacity animation added to them, so you won't be able to see anything except the background plate while the playhead is at the beginning (00;00;00;00) of the Timeline.

2   Choose File > Save As and navigate to the ae08lessons folder. Rename the file **SecretOfSuccess_Working.aep** and click Save.

3 With the Composition panel highlighted, choose View > Clear Guides to remove the onscreen guidelines.

The onscreen guides were used when this file was being created to help arrange the different layers.

4 Lock the Background layer to avoid accidentally editing it, by clicking the Lock button (🔒) to the left of the layer. If it is not already open, expand the Layer Switches pane in the After Effects Timeline panel by pressing the Expand/Collapse button (🔘) in the lower-left corner of the panel.

5 Click on the first layer to highlight it and press Ctrl+A (Windows) or Command+A (Mac OS) to select all the layers in the composition, then click the 3D Layer switch (🔵) to enable each layer's 3D properties.

You can use layer switches to enable effects such as 3D and Motion Blur.

6 Press Ctrl+Shift+A (Windows) or Command+Shift+A (Mac OS) to deselect all the layers in your composition.

7 Save your file by choosing File > Save.

Using multiple viewports

When working with layers in 3D space, it is very helpful to be able to change the native composition window from the standard single-view layout to a multiple-view layout. The multiple-view layout can split the composition area into either two or four viewports, each of which has several configurations. In preparation for working in 3D space, you will configure the Composition window with a two-view layout.

1   Click the Select View Layout drop-down menu located at the bottom of the Composition window.

As you work with 3D elements in After Effects, you will often change the viewport layout.

2   Choose the multiple-view layout named 2 Views-Horizontal from the drop-down menu. Keep in mind when working on your own that you may need to change the view configuration quite often; in these situations you will want to choose the specific multiple-view layout that fits your needs.

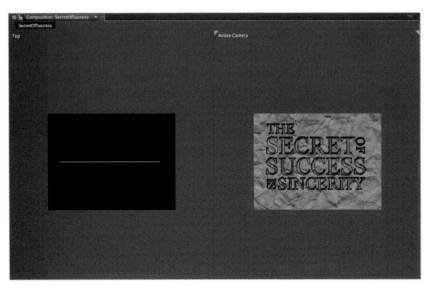

The default display of 2 Views-Horizontal is a Top and Active Camera view.

Understanding the different views

Located next to the Select View Layout drop-down menu is the 3D View popup menu. You use it to change the view of the active viewport. While it is available at any time in the program, it is only useful when working with 3D layers. You have a choice between the Active Camera view; Orthographic views such as Front, Top, and Left; and using camera layers that you have created as viewports.

The default view in After Effects is called Active Camera. This is a perspective view that allows you to interact with your content along all three axes (X, Y, and Z), and it shows the effects of perspective as well. Initially you can think of it as a virtual default camera. Once you add additional cameras, however, the effect of choosing Active Camera changes a bit. When working with camera layers, you have the choice of viewing through either the cameras lens or Active Camera. In this situation, the active camera view refers to the camera that is currently underneath the playhead.

In the figure above, as the playhead moves, the Active Camera view changes. At the beginning of the Timeline, Camera 1 is the Active Camera, but at 2 seconds (0;00;02;00) Camera 2 becomes the Active Camera view. As the playhead progresses and reaches the 4 second (0;00;04;00) mark, the third camera, named Camera 3, becomes active. What this means is that the viewports shift what they are viewing. This is important to be aware of because only the Active Camera view can be rendered, so controlling the start and end points of camera layers is a way of creating cuts to different cameras in After Effects.

In addition to camera layers and the Active Camera views, you can use a series of Orthographic views as well. These views — Front, Left, Top, Back, Right, and Bottom — provide an isolation of one specific angle. Each view is 90 degrees from the previous view, creating a virtual box that surrounds the composition. These views are very helpful when you must lay out content in three-dimensional space or if you simply need to isolate and move a single layer along a specified axis.

3   Select the left viewport and confirm that the 3D view popup menu is set to Top. When you click on a view, small triangular markers appear at its corners, indicating that it is the active viewport. Choose Fit Up To 100% from the Magnification drop-down menu.

4   Select the right viewport and confirm that the 3D view popup menu is set to Active Camera, and again choose Fit Up To 100% from the Magnification drop-down menu. This ensures that you have enough room to actually see the composition as you animate the text. If you are working on a smaller display, the magnification may not increase.

Understanding 3D Transform properties

Once you have enabled the 3D properties for any layer, you can immediately see a change in that layer's Transform properties. With the exception of Opacity, every property that formerly had two values (for X and Y) now has an additional Z property. In addition to these modifications, the rotation value has been completely altered. When converted to a 3D layer, the single Rotation property is split into X Rotation, Y Rotation, Z Rotation, and a fourth property that combines them all as a single keyframe-value Orientation.

Position, Anchor Point, and Scale

When a layer's 3D property is disabled, Position, Anchor Point, and Scale each have two numerical values, one for X and one for Y. As part of a 3D layer, each of these properties gains another value for the Z property. For example, Position is now seen in the property list as Position 00.0, 00.0, 00.0 where the first value represents the position of the layer along the X-axis, the second value represents its position along the Y-axis, and the third value its position along the Z-axis.

X Rotation, Y Rotation, Z Rotation and Orientation

When you disable a layer's 3D property, the single rotation value (which is actually Z Rotation) is split into three properties (X Rotation, Y Rotation , Z Rotation) and the Orientation property is added. The individual rotation properties allow you to create individual keyframes for each axis of rotation. This is helpful when you want to create rotational animations where the properties change by different values or have different timing, as you can create separate keyframes for each property. However, animation of the Orientation property creates a single keyframe that contains the values of all three rotation values.

Understanding Material Options

Once you have enabled the 3D switch for a layer, an additional property group named Material Options becomes available. A 3D layer's Material Options specify how that layer reacts when it receives light and casts shadows.

Cast Shadows: This option specifies whether a layer can cast shadows onto other layers. The position and angle of the cast shadows is determined by the relationship of the light that is creating the shadows to the layers that are casting and receiving the shadows. The density and diffusion of the shadows is determined by the light's options. The Cast Shadows option is turned off by default, but it actually has three settings: off, on, and only. The only setting removes the layer's content and just projects a shadow onto the receiving layers.

Light Transmission: This option specifies the translucency of a layer as a percentage. When you set the value to zero percent, the layer acts like an opaque wall casting a black shadow. A value of 100 percent allows the colors of a shadow-producing layer to be projected onto a receiving layer.

Accepts Shadows: This option specifies whether or not a layer can receive shadows that are cast by other layers. In order to see the effects of the Cast Shadows option in a scene, there has to be at least one 3D layer in that scene with the Accepts Shadows option enabled.

Accepts Lights: This option specifies whether or not the content of a 3D layer is affected by light layers in a composition.

Ambient: This option specifies the ambient reflectivity of a layer. The ambient reflectivity of a layer is non-directional, meaning it doesn't actually project light back toward the viewer. This setting is the most reflective at 100 percent, and the least reflective at zero percent.

Diffuse: This option specifies the diffuse reflectivity of a layer. The diffuse reflectivity is omnidirectional, meaning that light that falls on this layer is reflected in all directions. You can think of the diffuse reflectivity as the base or overall reflectivity of the layer. This setting is the most reflective at 100 percent, and the least reflective at zero percent.

Specular: This option specifies the specular reflectivity of a layer. The specular reflectivity is directional, reflecting back towards the source of light, the way a mirror would. Specular reflectivity is what causes the intense highlights that give shiny metals, such as gold and silver, their distinctive appearances. This setting is the most reflective at 100 percent, and the least reflective at zero percent.

Shininess: This option specifies the size of the highlight created (called the specular highlight) when you set the specular reflectivity to a value higher than zero percent. Smaller values produce a larger specular highlight, while higher values produce a smaller one. Materials, such as shiny metals and plastics, tend to have very small specular highlights.

Metal: This option specifies whether or not the layer's content affects the color of the specular highlight. The default value of 100 percent sets the color of the highlight to that of the layer's content, while a value of zero percent sets the highlight color to the light's color.

Animating 3D layers

Three-dimensional layer properties are animated in exactly the same fashion as two-dimensional layer properties. Once you have enabled animation for a specific property (by clicking on the Time-Vary Stopwatch (●) to the left of the property), any change to that property—either by changing the numerical values for the property in the Timeline, or by directly editing it in the Composition window—creates a new animation keyframe. Most of the properties for 2D and 3D layers are the same (Anchor Point, Position, and Scale) except they have an additional value for the Z-axis. However, the Rotation property is significantly different between these two types of layers.

When working with two-dimensional layers, there is a single rotation value; it doesn't say so, but this is a rotation along the Z-axis. Once you enable the 3D switch for a layer, it gains three isolated rotation values: X Rotation, Y Rotation, and Z Rotation. It also gains the Orientation property, which combines all three rotations into a single keyframe value.

In this exercise, you will animate the layers along their respective X and Y axes to give the impression that they are flipping towards the viewer, like a swinging door. In this exercise, the Anchor Point properties of the layers have been repositioned so that each layer will rotate properly.

The Opacity property is unchanged when dealing with 3D layers.

1   Select the first layer named "THE" and press **U** on your keyboard; this shows the Opacity property. You press the **U** key to reveal all layer properties that already have the Time-Vary stopwatch icon (●) enabled.

2   Hold down the Shift key on your keyboard and press **R** to reveal its Rotation properties (Orientation, X Rotation, Y Rotation, Z Rotation) as well. This ability to show multiple properties at once is helpful, especially when you want to create animation where different properties animate concurrently.

Learning the various keyboard commands in After Effects improves your speed and efficiency when using the program.

Use the Shift key to add properties to the display without replacing the ones that are currently displayed. You can also use the Shift key to hide individual properties if you press Shift+R; in this example, the Rotation properties would be hidden, but the Opacity property would remain.

3   If it is not already there, move your playhead to the beginning of the Timeline, where the first Opacity keyframe is located. Click the Auto-Keyframe button (●) at the top of the Timeline panel. Auto-Keyframe is a timesaving feature that allows you to enable animation for any property by simply changing its value.

4   Change this layer's Y Rotation to **0x -90** degrees; a keyframe is created. Because the Auto-Keyframe switch was enabled, you don't have to click on the property's Time-Vary stopwatch icon (●) first.

5   Press the **K** key on your keyboard to jump to the second opacity keyframe at 0;00;01;00. Change the Y Rotation value to **0x 00** degrees. This returns the layer to its forward-facing position. Scrub the playhead back and forth to test your animation. The text now appears to swing forward and fade in to view. If you look in the Top viewport on the left, you will notice a wireframe animation that shows the position of the layer in that view.

The orthographic views are helpful for determining the positional relationship of layers in 3D space.

6   With the first layer still selected, press Ctrl+~ on your keyboard to close all its visible properties. Then select layer 2, named "SECRET", and again press **U** on your keyboard to reveal all properties with animation enabled. Then hold down the Shift key and press R to reveal this layer's Rotation properties as well. The "SECRET" layer needs an X Rotation animation so that it can look like it swings down from the previous layer.

7 Click in any area of the viewport on the left side of the Composition panel to make it active and change the 3D View Popup menu to Left. Now move the playhead to the first opacity keyframe for this layer by pressing **J** (to move the playhead back) or **K** (to move the playhead forward) on your keyboard. Change the X Rotation to **90** degrees.

The 3D View Popup menu is used to change each view port independently.>>

8 Press **K** on your keyboard to jump to the last Opacity keyframe for this layer and change the X Rotation to **zero** degrees. Scrub the playhead, and you can see that the animations all run simultaneously.

With the layer selected, press Ctrl+~ to close all its visible properties.

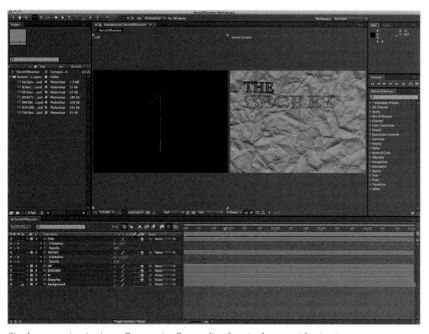

Simultaneous animation is usually more visually appealing than simple sequential animation.

9 Select layer 3 and press **T** on your keyboard to reveal its Opacity property. Then hold down the Shift key and press **R** to reveal this layer's Rotation properties as well. Hold down the Shift key and drag the playhead to the first keyframe in the Opacity property. The Shift key forces the playhead to snap to keyframes and layer in/out points.

10 Set the Y Rotation for layer 3 to **–90** degrees, move the playhead to the second opacity keyframe, and set the rotation value to zero degrees.

Now that you are familiar with this process, you can complete the other three layers yourself. The properties to animate and their values are listed in the following table. All the values below are for the first keyframe of the animation. The second keyframe is always 0 degrees.

LAYER NUMBER	LAYER NAME	PROPERTY	VALUE
4	SUCCESS	X Rotation	90 degrees
5	IS	X Rotation	90 degrees
6	Sincerity	X Rotation	90 degrees

Remember to place each pair of rotation keyframes so that they correspond with the position of each layer's opacity keyframes. The final Timeline should look like this when complete.

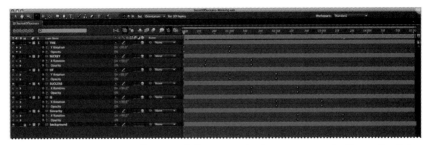

Making the rotation animation simultaneous with the opacity animation creates a more visually appealing design.

11 Save your file by choosing File > Save.

Creating and using lights

Lights in After Effects affect only three-dimensional layers, and you can use them to illuminate these layers and cast shadows. You can use lights to create appealing visual effects and enhance the sense of depth and volume in a scene. There are four types of lights that you can create in After Effects: Parallel, Spot, Point, and Ambient. Each light has specific editable properties and is intended to be used in a specific way. In this exercise, you will be creating a spotlight. The appearance of the shadows and highlights created by a spotlight are based on the position of the light and the layer it is shining on, as well their properties for Light and Material options.

Lights do not have an Anchor Point property like other layers do; instead, they have a point of interest. This Point of Interest property sets the point in the composition that the light looks at. When it is moved around the composition, the light always rotates to look at this point. This feature is called Auto-Orient Towards Point of Interest, and you can edit it from the Auto-Orientation dialog box by choosing Layer > Transform > Auto-Orient.

Unlike in the real world, lights in After Effects only cast shadows if you want them to. If you have ever tried to light a scene, you will be amazed at how different everything looks when you can actually turn off a light's ability to cast shadows, or for that matter a layer's ability to receive them, or even turn off a layer's ability to be affected by lights. In this exercise, you will set up the background layer so that it can receive shadows from the text layers above it.

1   Open the SecretOfSuccess_Working.aep file that you created earlier in this lesson. If you skipped that section, you can use the file named SecretOfSuccess-complete.aep that has been provided. Move the playhead to the 4 second (0;00;04;00) mark so that you can see the final position of the animation.

2   Choose File > Save As. If necessary, navigate to the ae08lessons folder. Rename the file SecretOfSuccess-lighting.aep and click Save.

3 Choose Layer > New > Light to open the Light Options dialog box. In the dialog box, set the light's properties as follows:

- Name: Spot Light 1

- Light Type: Spot

- Intensity: 100%

- Cone Angle: 90°

- Cone Feather: 50%

- Color: White (R:255, G:255, B:255)

- Cast Shadows: On

- Shadow Darkness: 100%

- Shadow Diffusion: 0%

Once you have set its properties, click OK to create the new light.

Spotlights are directional lights that project a cone of light at the subject.

The keyboard command for creating a new camera layer is Ctrl+Alt+Shift+C (Windows) or Command+Option+Shift+C (Mac OS).

The new spotlight has been created but you can see that it only affects the text layers. The middle of the layers where the light is actually hitting them is brightest, while the edges are much darker; this is caused by the light's Cone Angle and Cone Feather settings. Even though Cast Shadows has been enabled for the light, the layers need to have the Cast Shadows option enabled individually, and even then the shadows need to have a surface to be cast on. To receive shadows, you have to convert the background layer to 3D and enable it to receive shadows.

The effect of lights is only visible on the opaque parts of 3D layers.

4 In the Composition panel's Select View Layout drop-down menu, select 1 View.

In the Timeline panel, lock the Spot Light 1 layer; the background layer was locked prior to this in an earlier exercise of the lesson. Press Ctrl+Shift+A (Windows) or Command+Shift+A (Mac OS) to select the remaining text layers. Now that they are all highlighted, any change you make to the properties of one layer will affect them all.

On the layer named THE, click the reveal triangle to the left of the layer name to show its properties. Then click the reveal triangle next to Material Options to show them as well.

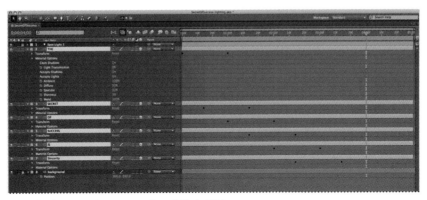

Remember that Material options are only available for 3D layers.

5 Click the Cast Shadows property to turn it on. This enables Cast Shadows for all selected layers, but you still see no effect because shadows have to be cast onto a three-dimensional background layer. Additionally, the layer that receives the shadows cannot be at the same Z position as the layers that are casting the shadows.

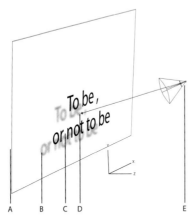

A. *Layer to receive the shadows.* **B.** *The shadow.* **C.** *Layer that casts the shadow.*
D. *Point of Interest.* **E.** *Light source.*

With all the text layers still selected, press Ctrl+~ (Windows/Mac OS) to hide all the currently visible properties.

Sometimes it is necessary to use the Ctrl+~ (Windows/Mac OS) *multiple times to close all the visible properties.*

6 Unlock the bottom layer named background. Click the layer's 3D switch; this immediately allows it to be affected by the spotlight. While the Accept Shadows property is enabled for this layer, the text layers can't cast shadows on it because they all occupy the exact same Z position. To correct this, you will adjust the depth of this layer.

Confirm that the playhead is still at the 4 second (0;00;04;00) mark n the timeline, and with the background layer still selected, press the **P** key on your keyboard to reveal its Position property and change the Z position to **150**. This makes the layer's position values 360.0, 240.0, and 150.0. You can now see the shadows being cast by the letters.

The shadows are dark and heavy due to the initial light settings, but they will be adjusted later.

7 Disable the visibility of the Spot Light 1 layer by clicking on the eye icon (👁) to the left of the layer name. This disables the lighting effect and returns the scene to the default lighting conditions where all layers receive a default ambient light. Now that you can see it, you will notice that the background layer appears much smaller than it did before. Due to the effect of perspective, objects that are farther away from the viewer appear smaller than objects that are closer.

Whenever you are working with 3D layers, you must take into account the effect of size distortion caused by perspective.

8 With the background layer still selected, hold down the Shift key on your keyboard and press **S** to reveal the Scale property.

Make sure the Constrain Proportions switch is enabled and change the layer's scale to **120.0**. This allows it to fill the entire composition background.

9 Re-enable the visibility of the Spot Light 1 layer and click the lock icon (🔒) to unlock it. Click the reveal triangle to the left of the layer name to show its properties, and then click the reveal triangle next to Light Options. Change the Shadow Darkness to **40** percent and the Shadow Diffusion to **20** pixels. Change the light's Cone Feather to **100** percent. This produces a softer, more subdued effect.

10 Press the **P** key on your keyboard to reveal the light's Position property and change its position values to **455.0**, **70.0**, **–375.0**.

The Position property stores the X, Y & Z positions as a single keyframe value.

11 Save your file by choosing File > Save or by pressing Ctrl+S (Windows) or Command+S (Mac OS) on the keyboard.

Understanding light options

When you create a new light, you always have access to the exact same properties but, depending on the light type you choose, some options will be disabled. In addition to being accessible in the Light Settings dialog box when you create a new light layer, these attributes are editable under the Light Options property group in the Timeline panel or when you double-click a light layer.

Light Type: Located in the Light Settings dialog box, this setting lets you specify the type of light you want to create. Point lights create directional unrestricted light, similar to that cast by the sun. The Spot light is a directional light that is restricted to a conical shape and increases in diameter the farther the source of light is from the layers that are receiving it. A Point light emits unrestricted omnidirectional light, similar to the way a household light bulb does. An Ambient light lacks a source and doesn't cast shadows, but instead adds to the overall brightness of a 3D scene.

Intensity: This setting specifies the strength of the light as a percentage. Values above 100 percent produce a burned-out effect on layers the light falls on, while negative values subtract from the colors of a layer.

Color: This setting specifies the color of the light source.

Cone Angle: For a spotlight, this setting specifies the angle of the cone that constrains the source of light. This affects the diameter of the light as it falls onto layers in your scene.

Cone Feather: For a spotlight, this setting specifies the softness of the cone's edge.

Cast Shadows: This setting specifies whether or not the light causes layers in a 3D scene to cast shadows onto other layers.

Shadow Darkness: If you enable the Cast Shadows option, this setting specifies the darkness of the shadow.

Shadow Diffusion: If you enable the Cast Shadows option, this setting specifies the shadow's softness. The amount of softness is based on the value you set and the shadow's distance from the layer casting it.

Animating light properties

Like nearly every other attribute in After Effects, the light options can be fully edited and animated in the Timeline. With the exceptions of the light type and whether or not it can cast shadows, you can animate every other property of a light to produce visually appealing graphics. In this exercise, you will use the SecretOfSuccess-lighting.aep file that you created previously and animate the light's Point of Interest and Intensity properties to create a more visually compelling design.

1   Open the SecretOfSuccess-lighting.aep file that you created earlier in this lesson. If you skipped that section, you can use the file named SecretOfSuccess-lighting-complete.aep that has been provided for you. Move the playhead to the 4 second (0;00;04;00) mark so that you can see the final position of the animation.

2   Choose File > Save As. If necessary, navigate to the ae08lessons folder. Rename the file **SecretOfSuccess-lighting-working.aep** and click Save.

3   Move the playhead to the 1 second (0;00;01;00) mark on the Timeline and click on the Spot Light 1 layer to highlight it. Press the Ctrl+~ keys (Windows/Mac OS) on your keyboard to reveal all the layer's properties.

Once a light is created it overrides the default light in a composition so that only what the lights in your scene illuminate is visible.

4   Click the Time-Vary stopwatch icon (🕑) for the Point of Interest property in the Transform group to create a keyframe for the final position of the animation. Move the playhead to the beginning (0;00;00;00) of the Timeline and change the Point of Interest property to 760.0, 510.0, 0.0. This moves it just outside of the lower-right corner, plunging the rest of the composition into darkness.

5　Preview the animation. It works, but it would benefit if the point of interest didn't move in a straight line. You can easily do this, as you can adjust its Motion Path just like any other. Click on the Point of Interest property to highlight it so that you can view its Motion Path. Position your Selection tool (⟨) over the direction handle at the end of the Motion Path and drag it down and to the left to the position shown in the following figure. Preview the animation to see the changes you made.

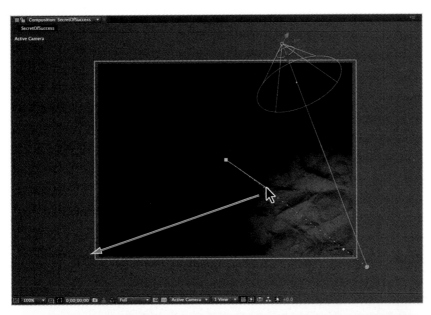

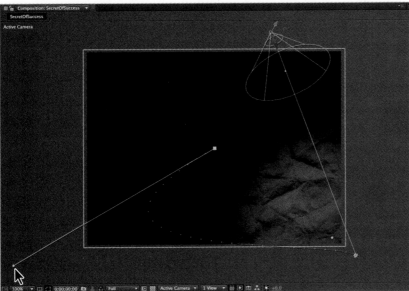

Motion Paths are visible for any positional animation such as Anchor Point, Point of Interest, and Position.

6 Move the playhead to the 4 second (0;00;04;00) mark, where the text animation ends. Click on the Time-Vary stopwatch icons (●) for Intensity and Cone Angle to create two keyframes. Because they are the first keyframes on the Timeline for this property, they will act as placeholders, locking their values in place until this time.

7 Move the playhead to the end of the Timeline. Change the Intensity to **700%** and the Cone Angle to **180°**.

While the Intensity value defaults to 100 percent, you can change it for visual effect.

This effectively whites-out the majority of the composition. You can combine this effect with a Dip to White (Fade to White) transition in an editing application such as Adobe Premiere Pro or Final Cut Pro to segue into another clip.

8 Save your file by choosing File > Save or by pressing Ctrl+S (Windows) or Command+S (Mac OS) on the keyboard.

Creating and using cameras

In After Effects, camera layers are designed to simulate the performance and behavior of film cameras in real life. As three-dimensional objects, cameras can be panned, tilted, and moved to create more engaging compositions. In addition to the ability to animate the transform (Position, Rotation, Point of Interest, and so on) properties of camera layers, you can also animate a set of additional properties called Camera Options that are unique to camera layers. You can use these properties, such as Zoom, Focus Distance, and Blur Level, to simulate effects found in real-world cameras such as Depth of Field and Rack Focus.

Like lights, cameras do not have an Anchor Point property like other layers; instead, they have a point of interest. This Point of Interest property sets the point in the composition that the camera looks at. If you move a camera, it always rotates to look at this point. This feature is called Auto-Orient Towards Point of Interest and you can edit it from the Auto-Orientation dialog box by choosing Layer > Transform > Auto-Orient.

1 As in the previous exercise, open the SecretOfSuccess-lighting.aep file that you created earlier in this lesson. If you skipped that section, you can use the file named SecretOfSuccess-lighting-complete.aep that has been provided for you. Move the playhead to the 4 second (0;00;04;00) mark so that you can see the final position of the animation.

2 Choose File > Save As. If necessary, navigate to the ae08lessons folder. Rename the file **SecretOfSuccess-camera-working.aep** and click Save.

3 Click on the Timeline panel to highlight it and choose Layer > New > Camera to open the Camera Options dialog box.

From the Type drop-down menu, select Two-Node Camera, and from the Preset menu, choose 50mm.

If it is enabled, uncheck the switch for Enable Depth of Field. Leave all other values unchanged and click OK to create the new camera layer.

4 Click on the new camera layer to highlight it and press Ctrl+~ on the keyboard to show its properties. Click on the Select View Layout drop-down menu and choose 2 views-Horizontal from the list.

Click on the left viewport and choose Top from the 3-D View Popup menu.

Click on the Hand Tool (✋) in the Tools panel to activate it. Click and drag in the Top view until you can see the rectangular camera icon. Depending on your screen size and monitor resolution you may need to change the lower the magnification amount for this view as well.

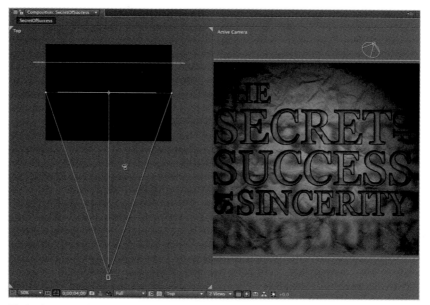

The hand icon is used to pan around a viewport.

5 Click on the Selection tool (▸) in the Tools panel to make it active and then click in the viewport on the right (the one labeled Active Camera) to make it active and change its Magnification to Fit up to 100%.

6 With the camera layer selected in the timeline place your Selection tool on top of the rectangular camera body symbol in the top view. Click and drag the camera to the left side of the viewport and notice how the Active Camera view changes as well.

The Camera, like all 3D layers has a Red, green and blue gizmo when selected. If you position the Selection tool over one of these arrows it allows you to constrain the movement of the layer to a specific axis. If you place the Selection tool over the actual camera icon, as you do here, it allows you to move the layer along any axis.

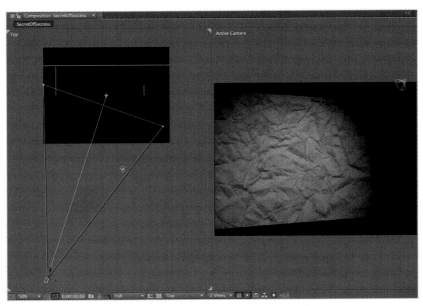

Any Active Camera view will update in real time as you move the camera in another viewport.

When working on your own, you will usually position layers by dragging them around the viewport. However, for the purposes of this exercise, change the camera's position value to **19.0**, **240.0**, **–910.0**.

7 Moving the camera has changed the relationship of the layers on your screen. The background no longer covers the entire composition space when viewed from the camera's new position.

Click on the background layer to make it active and press the **S** key on your keyboard to reveal its Scale property. Hold down the Shift key and press the **P** key to reveal the Position property as well.

8   Make sure the Constrain Proportions switch is enabled and change the background layer's Scale property to **145**. Then change the layer's X position to **490.0**.

9   Press the spacebar to begin building a preview to review the animation.

10 Save your file by choosing File > Save or by pressing Ctrl+S (Windows) or Command+S (Mac OS) on the keyboard.

Understanding camera options

Cameras in After Effects are designed to mimic real-world video cameras. Like real cameras, they have properties such as position and rotation that can be animated to duplicate camera movements like panning and dollying. In addition to these physical properties like all layers possess there are specialized Camera options that can be manipulated to produces effects like zooms and focus changes.

Zoom: This specifies the distance from the camera lens to the subjects in the 3D scene. This setting affects the relative size distortion of objects caused by perspective. A layer that is at the zoom distance appears at its normal size, while one that is double that distance from the camera appears to be half its actual size.

Depth of Field: Toggle this setting to enable or disable depth of field. When enabled, layers that are outside of the focus distance of the camera can appear blurry.

Focus Distance: This specifies the distance from the camera lens at which a layer is perfectly in focus. You can manipulate the Focus Distance value to produce depth-of-field effects like those seen in standard photography and films.

Aperture: This specifies the size of the opening in a camera lens, and affects the camera's depth of field. Smaller Aperture settings decrease the blur produced by depth of field, while larger settings increase it.

Blur Level: This specifies the amount of blur produced by a camera's Depth of Field effect.

Animating camera properties

Like all layers, cameras possess a variety of properties that you can animate. In addition to the familiar Position, Orientation, and X, Y, and Z Rotation properties, camera layers have a Point of Interest property. The point of interest is a target on screen that the camera always looks at. By default, all camera layers are set to automatically orient to their point of interest, but you can override this setting to allow them to move and rotate freely or to turn and bank following their motion paths during animation. In this exercise, you will work with the project you opened previously to create a camera fly-through animation. You will add a camera to the project and animate its position over time.

1 Choose File > Open Project. In the Open Project dialog box, navigate to the ae08lessons folder, click on Camera FlyIn.aep to highlight it, and click Open. This file is composed of a total of ten layers. Seven of the layers (Strip01 to Strip06 and Textured Background) contain images, the Background Text layer is a composition, and there are two light layers as well.

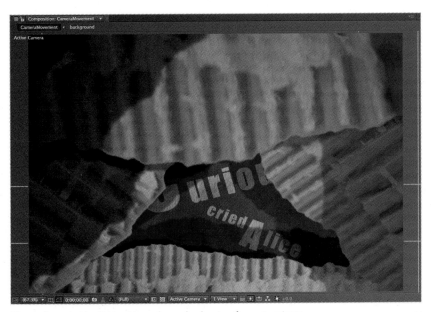

The starting project has light and image layers already set up for you to animate.

The keyboard command to open an existing project is Ctrl+O (Windows) or Command+O (Mac OS).

2 Choose File > Save As. If necessary, navigate to the ae08lessons folder. Rename the file **Camera FlyIn-working.aep** and click Save.

3   Click on the Select View Layout drop-down menu at the bottom of the Composition panel and choose Two views–Horizontal from the list.

The viewport on the right should be the Active Camera view; change its Magnification to Fit Up To 100%.

The viewport on the left should be a Top view; if not, you can use the 3D View popup menu to change it. Change this view's magnification until you can see the entire composition on screen. In the following example, the window is set to 12.5 percent, but yours may be different.

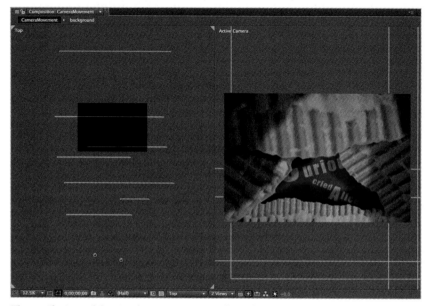

The magnification needed to view the entire composition will vary from computer to computer, based on monitor size and resolution.

4 With the Composition panel highlighted, create a new camera by choosing Layer > New > Camera to open the Camera Settings dialog box.

Leave the default name, Camera 1, unchanged. From the Type drop-down menu, select Two-Node Camera. Then from the Preset drop-down menu, choose 50mm, disable the Depth of Field switch, and click OK.

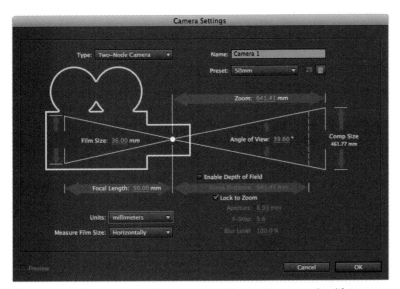

When working with cameras, it is usually easiest to start with an existing preset and modify it.

5 With the new camera layer highlighted, press **P** on your keyboard to reveal its Position property and change its Z position to **-2550**. Its Position values should now be 720.0, 480.0, -2550.

When working with Z position values, zero represents the origin point in the middle of the composition. Negative numbers are closer to the viewer than this point and positive numbers are farther away.

6 Move the playhead to the beginning of the Timeline (0;00;00;00) and click the Time-Vary stopwatch icon (⏱) for the camera's Position property to enable animation and create a keyframe.

7   Move the playhead to the 8 second (0;00;08;00) mark on the Timeline and change the camera's Z position to **-750.0**.

Scrub the playhead to preview the animation.

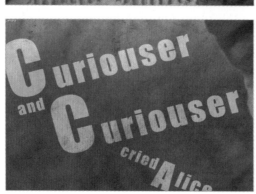

Animating the position of the camera creates a change in the positional relationship of the layers in the composition and can create an interesting visual effect.

This animation might benefit from some rotational animation in addition to what you have just done.

8   Press and hold the Shift key and then press the **R** key to display the rotation properties on the Timeline display; then click on the viewport on the left and change it from the Top view to the Front view.

Change the Front view's Magnification to Fit Up To 100%.

9 Again move the playhead to the beginning of the Timeline and click the Time-Vary stopwatch icon (⏱) next to the Orientation property to enable its animation and create the first keyframe. This creates a keyframe for Orientation with a value of 0.0°, 0.0°, 0.0°.

10 In the Timeline panel, click on the lock icon (🔒) of all the layers in the composition except the camera layer. Then click on the Camera layer to select it and make it active.

Locking layers is very helpful to avoid accidentally transforming the wrong layer when working in the Composition panel.

Move the playhead to the 3 second (0;00;03;00) mark and click the Rotation tool (↻) in the Tools panel to make it active.

11 In the Front view, position the Rotation tool in the exact middle of the camera icon right on top of the blue circle so that the tool becomes a capital Z. This indicates that your rotation will be constrained to the Z-axis.

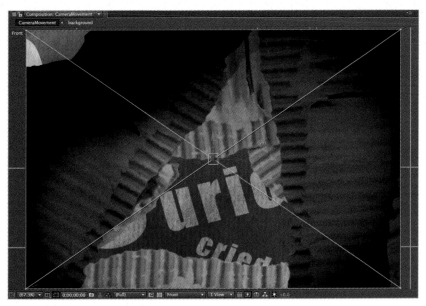

All 3D layers have a Red, Green and Blue arrow gizmo that allows you to constrain their transformations to a single axis.

 If you were to position the Rotation tool over the red or green arrows on the camera, this would constrain its movement to the X and Y axes, respectively.

Click and drag toward the bottom of the screen until the Z value of the Orientation property in the Timeline reads 50 degrees. When you first begin to click and drag on the camera a warning dialog box will appear. This dialog warns you that the camera is auto-orientated towards its point of interest and changing the rotation value may cause it to point away from it.

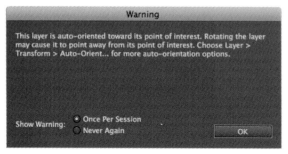

The dialog box warns you that the layer is auto-oriented toward its point of interest.

Click OK to close the dialog and continue to change the Camera's orientation value. If you cannot stop exactly at 50 degrees, you can just type the value in the Timeline. The completed Orientation property should read 0.0°, 0.0°, 50.0°.

When viewing the Orientation property the first value represents the X Rotation, the second value represents the Y Rotation and the third value represents the Z Rotation.

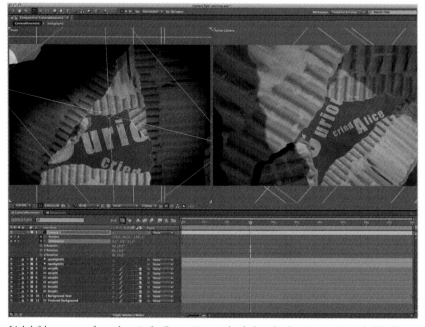

It's helpful as you transform a layer in the Composition panel to look at that layer's properties in the Timeline panel.

By default both camera and light layers are auto orientated towards their own point of interest. This is very useful in many situations such as when a light or camera must follow an object around the screen, but can be detrimental when you require a completely free range of movement. There are three choice for Auto Orient: Off, Orient Along Path, and Orient Towards Point of Interest. The can be adjusted from the Auto-Orientation dialog box by choosing Layer > Transform > Auto-Orient.

12 Move the playhead to the 6 second (00;00;06;00) mark on the Timeline and rotate the camera until the Orientation's Z value is 300.0°.

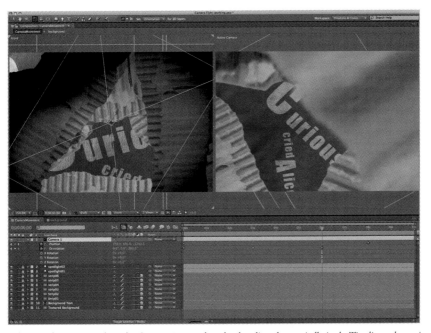

Often transformations made in the Composition panel need to be adjusted numerically in the Timeline to be precise.

13 Press the **K** key on the keyboard to move the playhead to the next visible keyframe; this is the last position keyframe that you created in the beginning of this exercise.

Click on the first Orientation keyframe to highlight it (it becomes yellow) and choose Edit > Copy. This copies the keyframe's values so you can apply them later.

14 Choose Edit > Paste to add the copied keyframe to the Timeline. The keyframe is placed at the current position of the playhead. The ability to copy and paste keyframes is very helpful when you want to have the exact same property values at different points along the Timeline.

Instead of using the menu commands, you can use the standard copy-and-paste keyboard shortcuts: Ctrl+C and Ctrl+V (Windows) or Command+C and Command+V (Mac OS) .

15 Scrub the playhead to preview the animation, and then save your file by choosing File > Save or by pressing Ctrl+S (Windows) or Command+S (Mac OS) on the keyboard.

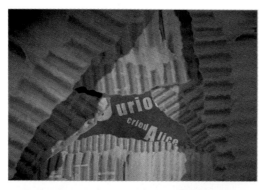

Animating multiple properties simultaneously usually creates a more interesting effect.

Creating the depth-of-field effect

Depth of field is a classic effect used in both still photography and filmmaking. The effect involves setting up a specific focal distance for the camera, the distance from the camera at which objects are in focus, and then moving the camera along the Z-axis. This effect is extremely appealing when animating the position of the camera; as it moves closer to or farther away from the layers in the composition, they appear to be more or less in focus, thus creating a more believable sense of movement and depth.

1 With Camera Flyin-working.aep still open, move the playhead to the beginning of the Timeline (0;00;00;00).

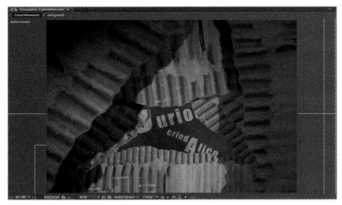

You can create the Depth of Field property of a camera when you create the camera or at any time after.

2 Highlight the camera layer in the Timeline, click the reveal triangle to the left to show the Camera Options, and click the Camera Options reveal triangle to show its properties.

3 The camera's Depth of Field property is currently disabled; click the Off switch to On to enable it.

4 Even though it has been enabled, the effect is usually too subtle to be useful at its default settings. There are three properties that affect depth of field: Focus Distance, Aperture, and Blur Level.

- Set the Focus Distance to **2250.0**

- Set the Aperture to **300**

- Set the Blur Level to **100**

The settings above work for this particular animation only. They are intended to show the effect of depth of field while the camera is moving, but to keep the final image of the text clear. Notice that all three properties above could be animated if you wanted to achieve an effect with varying depth-of-field blurring. Feel free to experiment with different settings to achieve an effect that you are happy with.

5 Move the playhead to the beginning of the Timeline and press the spacebar to build a preview of your animation. The rendering of this preview may take some time as the Depth of Field effect can be quite memory-intensive.

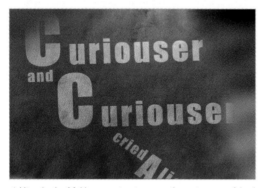

Adding depth of field to an animation can enhance its sense of depth and space.

6 Save your file by choosing File > Save or by pressing Ctrl+S (Windows) or Command+S (Mac OS) on the keyboard.

Creating a Rack Focus shot

Rack Focus is an effect used in television and video production. This technique is used to shift the attention of the viewer by changing the focus of the camera from a subject in the foreground to a subject in the background, or vice versa. In After Effects, you can do this by animating the focal distance of the camera. In this exercise, you will work with a project that has three layers, each at different positions along the Z-axis. You will create a camera and animate its focus distance to create the effect.

1   Choose File > Open Project. Navigate to the ae08lessons folder and open Understanding Rack Focus.aep. The file has three layers: This is, Rack, and Focus.

Each of the three layers in this composition is given a different Z position. The layer with the *This is* text is positioned at 0.0 on the Z axis, while the Rack text layer is further away from the viewer at 233.0 and the Focus layer is closer to the viewer at -240.0. These difference in depth are what allow you to create the Rack Focus effect.

Choose File > Save As. Navigate to the ae08lessons folder and save the file as **Understanding Rack Focus_Working.aep**.

2   With the Composition panel highlighted, create a new camera by choosing Layer > New > Camera to open the Camera Settings dialog box.

3   From the Preset drop-down menu, choose 50mm. Click the switch to Enable Depth of Field and then disable the Lock to Zoom option. Click OK.

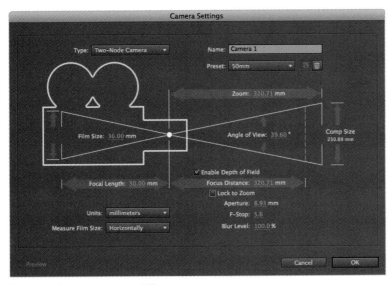

You can use the camera presets to quickly create new cameras.

4   When a camera layer is first created, it is often difficult to see its position in relation to the other layers in your composition. This can be fixed by zooming and panning the views in the Composition panel. Click in the left viewport, the one labeled Top, and change the Magnification to **50** percent. Press and hold the spacebar to activate the Hand tool (🖐). Use it to pan the viewport until you can see the camera body as well as its cone. You may need to use a different magnification value depending upon the size and resolution of your monitor.

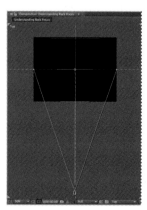

An Orthographic view such as Top is very helpful when trying to animate objects moving along the Z-axis.

5   In the Timeline panel, select the new camera layer and press Ctrl+~ (Windows/Mac OS) to reveal its properties. The Focus Distance property should already be set to 909.1, which places it in the middle of the composition, exactly at the 0 Z position.

    If it is enabled, click the Auto-Keyframe Timeline switch to turn it off. Then change the Aperture property to **150** and the Blur Level to **200**. The text *This is* remains clear, but the rest becomes blurry.

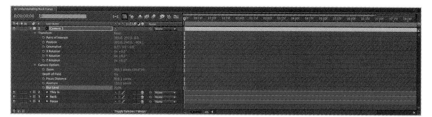

At this point, your settings should match those shown here.

6   Move the playhead to the 1 second (0;00;01;00) mark. Click the Time-Vary stopwatch icon (⏱) next to the Focus Distance property to enable its animation.

7   Move the playhead to the 2 second (0;00;02;00) mark. Change the Focus Distance property to **1144**. The word Rack is now in focus.

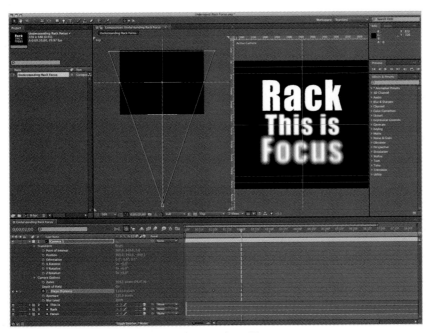

As the Focus Distance changes, different layers move in and out of focus.

8   To hold the word Rack in focus for a time, you will create a second keyframe as a placeholder. Move the playhead to the 3 second (0;00;03;00) mark. Click on the Add or Remove Keyframe icon (◆) to the left of the Focus Distance property to create a new keyframe to act as a placeholder.

9   Move the playhead to the 4 second (0;00;04;00) mark. Change the Focus Distance property to **670**. This completes the animation.

To enhance the blur effect, try raising the Aperture and/or Blur Level values.

10   Save your file by choosing File > Save or by clicking Ctrl+S (Windows) or Command+S (Mac OS) on the keyboard.

Working with Live Photoshop 3D

Photoshop Extended supports importing 3D files in a variety of popular formats and also the native creation of 3D content directly from flat layers or vector paths. If you are using After Effects CS4 or later, you can import live Photoshop 3D layers. In fact, the only type of direct 3D object import is through the Photoshop 3D format. The process of importing 3D objects into After Effects is a little bit difficult, but it can often be well worth the effort. This process involves the following steps:

1   A three-dimensional object can be created in a variety of dedicated 3D modeling applications such as Maya and 3D Studio Max.

2   From these applications, the 3D model is then exported to a generic interchange format such as .obj and .3ds.

3   The model is then imported into Photoshop as a 3D layer, where it can be manipulated in three-dimensional space.

4   The native .psd file is saved and then imported into After Effects as a Live Photoshop 3D layer. The .psd file is converted into an After Effects 3D composition, which preserves the features of your three-dimensional content.

In addition to the ability to import complex geometric models from popular 3D modeling programs, with the creation of Photoshop CS5, you now have the ability to create three-dimensional extruded and beveled models directly from any path, shape layer, or text object. In the following exercise, you will work with a 3D logo that has been rendered using the new Photoshop CS5 Repoussé effect. The model will be imported into an existing After Effects composition and its built-in camera will be animated.

Importing Live Photoshop 3D effects

1   Choose File > Open > Project. Navigate to the Lesson 8 project folder that you copied to your hard drive, and double-click on the file Working with Photoshop 3D.aep to open it in After Effects.

You can only have one After Effects project open at a time. If you try to open or create a new project, your current one will automatically be closed. If the current project has not been saved, After Effects will prompt you to save it, discard your changes, or cancel.

2   Choose File > Save As. Navigate to the ae08lessons folder, rename the project **Working with Photoshop 3D_working.aep** and click Save.

3   Double-click on an empty area of the project panel to open the Import File dialog box. Navigate to the ae08lessons folder and click once on the file named Pixel Juice Motif.psd to highlight it.

From the Import As drop-down menu, choose Composition and click Open to view the import options for this Photoshop file.

You can also open the Import File dialog box by choosing File > Import > File or by pressing Command+I (Mac OS) or Ctrl+I (Windows) on your keyboard. You can also open it by right-clicking on any empty space within the Project panel and choosing Import > File from the context menu that pops up.

4   Confirm that the Import kind is set to Composition and the Editable Layer Styles and Live Photoshop 3D switches are set in the Layer Options section of the dialog box.

Click OK to import the file.

The Live Photoshop 3D switch must be enabled to preserve the 3D objects in the Photoshop file.

5   Drag the Pixel Juice Motif composition into the Working with Photoshop 3D composition on the Timeline. Make sure to place it above the Spectral Background layer.

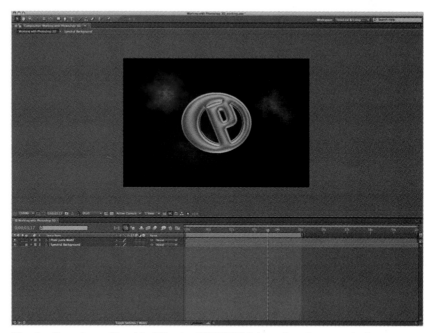

Photoshop files are imported into After Effects in a WYSIWYG fashion, where what you see is what you get.

In the next exercise, you will learn how to work with Live Photoshop 3D compositions in the After Effects Timeline.

6   Save your file by choosing File > Save or by pressing Ctrl+S (Windows) or Command+S (Mac OS) on the keyboard.

Animating Photoshop 3D compositions

When Photoshop files are imported with the Live Photoshop 3D switch enabled, they are converted into two-dimensional compositions. This may seem counter-intuitive but it is actually the content inside of the composition that preserves the 3D nature of the graphics. The imported composition is composed of four layers: Camera 1, Motif Controller, Motif, and Motif Glow, which is hidden. The camera layer is used to set the visible content of the Pixel Juice Motif composition. The Motif layer is the actual 3D object that was imported from Photoshop. It has an effect named Live Photoshop 3D that allows you to treat it as a three-dimensional object. Because it can be very difficult to control 3D objects directly, you can use the Motif Controller to control the transformation that will be applied to the Motif layer.

The Motif Glow layer is hidden and is intended to be used to apply a background glow effect to the composition.

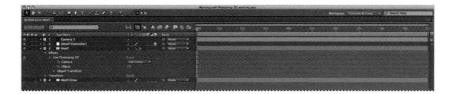

When working with Photoshop 3D layers in After Effects, all three-dimensional transformations are made inside of the nested composition by adjusting the controller layer or the camera. In this exercise you will animate the camera in the logo layer so that it creates a 3D spin effect, and then add a few embellishments to really make the logo pop.

1 With the Working with Photoshop 3D_working.aep file still open, double-click on the Pixel Juice Motif composition in the Timeline to open it.

2 From the Select View Layout drop-down menu, select 2 Views - Horizontal. Set the left viewport to the Top view and adjust its magnification until you can see the camera icon.

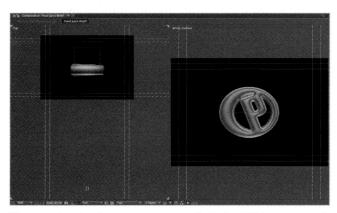

If you are using a three-button mouse, you can scroll with the middle button to zoom in and out of a composition viewer.

3 The easiest way to make a camera or any layer orbit around a fixed point is to parent it to a null object. Choose Layer > New > Null Object. A new layer named Null 1 is created at the top of the layer stack.

4 Click on the new layer to highlight it, press the Enter (Windows) or Return (Mac OS) key on the keyboard, and rename it to **Camera Controller**.

With the layer still highlighted, press the **A** key to reveal the layer's Anchor Point property.

Change the layer's Anchor Point property to **50.0, 50.0**. This positions it toward the middle of the 3D object.

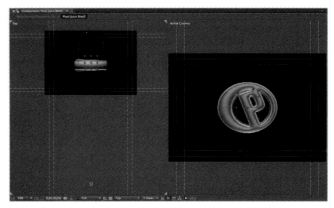

Null objects are always created with a with and height of 100 pixels each so placing the Anchor Points at 50.0.50.0 will reposition it in the middle of the Null.>

5 In the Parent drop-down menu, change the parent for the Camera 1 layer from None to 1. Camera Controller.

Parenting affects all properties except Opacity.

6 Convert the Camera Controller layer to a 3D layer by enabling its 3D switch, and press the **R** key on your keyboard to view its Rotation properties.

7 Move the cursor to the beginning (0;00;00;00) of the Timeline and click the Time-Vary stopwatch icon (●) next to the Y Rotation property to enable its animation.

Move the playhead to the 3 second (0;00;03;00) mark and change the Y rotation to **–1** x **–30.0**.

8 In the Timeline, click on the tab for the Working with Photoshop 3D composition to return to it.

9 Click the RAM Preview button in the Preview panel to begin rendering the Timeline.

10 After the preview has concluded, save your file by choosing File > Save or by pressing Command+S (Mac OS) or Ctrl+S (Windows) on the keyboard.

Creating 3D objects in Photoshop CS5

There are two ways of creating 3D layers in Photoshop. Files created in third-party 3D modeling and animation programs can be imported as Photoshop 3D layers using the 3D menu command, 3D > New Layer from 3D File. This imports a variety of generic file types and converts them into a Photoshop 3D layer, complete with their lights and textures. If you are not currently familiar with any 3D modeling software, two very good and free applications that you might want to look at are Blender (www.blender.org) and Google Sketch Up, *http://sketchup.google.com*.

Photoshop CS5 also has the ability to create 3D layers from existing two-dimensional layers in your document. This includes a series of object primitives such as spheres, cubes, and cylinders, as well as image planes called postcards that you can manipulate in 3D space. While these features have existed in older versions of Photoshop, CS5 adds a new feature set called Repoussé. This effect allows you to create three-dimensional objects by extruding and beveling any path or text layer.

Importable 3D formats

There are a limited number of importable 3D formats: 3DStudio (.3ds), COLLADA (.dae), Wavefront (.obj), Google Earth 4 (.kmz), and Universal 3D (.u3d). Most current applications can produce at least one of these formats and will usually give you the option of preserving both the geometry (that's your model) and the lights and textures added to the scene.

Photoshop Repoussé

You can use the Photoshop CS5 Repoussé effect on any vector-based object: text, shape layer, or path. Using the Repoussé dialog box, you can create extruded and beveled 3D shapes.

The dialog box has built-in controls for setting the extrusion depth and bevel amount of the edges, and the materials used on the back, front, and sides as well as for each beveled edge. Photoshop comes with a library of available textures, and additional ones can be downloaded and loaded as a program extension using the Adobe Extension Manager.

Roundtrip editing Photoshop 3D files

The major advantage to using native Photoshop and Illustrator files is the ease with which they can be updated in After Effects. You can also update Photoshop 3D files by selecting the file in either the Timeline or Project panel and using the Edit > Edit Original command to open it in Photoshop. Once in Photoshop, you can make your changes, save the files, and return to After Effects to see the results of your edits.

For a full explanation of how to create and work with 3D graphics in Photoshop CS5, check out the Photoshop CS5 Digital Classroom *from Jennifer Smith, published by AGI and Wiley.*

Adding a Glow and Lens Flare effect

The graphic that was created in Photoshop using the Repoussé effect is interesting but does appear a little flat. You can increase the contrast between the highlights and shadows a bit to improve the texture of the design. As its name implies, the Glow effect creates a colored glow around or in an object. This glow can be based either on the color of the layer it is applied to or on an arbitrary set of colors you decide upon. The Lens Flare effect attempts to replicate the effect of light hitting a camera lens. This creates a recognizable pattern that can enhance the sense of depth and movement in a scene. In this exercise, you will add a glow and lens flare to the nested composition to enhance the overall visual appeal of the animation.

1 With the Working with Photoshop 3D composition active in the Timeline panel, click on the Pixel Juice Motif layer to highlight it.

2 In the Effects & Presets panel, type **glow** into the search field. This limits the panel's display to only the effects with that word in their names.

If you know the name of the effect or preset you are looking for, the search text field can be a very good way of locating it without knowing its folder grouping.

3 With the Pixel Juice Motif layer still highlighted, double-click on the Glow effect found under the Stylize folder in the panel. This immediately applies the effect and opens the Effect Controls panel.

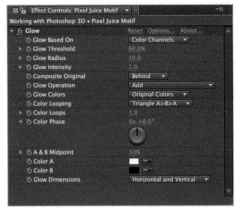

You can edit all effects simultaneously from the Timeline or Effect Controls panel.

One of the things about After Effects that many new users find intimidating is the sheer number of properties that can be animated. In addition to the built-in transform properties of layers, all effects have properties that can be animated as well. As you can see in the Effect Controls panel above, even effects that are not based on numerical values, such as Glow Colors and Glow Dimensions, have Time-Vary stopwatch icons (●) to enable you to change their values over time.

4   In this section of the exercise, you will animate the Glow Intensity so that it grows and fades as the logo spins.

Move the playhead to the beginning of the Timeline (0;00;00;00) and, in the Effect Controls panel, click on the Time-Vary stopwatch icon (●) next to Glow Intensity to enable animation and create the first keyframe at the current position of the playhead.

Even though you can't see it in the Effect Controls panel, a keyframe has been created. Keyframes are visible only on the Timeline.

5   On the Timeline, click on the Pixel Juice Motif layer to highlight it and press **U** on your keyboard. This reveals only the layer properties that have the Time-Vary stopwatch icon (●) enabled, revealing the Glow Intensity property of the Glow Effect.

6   Click on the Current Time field, type in **114**, and press the Enter (Windows) or Return (Mac OS) key on your keyboard to jump to the 1 second 14 frames (0;00;01;14) mark of the Timeline. This is the center point of the spin animation in the nested composition. Click on the value of the Glow Intensity property in the Timeline and change it to **3.0**.

Because the current time field can only accept time code values, entering any set of numbers automatically results in them being converted into their time code equivalent.

7   Again click on the Current Time field, and this time type in **300** and press Enter/Return on your keyboard to jump to the 3 second (0;00;03;00) mark of the Timeline.

Click on the first keyframe to highlight it, choose Edit > Copy, and then choose Edit > Paste to copy and paste the first keyframe to the current position of the playhead.

Any number of keyframes can be selected, copied, and pasted. The first keyframes are always pasted at the current position of the playhead.

8   Render a RAM preview of the animation by clicking the RAM Preview button on the Preview panel. It takes a moment to build and play.

9   Choose Layer > New > Adjustment Layer. Adjustment layers are used as the target of effects. Effects applied to these layers actually affect all the layers below them.

Click on the new adjustment layer in the Timeline panel to highlight it and press the Enter (Windows) or Return (Mac OS) key on your keyboard to make the name text field editable.

Change the name of this layer to **Lens Flare**.

It is important to click on the layer to highlight it before pressing the Return (Mac OS) or Enter (Windows) keys. If you don't, then instead of editing the name field, you will open the layer in a new layer window.

10   In the Effects & Presets panel, type **lens flare** into the search field. When the Lens Flare effect pops up under the Generate folder, drag and drop it onto the Lens Flare layer in the Timeline.

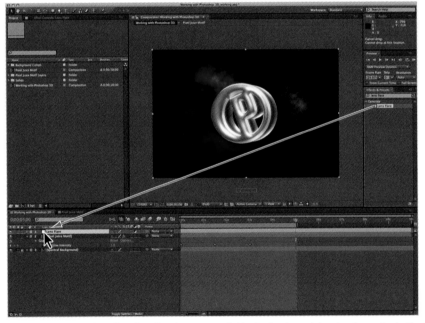

You can add effects to a layer from the Effects & Presets panel either by dragging and dropping them or by double-clicking on them.

11 Move the playhead to the beginning of the Timeline.

In the Effect Controls panel, click on the Time-Vary stopwatch icon (●) next to the Flare Center property and change its values to **250.0**, **175.0**. This positions it at the upper-left corner of the logo.

12 Highlight the Lens Flare layer on the Timeline and press **U** on your keyboard to view the properties that have the Time-Vary stopwatch icons enabled.

With the keyframes for the Pixel Juice Motif layer's Glow Intensity property also visible, press the **K** key on your keyboard to jump to the next visible keyframe. This is the one at 1 second 14 frames (0;00;01;14).

You can use the J and K keys on the keyboard to move the playhead from one visible keyframe to the next.

13 Change the Flare Center property to **370.0**, **135.0**.

Press the **K** key again to jump to the last keyframe at 3 seconds (0;00;03;00) and change the Flare Center property to **425.0**, **125.0**.

14 Render a RAM preview of the animation by clicking the RAM Preview button on the Preview panel. It takes a moment to build and play.

15 After the preview has concluded, save your file by choosing File > Save.

Self study

Create your own 3D scene in After Effects and animate the camera's position to make it move through and around the layers in your composition.

Enable a camera's Depth of Field property and animate its properties to create a scene that has a varying depth-of-field effect.

Review

Questions

1   Once a layer's 3D switch is enabled, what are the fours properties it gains for rotation?

2   Which three properties affect the strength of a camera's depth of field?

3   When working with imported Photoshop 3D layers, how do you animate their appearance?

Answers

1   X Rotation, Y Rotation, Z Rotation, and Orientation. Each of the rotation properties allows you to isolate the property along a single axis, while the Orientation property creates a single keyframe for all three rotational axes.

2   Focus Distance, Aperture, and Blur Level are the three properties that affect depth of field.

Focus Distance specifies the distance from the camera lens at which a layer would be perfectly in focus. You can manipulate the Focus Distance value to produce depth-of-field effects like those seen in standard photography and films.

Aperture specifies the size of the opening in a camera lens, and affects the camera's depth of field. Smaller Aperture settings decrease the blur produced by depth of field, while larger settings increase it.

Blur Level specifies the amount of blur produced by a camera's depth-of-field effect.

3   When working with imported Photoshop 3D layers, you animate the camera that is automatically created inside the imported composition. This camera controls what the composition displays when nested on the Timeline.

What you'll learn in this lesson:

- Animating with effects
- Applying and modifying effects presets
- Saving your own presets
- Using the Graph Editor

Advanced Animation

The animation you have created so far is just the tip of the proverbial iceberg. In addition to animating the native properties of layers, you can add additional properties and complexity to any animation by adding and animating effects, and when you want even more control of your animation, you can use tools such as Smoother, Wiggler, and the Graph Editor to enhance your work.

Starting up

You will work with several files from the ae09lessons folder in this lesson. Make sure that you have loaded the aelessons folder onto your hard drive from the supplied DVD. See "Loading lesson files" on page 4.

See Lesson 9 in action!

Use the accompanying video to gain a better understanding of how to use some of the features shown in this lesson. The video tutorial for this lesson can be found on the included DVD.

Setting up

As you work in After Effects you will inevitably open and close many panels, depending on the type of project you are creating. However, when working through the projects in this book, it is important to have an interface that matches the lessons. To this end, you should always reset your workspace to the preset Standard configuration.

1   Choose Window > Workspace > Standard to set your current workspace configuration.

2   Choose Window > Workspace > Reset "Standard" to reset the standard workspace in case you have modified it at some point.

Animating with effects

There is a reason this program is called After Effects. In fact, the number of built-in effects that can be animated is something that new users often find surprising and perhaps a little intimidating. Unlike other programs you may be familiar with, this is not a heavily tool-based application, but it is very reliant on manipulating the properties of these effects. In order to create compelling motion graphics, you need to become comfortable working with the wide range of built-in effects plugins that are available to you.

In this lesson, you will animate a layer so that it explodes and blows away like stardust. The project contains a text layer that has been converted to shapes using the Layer > Create Shapes from Text command. This converts a text layer into a vector shape layer; it isn't necessary to do this for the effects to work but it is useful in a situation like this when you must give a file to someone who may not have the same fonts installed on their computer as you do.

Applying effects to layers

The Effects & Presets panel is a library of the effects you have access to in the application. Effects are similar to filters in Adobe Photoshop because they allow you to apply special effects such as glows and blurs or add noise or color-correct a layer.

In this section of the lesson you will apply an effect to an existing layer and edit some of the default properties of the effect.

Depending on the speed of your computer rendering even single frames, previews of the Shatter effect you are going to use in this lesson can take considerable time. If you experience a delay while waiting for individual frames to preview when moving the playhead around the Timeline, you may want to change the Resolution/Down Sample factor to Half or Quarter to speed up the process.

1 Choose File > Open Project and navigate to the ae09lessons folder. Locate the project named Animating with Effects.aep and double-click it to open the file.

2 In the Effects & Presets panel, type **shatter** into the search field. When the Shatter effect appears, drag it onto the layer named Up Next in the Timeline. The Shatter effect is a great one to use when you want to explode a layer. It can simulate a wide range of common shatter patterns such as glass or bricks, and with a few adjustments it can produce a variety of different looks.

As a result of applying the effect, the Effect Controls panel appears and the entire layer enters a wireframe display mode. The rendered Shatter effect requires a great deal of processing power to preview on the Timeline, and as a result, it is set to use the wireframe display mode as a default view setting.

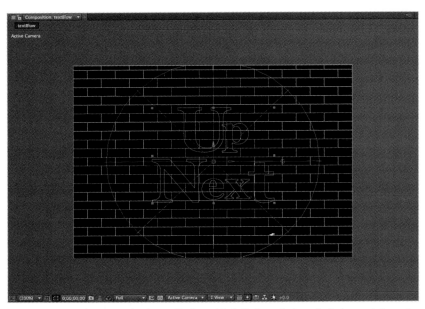

In order to speed up the preview, the Shatter effect has a default display mode that only displays a wireframe view of the layer.

3 Move the playhead to the 5 frame (0;00;00;05) mark on the Timeline and in the Effect Controls panel, change the view property pull-down menu to Rendered; this returns the layer's appearance to normal.

4 The default settings of the Shatter effect resemble bricks that fall toward the bottom of the screen. The first thing you must do is to modify the effect's properties so that the layer will look more like particles of dust or sand and fly off the side of the screen.

In the Effect Controls panel, click on the reveal triangle to the left of the Shape property group and adjust the settings as follows:

PROPERTY	VALUE
Pattern	Eggs
Repetitions	200
Direction	0 x 0.0°
Extrusion Depth	0.0

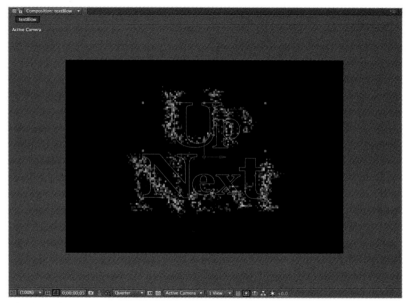

The Shatter effect will automatically animate, so positioning the playhead at frame 5 allows you to see the effect of your adjustments.

These settings will produce particles that look more like sand.

5 Click on the reveal triangle to the left of the Force 1 and Force 2 property groups and adjust their settings to match those below:

FORCE 1	
PROPERTY	**VALUE**
Position	176, 234
Depth	0.0
Radius	0.0
Strength	3.75

FORCE 2	
PROPERTY	**VALUE**
Position	743, 247
Depth	0.0
Radius	0.0
Strength	0.0

When you select the shape layer, a blue outline appears around the text, but when you deselect the layer, the blue outline vanishes.

These settings, specifically the ones for Force 1, will return the layer to the appearance it had before the effect was applied. Later in the lesson you will animate this property group to blow the text away.

6 Click on the reveal triangle to the left of the Physics property group and adjust its settings to match the ones below:

PROPERTY	VALUE
Rotation Speed	0.20
Tumble Axis	Free
Randomness	0.10
Viscosity	0.00
Mass Variance	30%
Gravity	0.00
Gravity Direction	0 x +90.0°
Gravity Inclination	0.00

The adjustments to the Physics property group do not produce a noticeable change at this time but they are used to control the force of gravity, which will control the direction of movement of the particles created by the effect, once you animate the Force 1 property group.

In the next part of the lesson you will animate the properties of the Effect you have just applied.

7 Choose File > Save As and navigate to the ae09lessons folder. Rename the project **Animating with Effects-working.aep** and click the Save button. Do not close this file, as you will need it in the next part of this lesson.

Animating effect properties

Many novice After Effects users are surprised by the sheer number of animatable effects they have access to. Nearly every property of every effect can be keyframed, even switches and pull-down menus. In this section of the lesson, you will animate the properties of the Shatter effect to blow away the text.

Up until this point, your preview and the speed at which the composition panel refreshes when you move around the timeline have probably been pretty smooth. When animating properties you may experience longer delays while the application builds a preview for you. This is due to both the speed of your computer and the power needed to build and preview some effects.

1 With the Animating with Effects-working.aep file open, move the playhead to the beginning (0;00;00;00) of the Timeline.

2 In the Effect Controls panel, locate the Force 1 property group and click the time-vary stopwatch for the Radius property. This enables animation for this property and sets the first keyframe at the beginning of the Timeline for the current values.

If the Effect Controls panel is not open already, you can choose Window > Effect Controls to reveal it.

3   Move the playhead to the 3 second (0;00;03;00) mark of the Timeline. With the Up Next layer selected, press the **U** key on the keyboard to reveal all animated properties on this layer. In the Effect Controls panel, change the Radius property of Force 1 to **5.00**.

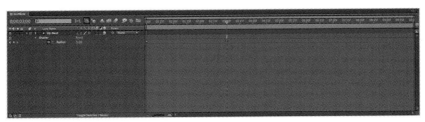

Because you have revealed the Radius property on the Timeline, you can also change the property value there if you prefer.

4   Move the playhead to the 4 second (0;00;04;00) mark on the Timeline and press the **N** key on your keyboard. This moves the end of the work area bar to the current position of the playhead. Depending upon the speed of your computer, this could take a moment.

RAM preview the animation. When the last keyframe of the animation is located at 4 seconds (0;00;04;00) on the Timeline, this signals the end of the animation, the point at which the layer has been completely removed from the screen.

*You can move the beginning and end of the work area bar either with the cursor by clicking and dragging the end markers or by using the keyboard. Pressing the **B** key on the keyboard moves the beginning of the work area bar to the current position of the playhead, while pressing the **N** key on the keyboard moves the end of the bar to the playhead's current position.*

5   The text blows away as the Radius of Force 1 increases, but you can enhance the effect and make it more dynamic by animating the Camera Position property group as well.

From the Resolution/Down Sample Factor Popup menu at the bottom of the Composition panel, choose Quarter. This reduces the quality of the panel's preview by rendering only every fourth pixel, but it also produces faster previews.

Press the **J** key on the keyboard until the playhead is at the position of the first Radius keyframe.

If you experience a delay while the Composition panel preview renders, you may want to press the Caps Lock key on the keyboard. This disables the preview and prevents it from refreshing, allowing you to move around the Timeline and edit properties. You have to press the Caps Lock key again to turn it off and re-enable screen refreshing.

6 In the Camera Position property group, confirm that the Y Rotation property is set to 0 x 0.0°. Then click this property's Time-Vary Stopwatch (●) to create a keyframe and enable animation.

7 Press the **K** key on the keyboard to move the playhead to the position of the second Radius keyframe and change the Y Rotation property to **0 x 80.0°**.

Press the **U** key on the keyboard to hide the layer's properties, and then press it again to reveal both Radius and Y Rotation. RAM preview the animation.

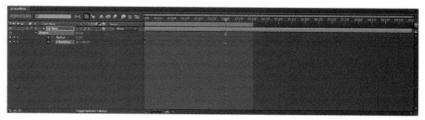

*If properties are visible on the Timeline, pressing the **U** key on the keyboard hides them, and pressing it again reveals only the currently animated properties.*

8 If it is not already there, move the playhead to the beginning (0;00;00;00) of the Timeline and in the Composition panel, change the Resolution/Down Sample Factor Popup menu to Auto. In the Effect Controls panel, click the reveal triangle next to Shatter to hide its properties. In the Effects & Presets panel, type **glow** into the search field. When it appears, drag the Glow effect onto the Up Next layer in the Timeline panel.

9 You use the Glow effect to make layers appear as if they are illuminated by an internal light, and when you combine it with the Shatter effect used here, it is applied to each shattered piece separately. In the Effect Controls panel, set the Glow effects properties to the following values:

PROPERTY	VALUE
Glow Based On	Color Channels
Glow Threshold	25.0%
Glow Radius	10.0
Glow Intensity	2.0
Composite Original	Behind
Glow Operation	Add

PROPERTY	VALUE
Glow Color	A & B Colors
Color Looping	Triangle A>B>A
Color Loops	1.0
Color Phase	0 x 0.0°
A & B Midpoint	50%
Glow Dimensions	Horizontal and Vertical

Click on the color box for the Color A property and in the Color A dialog box, change the hexadecimal value to **FFA200** and then Click OK to close the dialog. This changes Color A to a light orange.

You can enter colors numerically in After Effects using HSB, RGB, or hexadecimal values.

Click on the color box for the Color B property and in the Color B dialog box, change the hexadecimal value to **FFFF00** and then click OK to close the dialog. This changes Color B to a very bright yellow color.

RAM preview the animation. You may need to change the Resolution/Down Sample Factor Popup menu (located at the bottom of the Composition panel) to Half, Third, or Quarter to speed up your rendering time.

As you can see, the Glow effect adds a sparkle to the animation and really makes it appear more vibrant.

10 One last effect to add a greater sense of movement and depth to the animation, and it will be complete. Move the playhead to the 15 frame (0;00;00;15) mark on the Timeline. In the Effect Controls panel, click the reveal triangle next to Glow to hide its properties. In the Effects & Presets panel, type the word **fast** into the search field. When it appears, drag the Fast Blur effect onto the Up Next layer in the Timeline panel.

11 In the Effect Controls panel, click the Time-Vary Stopwatch (●) next to the Blurriness property of the Fast Blur effect to create a keyframe for this property.

12 Press the letter **K** on the keyboard to move the playhead to the next visible keyframe at 3 seconds (00;00;03;00) on the Timeline. Change the value of Blurriness to 10.0. RAM preview the animation. As you can see, the text now starts the animation completely sharp and becomes progressively more blurry over time.

13 Choose File > Save to save these changes to your After Effects project. Do not close the file, as you will need it again in the next part of the lesson.

Saving animation presets

Presets are shipped with the application and are intended to make using and learning effects easier. Originally called favorite effects, presets are stored groupings of effects with their settings and keyframes intact. They are fully editable, and you can apply them to a layer and customize them to fit the needs of your animation. You aren't limited to just using the animation presets that ship with After Effects. You can, of course, also create your own. This makes it very easy to reuse favorite effects that you have taken the time and effort to develop. In addition to the effects and their properties, the preset also includes any keyframes and expressions that you may have created.

1   With the Animating with Effects-working.aep file open, move the playhead to the beginning (0;00;00;00) of the Timeline.

2   In the Effect Controls panel, click on the Shatter effect to select it. Press and hold the Shift key on your keyboard and click on the Glow and Fast Blur effects to select them as well.

3   With all three effects selected, choose Animation > Save Animation Preset.

4   In the Save Animation Preset As dialog box, change the default name to **Exploding Stardust**. Confirm that the Save As location is set to the default User Presets folder and click the Save button. You can now access the animation preset in any project from Animation Presets > User Presets > Exploding Text in the Effects & Presets panel.

5   Choose File > Save to save these changes to your After Effects project. You may now close this project, as you are finished with it.

Applying and modifying effects presets

In addition to the presets found in the Effects & Presets panel, some effects have presets that you can apply and modify from the Effect Controls panel. Presets themselves are great, as they provide you with a place to start your animations, but the weakness of relying too much on presets is that everyone else who buys the program has access to the exact same ones. In order to create greater variety in your animation, you will inevitably want to customize the existing presets by editing the Effects properties.

In this part of the lesson, you will apply the Exploding Stardust preset that you just created to a composition in another project and modify its settings. In this project you will work with an animated logo; the goal is to have the logo materialize from a hail of stardust.

Depending on the speed of your computer, rendering even single–frame previews of the Shatter effect can take considerable time. If you experience a delay while waiting for individual frames to preview when moving the playhead around the Timeline, you may want to change the Resolution/Down Sample factor to Half or Quarter to speed up the process.

1   Choose File > Open Project and navigate to the ae09lessons folder. Locate the project named Bad Robot Animated Logo.aep and double-click it to open the file. Scrub the playhead to preview the Animated Logo composition.

This project contains two compositions: Bad Robot and Animated Logo. The Bad Robot comp contains the animation of the two halves of the robot head separating and revealing the logo; it is nested inside the Animated Logo composition.

In Animated Logo, there is a marker on the Bad Robot Comp layer at the 4 second (0;00;04;00) mark that reads "Animation Starts Here." Markers that are placed inside compositions are visible when they are nested and are helpful tools for synchronizing animations.

2   Hold down the Shift key on your keyboard and drag the playhead to the marker until it snaps into position at the 4 second (0;00;04;00) mark on the Timeline.

The easiest way to apply an effect or preset to only part of the duration of a layer is to split it to produce two separate layers and then apply different effects to each layer.

3   With the Bad Robot composition layer selected, choose Edit > Split Layer. The top layer is still selected after you split the layer. Press the Return (Mac OS) or Enter (Windows) key on the keyboard to make the layer name editable and rename it **Bad Robot–Animation**.

Click on the lower layer, the one still named [Bad Robot], press the Return (Mac OS) or Enter (Windows) key on the keyboard to make the layer name editable, and rename it **Bad Robot–Stardust Effect**.

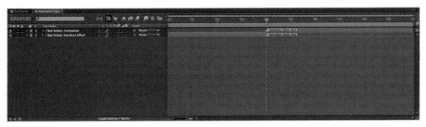

The Split Layer command actually creates two exact copies of the layer and trims the in and out points of each copy to adjust their lengths.

4   Move the playhead to the beginning (0;00;00;00) of the Timeline and in the Effects & Presets panel, type **stardust** into the search field.

When it appears, drag the Exploding Stardust preset onto the Bad Robot–Stardust Effect layer in the Timeline panel.

It is very important that you know where the playhead is before you apply any saved animation presets. Any keyframes that are saved with the animation preset are added to the Timeline; the first keyframe in the preset is placed at the current position of the playhead, and any others are placed relative to that keyframe to maintain the timing of the overall animation.

RAM preview the animation. Notice that the glow effect isn't working; this is because the effect's settings need to be adjusted for the fact that this layer's artwork is black while the original one that it was created for was white.

5   Make sure the Bad Robot-Stardust Effect layer is selected and in the Effect Controls panel, locate the Glow effect. Change the Glow Based On property to Alpha Channel. This will allow it to create a glow around the opaque areas of the layer. The problem now is that the effect is very overpowering; to correct this, change the Glow Operation property to Normal.

 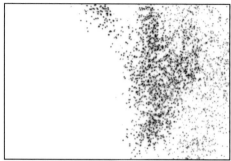

The first image is from the beginning (0;00;00;00) of the Timeline; the second is from 1 second (0;00;01;00).

6   RAM preview the animation.

Choose File > Save As and navigate to the ae09lessons folder. Rename the project **Bad Robot Animated Logo-working.aep** and click Save.

Do not close this file. You will need it in the next part of this lesson where you will change the layer's property so that it plays from the end to the beginning and gives the impression that the layer is being created from stardust.

Time-reversing a layer

In real life, time flows in a straight line from beginning to end, but with After Effects you are not constrained to this linear approach. Using the variety of advanced time remapping features built into the program, you can reverse, speed up, slow down, and pause video footage to fit your project's needs.

Depending on the speed of your computer rendering even single frames, previews of the Shatter effect can take considerable time. If you experience a delay while waiting for individual frames to preview when moving the playhead around the Timeline, you may want to change the Resolution/Down Sample factor to Half or Quarter to speed up the process.

1 With the Bad Robot Animated Logo-working.aep file still open, click on the Bad Robot-Stardust Effect layer to select it.

2 Choose Layer > Time > Time-Reverse Layer. This swaps the layer's In and Out points and allows it to play from beginning to end.

You can achieve the same effect from the In/Out/Duration/Stretch pane by setting the layer's Stretch percentage to -100 percent.

3 You may not have noticed it before you time-reversed the layer, but the position of the robot graphic changes from one layer to the next. This distortion is caused by the application of the Shatter effect. You can easily compensate for this by changing the position of the Bad Robot-Stardust Effect layer.

With the Bad Robot-Stardust Effect layer selected, press the **P** key on the keyboard to reveal the Position property. Change the value for Position to 396.0, 240.0. This corrects the distortion.

4 Because the Bad Robot-Animation layer does not have a glow effect on it, there is a slight disorienting jump when the layers switch. Animating the Glow property will correct this and help to create a more seamless changeover.

With the Bad Robot-Stardust Effect selected, press the letter **E** on your keyboard. This reveals the layer's effects in the Timeline panel.

5 Move the playhead to the 3 second (0;00;03;00) mark on the Timeline and click the reveal triangle for the Glow effect in the Timeline panel to show all its properties.

Click the time-vary stopwatch for the Glow Intensity property to enable animation and create a keyframe for the current value of 2.0.

6 Move the playhead to the 4 second (0;00;04;00) mark on the Timeline and change the value of the Glow Intensity property to 0.0.

7 RAM preview the animation; it should now appear to have a more seamless blend from one layer to the next.

Choose File > Save to save these changes to your After Effects project. You may now close this project, as you are finished with it.

Using the Motion Sketch panel to capture motion

Some artists find working with positional keyframes in After Effects to be tedious and non-intuitive. And truthfully, dragging objects around the screen or changing property values in the Timeline panel is a foreign concept to most people. To offer another and perhaps more intuitive solution to animation, After Effects has the Motion Sketch feature. Motion Sketch allows the animator to draw motion paths onscreen and apply them to objects in the Timeline. It can be a quick and easy way to create organic, free-flowing movement.

In this part of the lesson, you will work with a pre-assembled project that contains footage created in Adobe Photoshop and Illustrator. You will use the Smoother and Wiggler panels to add animation to the layers and create both smooth and frenetic movements that complement one another.

1   Choose File > Open Project and navigate to the ae09lessons folder. Locate the project named Empire of the Ants.aep and double-click it to open the file.

2   Move the playhead to the beginning (0;00;00;00) of the Timeline and click on the first layer, the one named ant. This layer is a nested composition; the ant graphic was created in Illustrator and the legs have been animated here.

Press the **P** key on the keyboard to reveal the Position property of the layer and change its values to **-95.0, 530**. This places the layer outside of the lower-left corner of the composition.

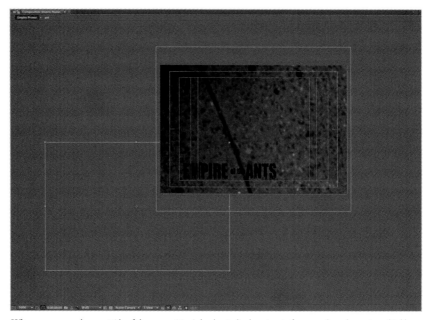

When you move a layer outside of the composition's border, it displays in wireframe mode and remains editable.

3 Choose Window > Motion Sketch to reveal the Motion Sketch panel. It opens in the lower-right corner of the Standard workspace.

Motion Sketch: Allows you to draw motion onscreen; the panel contains options to make this easier as well as to begin the capture process. There are five properties in the panel:

Capture Speed At: Sets the ratio of the speed that motion is recorded at (effectively the speed the cursor is moving on the screen) to the speed that it plays back at. A value of 100 percent means that the motion plays back at the same speed it was recorded at; a value lower than 100 percent plays back faster; and values above 100 percent play back more slowly.

Smoothing: Smoothes the path of motion by removing extraneous keyframes. Higher values producer a smoother motion path.

Show: The Wireframe switch shows a wireframe view of the layer onscreen as you are capturing motion, while the Background switch shows a static image of the frame where you started capturing motion.

Start: Displays the timecode where the Motion Sketch operation will begin capturing. The Start value corresponds to the start marker of the work area bar.

Duration: Specifies the overall duration of the capture operation.

4 Adjust the settings of the Motion Sketch dialog box to match the properties below:

PROPERTY	VALUE	PROPERTY	VALUE
Capture speed at	100.00%	Show Background	Checked
Smoothing	1	Start	0;00;00;00
Show Wireframe	Unchecked	Duration	0;00;10;00

Click the Start Capture button at the bottom of the panel.

5 Place your cursor, which now resembles a cross-hair, near the anchor point of the ant layer. Click and drag the cursor across the screen towards the upper-right corner, and then loop around as if making a large figure eight. When finished, you should have a path similar to the one in the figure below.

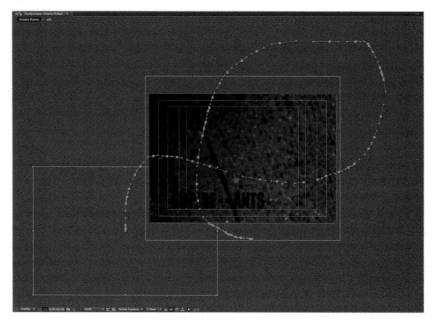

Motion Sketch is intended to create unique motion paths so there is no way to capture the exact same path twice.

6 As you draw the layer's motion path onscreen, Motion Sketch adds keyframes to the Position property. You may have a very different total number of keyframes and different animation duration than the figure below. The number of keyframes and duration of the animation are dependent on how long it took you to draw the motion path.

Drawing motion paths with the Motion Sketch feature creates unique paths that are nearly impossible to replicate.

RAM preview the animation. The two factors that are taken into account when motion is captured are the position of the mouse and the speed at which it moves. You will notice that the ant moves more slowly in certain points than in others; this is due to how quickly you may have moved the mouse onscreen. The motion is a little jagged and rough, and the ant doesn't actually look like it is following the motion path; you will correct this later in the lesson.

7 Choose File > Save As and navigate to the ae09lessons folder. Rename the project **Empire of the Ants-working.aep** and click the Save button. Do not close this file, as you will need it in the next part of this lesson.

Controlling layer orientation

As you preview the animation created in the previous exercise, you will notice that while the ant layer moves across the screen, it continues to face toward the top of the screen. This makes the movement seem unnatural. In reality, an ant, or an airplane, or any moving object must face the direction it is traveling.

All layers have a property named Auto-Orient but by default, footage layers are set to auto-orient toward nothing. This is usually a benefit as it allows the animator to freely rotate the layer as needed, but here this same setting makes the animation seem strange. To correct this, you will change the layer's Auto-Orient setting so that it follows its motion path.

1 With the Empire of the Ants-working project still open, move the playhead until you can see the ant graphic appear on your screen. Notice that the ant layer is pointing straight up toward the top of the composition. You must adjust this to add a sense of realistic movement to the animation.

2 With the ant layer highlighted, hold down the Shift key and press the **R** key on your keyboard so that the Rotation property displays along with the Position property.

Place your cursor over the property value and use the text slider to change the layer's rotation until the ant faces towards the motion path. In the image below, the value used is 0x +96.0 but your specific value will differ, as your direction path may vary.

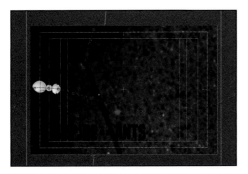

Positive values produce clockwise rotation, while negative values produce counter-clockwise rotation.

3 With the ant layer still selected, choose Layer > Transform > Auto-Orient to open the Auto Orient dialog box. Click the radio button next to Orient Along Path to enable this option, and click the OK button.

4 RAM preview the animation. Notice that the ant now seems to be following the motion path. Choose File > Save to save these changes to your After Effects project. Do not close this file, as you will need it in the next part of this lesson.

Using the Smoother panel to soften movement

The Smoother panel is used to modify the keyframes in an animation to make it appear smoother and more flowing. It does this by removing extraneous keyframes based on values that you set. When combined with the Motion Sketch feature, it can help produce a less jagged motion path. In this part of the lesson, you will use the Smoother panel to soften the ant's motion path.

1   With the Empire of the Ants-working project still open, scrub the playhead back and forth. Pay attention to the movement of the ant; notice that the movement seems jagged and perhaps a little wobbly. You can correct the motion path by using the Smoother panel to reduce the number of keyframes.

2   Choose Window > Workspace > Animation to switch to a workspace designed to aid in animation tasks. If you have amended the default animation workspace, choose Window > Workspace > Reset "Animation" to return it to its default appearance. Notice that in this workspace the Smoother panel is to the right of the Composition panel.

When resetting a workspace to its default configuration, a dialog box appears, asking if you are sure that you want to reset. You have to confirm that you are by clicking the Yes button to proceed.

The Smoother panel only has two options: Apply To and Tolerance. The Apply To pull-down menu allows you to choose between applying the smoothing result to either a spatial or temporal path. Because you are dealing with the Position property in this lesson, you can only affect the spatial path.

You can use the Tolerance property to control the strength of the effect. Higher values produce a more noticeable smoothing result but may remove more detail than you want.

3   In the Timeline panel, click on the ant layer's Position property. Clicking any property name selects all the keyframes belonging to that property. In order to use the Smoother panel, you must select a minimum of three keyframes.

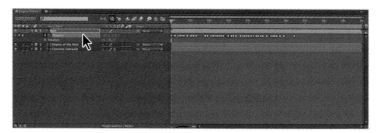

Clicking any property name selects all its keyframes simultaneously.

4 In the Smoother panel, set the Tolerance property to 8 and click the Apply button to produce a smoother path.

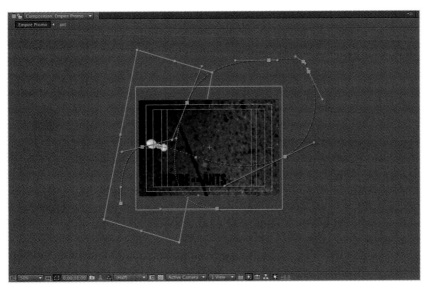

The specific path that you create will vary, depending on your smooth settings and the initial path you start with.

5 RAM preview the animation. Choose File > Save to save these changes to your After Effects project. Do not close this file, as you will need it in the next part of this lesson.

Using the Wiggler panel to add frantic motion

The Wiggler panel is the mirror opposite of Smoother. They both operate on the keyframes of an animation but instead of reducing keyframes, the Wiggler effect adds them. Wiggler is a great tool when you want to add random, frenetic movement to an animation without having to manually add extra keyframes.

In this exercise, you will use the Wiggler panel to add randomness to the Position property and apply a more frenetic sense of movement to the logo animation of Empire of the Ants. The logo animation that you have seen while previewing this project is inside of the Empire of the Ants comp. It is caused by keyframes and an expression on the layers named EMPIRE and ANTS. The up and down movement is caused by a series of three keyframes each: one at the beginning of the Timeline (0;00;00;00), another at 15 frames (0;00;00;15), and the final one at 1 second (0;00;01;00).

1 With the Empire of the Ants-working project still open and the Empire Promo composition active, double-click on the Empire of the Ants composition to open it.

2 Now in the Empire of the Ants comp, scrub the playhead to preview the animation. Notice that the words Empire and Ants repeat an animation where they move up and down.

   Select layers 1 (EMPIRE) and 4 (ANTS) and press the **U** key on the keyboard to reveal the keyframes and expressions on them. The animation on these layers is regular and even, but you can create a greater sense of frantic movement by adding randomness to the position keyframes with the Wiggler panel.

3 Move the playhead to the beginning (0;00;00;00) of the Timeline and if you are not currently in the Animation workspace, choose Window > Workspace > Animation to switch. If you have amended the default animation workspace, choose Window > Workspace > Reset "Animation" to return it to its default appearance. In this workspace, the Wiggler panel is located right below the Smoother panel on the right. The Wiggler panel contains the following options:

   Apply To: Specifies whether the Wiggler will change the spatial graph to add randomness to the motion of a layer, or the temporal graph to Add deviations to the velocity of a layer.

   Noise Type: Smooth Noise produces a gradual change that is free from sudden variations in the property, while Jagged Noise produces sudden, quick variations.

   Dimensions: Specifies whether to add deviations to a single dimension (x,y,z) or all dimensions simultaneously. If you use one of the all dimensions settings, you can specify whether to apply the same deviations to all the dimensions or to calculate individual values for each one.

   Frequency: Sets the number of deviations per second.

   Magnitude: Sets the maximum size of the deviation using the unit of measure of the selected property.

4 Click on the Position property of the EMPIRE layer to highlight all its keyframes; this also activates the Wiggler panel. Set the Wiggler as follows:

PROPERTY	VALUE
Apply To	Spatial Path
Noise Type	Jagged
Dimensions	Y
Frequency	10
Magnitude	10

Click the Apply button. The Wiggler adds a series of keyframes to the property. Preview the animation; notice that the word EMPIRE seems to jump up and down randomly.

The Wiggler can randomize values between existing keyframes.

5 Click on the Position property of the ANTS layer to highlight all its keyframes. The Wiggler panel maintains the previously used settings. Click Apply.

6 Double-click on the Empire Promo composition in the Project panel to make it active in the Timeline and Composition panels. RAM preview the composition.

7 Choose File > Save to commit these changes to your After Effects project. You may now close this project, as you are finished with it.

Understanding Keyframe Interpolation

You may ask yourself, what is interpolation? It is actually a very integral part of all keyframe-based computer animation, but many novice After Effects users don't completely understand how it works. When you create keyframes on the Timeline, you are setting the values of a specific property at a specific time. When you have two keyframes with different values, After Effects fills in the intermediate values between them (a process sometimes called tweening), thus creating animation. The technical term for this fill-in process where the program figures out the change in the keyframes and sets the intermediate values between them is called interpolation.

There are two types of keyframe interpolation in After Effects: spatial and temporal. Spatial involves the interpolation of values in space such as position, while temporal involves the interpolation of values in time to control velocity. Some properties such as Opacity only have temporal interpolation — that is, After Effects only has to interpret changes in the property over time — while other properties such as Position have both a temporal and spatial component.

Linear interpolation

The diamond-shaped keyframe icons that you have created in your animations throughout the projects in this book actually represent a very specific type of keyframe interpolation called linear interpolation. This type of interpolation creates a uniform rate of change between the keyframes. For example, if you have a layer moving 100 pixels across the screen over a duration of 10 seconds using linear interpolation, then the layer will move 10 pixels per second. Linear interpolation can lead to animation that seems stiff or mechanical. When dealing with spatial interpolation, a keyframe using linear interpolation creates a motion path in which the layer moves in a straight line.

Bézier interpolation

Bézier interpolation provides the most precise control of the value graph or motion path segments on either side of the keyframe. Bézier keyframes have two direction handles that operate independently on both the value graph and motion paths. If you apply Bézier interpolation to all the keyframes of a layer property, After Effects creates a smooth transition between these keyframes. Bézier interpolation allows you to create any combination of curves and straight lines along the motion path. Because each of the Bézier handles operates independently, a curving motion path can suddenly turn into a sharp corner.

Auto Bézier and Continuous Bézier interpolation

Auto Bézier interpolation creates a smooth rate of change, and is the default setting for spatial interpolation. As you change the values of keyframes using Auto Bézier interpolation, the positions of Auto Bézier direction handles change automatically to maintain a smooth transition between them.

Similar to Auto Bézier, Continuous Bézier interpolation also creates a smooth rate of change throughout a keyframe. However, the positions of direction handles in a Continuous Bézier keyframe are adjusted manually. When you manually adjust the direction handles of a keyframe using Auto Bézier interpolation, After Effects converts it into Continuous Bézier interpolation.

Hold interpolation

Hold interpolation is available only as a temporal interpolation method. You can use it to change the value of a layer property over time without a gradual transition. If you apply Hold interpolation to a property's keyframe, the value of the first keyframe holds steady until the next keyframe, at which point the values change immediately. This interpolation is very useful when you want to create strobe effects or have layers appear or vanish suddenly.

Create acceleration and deceleration using Easy Easing

The different types of keyframe interpolation are important because they give you a choice of how your animations look. Linear is the default interpolation type for temporal keyframes; this is what gives your animation a consistent change in the value of a property over time. Spatial keyframes, on the other hand, default to the Auto Bézier interpolation. This interpolation is what produces the curved or Bézier motion paths, what you have become used to seeing when animating the Position properties of objects. These different interpolation methods create different types of motion, both when animating onscreen movement such as that created by a motion path and when controlling the timing of animation to simulate acceleration or deceleration.

You are not limited to using the default interpolation method; you can change both spatial and temporal interpolation at any time to fit the specific needs of any project. In this part of the lesson, you will be working with an existing project that contains an animation of a bouncing ball. While the animation has already been built, it requires some modification to both the spatial and temporal keyframe interpolation to look more realistic.

Changing spatial interpolation

Spatial interpolation is the easiest one to adjust for most users because it is very similar to the way that you work in programs such as Photoshop and Illustrator. You can directly manipulate vertices and direction handles in the Composition panel in much the same fashion that you change mask shapes.

1   Choose File > Open Project and navigate to the ae09lessons folder. Locate the project named Using Easy Easing.aep and double-click it to open this file.

RAM preview the file to view the animation. As you can see, the project consists of a graphic of a ball bouncing up and down and there is also a shadow that follows the ball as it connects with the floor.

2   Move the playhead to the 2 second 15 frame (0;00;02;15) mark on the Timeline (this places you in the middle of the animation) and click on the Ball layer to highlight it. Then press the **U** key on your keyboard to reveal the layer's animated keyframes.

When you previewed the animation you may have noticed that the ball seems to float or slide as it makes contact with the table. This is due to the fact that the second keyframe is set to use Continuous Bezier for its spatial interpolation; however you can easily correct this by changing it so that is uses Linear interpolation.

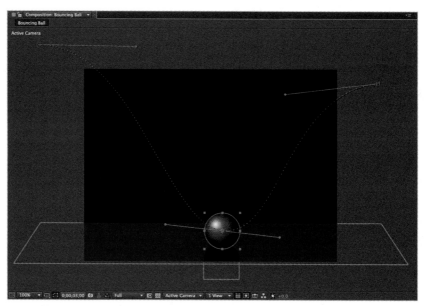

Changing spatial interpolation in After Effects is much like editing anchor points in graphics programs such as Adobe Illustrator and Photoshop.

3 In the Composition panel, right-click on the second keyframe; this is the one at which the ball connects with the floor graphic. In the menu that appears, choose Keyframe Interpolation to open a dialog box that allows you to control both temporal and spatial interpolation.

You can use the Keyframe Interpolation dialog box to set temporal and spatial interpolation simultaneously.

If you want to change the shape of the motion path now, you can do so by editing the handles of the first or last keyframes.

4 In the Keyframe Interpolation dialog box, change the Spatial Interpolation pull-down menu to Linear and click OK. The shape of the motion path changes to resemble two upward-facing curves.

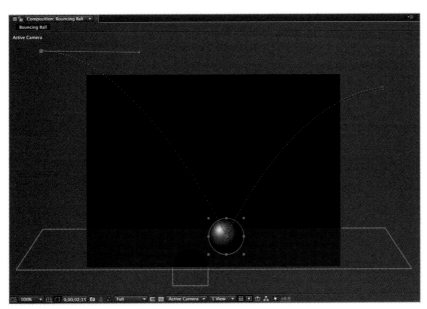

Motion paths in After Effects are similar to Bézier paths in other graphics programs.

5 Choose File > Save As and navigate to the ae09lessons folder. Rename the project **Using Easy Easing-working.aep** and click the Save button. Do not close this file, as you will need it in the next part of this lesson, where you will change the easing to the keyframes to simulate acceleration and deceleration.

Adding easing to keyframes

Easing is a technique that changes the rate of change or speed of an animated property to create the impression of acceleration or deceleration. If you are familiar with the principles of traditional cell animation, you may know this concept as slow-in and slow-out. After Effects makes it very simple to create this effect using Easy Ease In, Easy Ease Out, and Easy Ease, which you can use to quickly add easing with a simple right-click.

In this animation, the ball should gradually accelerate as it falls, attain its greatest speed just before it makes contact with the floor, and then decelerate as it approaches the top of its movement arc as it bounces away from the floor.

1 With the Using Easy Easing-working project still open, move the playhead to the beginning (0;00;00;00) of the Timeline. If the Position property of the ball layer is not visible, select the layer and press the **P** key on your keyboard to reveal it.

2 To create the sense that the ball is accelerating as it approaches contact with the floor, you will add Easy Ease Out to the first keyframe. In the Timeline panel, right-click on the first keyframe of the Position property and choose Keyframe Assistant > Easy Ease Out from the menu that appears.

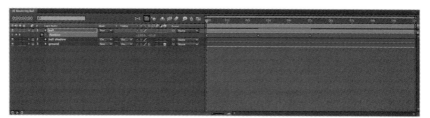

Adding easing to any keyframe means that it is no longer a simple linear keyframe.

3 Right-click on the last keyframe and choose Keyframe Assistant > Easy Ease In from the menu. This creates the deceleration effect as the ball bounces away from the point of contact with the floor.

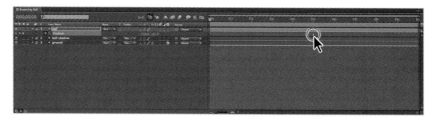

You can use Easy Easing to create quick acceleration and deceleration effects.

4 RAM preview the animation and you see that the speed at which the ball moves from keyframe to keyframe is no longer constant. Choose File > Save to save these changes to your After Effects project. Do not close this file, as you will need it in the next part of this lesson where you will add a few finishing touches to the animation to make it seem more realistic and engaging.

Using squash and stretch to enhance the animation

The Easy Easing you applied in the previous section of this lesson can enhance the sense of realistic movement in animations by creating acceleration or deceleration where you need it. Another principle of animation than you can also use to improve the visual appeal and sense of realism in an animated work is squash and stretch. Many animators consider it to be the most important element of an animation project and also one that is often overlooked in computer-based animation. You can use squash and stretch to convey a sense of weight and flexibility to objects by showing how they react to making contact with other objects.

In this animation, the ball should react to hitting the floor object. At its point of contact, the ball will squash vertically as it reacts to the force with which it hits the ground and also stretch horizontally to maintain its overall volume. Adding a motion blur to the animation should also help to establish the impression of a realistic movement through space.

1   With the Using Easy Easing-working project still open, move the playhead to the 2 second 15 frame (0;00;02;15) mark on the Timeline. Notice that the ball is still a perfect sphere at the point where it makes contact with the floor. This is actually the point at which it should squash and stretch.

2   With the ball layer selected, hold down the Shift key on your keyboard and press the letter **S** on the keyboard to add Scale to the currently displayed properties in the Timeline panel.

Then press the Page Up key on your keyboard (this moves the playhead back one frame to 0;00;02;14) and click the Time-Vary Stopwatch (●) for the Scale property. After Effects creates a keyframe at this point to preserve the ball's current scale value.

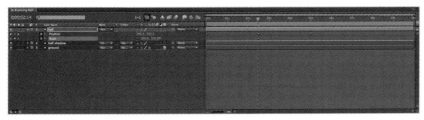

The Page Up and Page Down keys are very helpful when you must navigate the Timeline frame by frame.

3   Press the Page Down key on your keyboard to return to 0;00;02;15 or just press the letter **K** on the keyboard to move the playhead to the next visible keyframe, which is the one for the contact position of the ball.

4   Disable the Constrain Proportions switch to the left of the Scale property's values. Change the property values to 120.0%, 90.0%. This gives the spherical ball a more elliptical appearance.

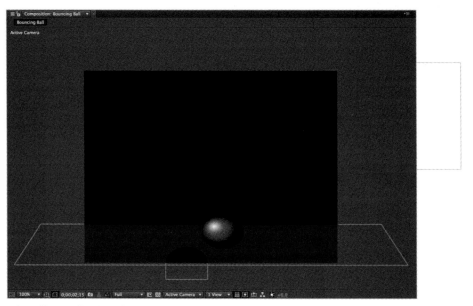

When adding squash and stretch, it is important to maintain the overall volume of the object.

5   Press the Page Down key on your keyboard five times to move to the 2 second 20 frame (0;00;02;20) mark on the Timeline. Change the Scale property values to 100.0%, 100.0% to restore the original appearance of the ball.

6   Enable the ball layer's Motion Blur switch and then click the Enable Motion Blur switch at the top of the Timeline panel to preview the motion blur effect in the composition.

7   Choose Edit > Deselect All and then RAM preview the animation. The overall effect is much more realistic than when you started.

     Choose File > Save to commit these changes to your After Effects project. You may now close this project, as you are finished with it.

Animating with the Graph Editor

Throughout this book you have created your animations either by manipulating property values in what is called the layer bar mode of the Timeline panel, or by directly moving your layers around in the Composition panel. While both of these methods can be very successful, there is another tool available to you called the Graph Editor that is intended to give you additional control over your animations. The Graph Editor represents property values along a two-dimensional graph, where composition time is represented horizontally while speed or value is represented vertically.

While you can use the Graph Editor to adjust the values of animated properties or to add additional keyframes, its primary function for most users is to control the speed of animations to create acceleration and deceleration. Like the Easy Easing you applied previously, you can use the Graph Editor to control the rate of change or speed of an animated property to create the impression of acceleration or deceleration. The difference is that the Graph Editor allows for much greater control and fine-tuning of the effect.

In this exercise, you will work with a pre-built After Effects project and use the Graph Editor to create a more realistic motion by adding acceleration to an animation.

1 Choose File > Open Project and navigate to the ae09lessons folder. Locate the project named Creating Acceleration with the Graph Editor.aep and double-click it to open this file.

RAM preview the Rocket composition. As you can see, it contains an animation of a rocket ship blasting off into space. The rocket moves up at a constant rate but this is unrealistic; it should start off slower and then accelerate upwards.

2 Click on layer 2, the one named Rocket, to select it and press the **U** key on your keyboard to reveal its animated properties.

Pressing the U key with any number of layers selected reveals only the properties that have animation enabled on those layers.

As you can see, this animation consists of two keyframes for the position of the rocket. The first keyframe at the 1 second (0;00;01;00) mark establishes the resting position and corresponds with the In points of the four layers that give you the rocket exhaust and flame trail. The second keyframe at the 5 second (0;00;05;00) mark places the rocket beyond the top border of the composition.

3   Click the switch that looks like a little graph to the right of the Time-Vary stopwatch (●) to include the Position property in the Graph Editor display.

Properties can be added or removed from the Graph Editor display by enabling or disabling this switch.

You must first add properties to the Graph Editor display before you can work with them. You can add and manipulate them individually, or in groups, depending on your needs.

4   Click the Graph Editor switch at the top of the Timeline panel to change the panel's default layer bar mode to the Graph Editor view.

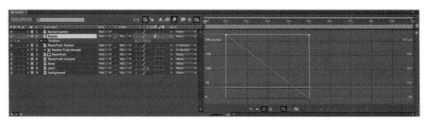

The Graph Editor displays composition time horizontally along the top of the Timeline and property values vertically along the right.

Understanding the Graph Editor

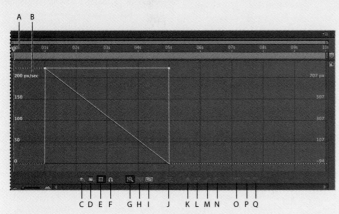

A. *Composition time ruler.* B. *Property values.* C. *Choose which properties are shown in the Graph Editor.*
D. *Choose graph type and options.* E. *Show transform box.* F. *Snap.* G. *Auto-zoom graph height.* H. *Fit selection to view.*
I. *Fit all graphs to view.* J. *Separate dimensions.* K. *Edit selected keyframe.* L. *Convert selected keyframe to hold.*
M. *Convert selected keyframe to linear.* N. *Convert selected keyframe to Auto Bézier.* O. *Easy Ease.* P. *Easy Ease In.*
Q. *Easy Ease Out.*

The Graph Editor displays composition time horizontally along the top of the Timeline and
property values vertically along the right. When working with the Graph Editor, there are two
different types of graphs available to you: value graphs and speed graphs. Value graphs show the
actual value of the animated properties that you have added to the editor, while speed graphs
show rates of change of the property values. For spatial properties such as Position, the Graph
Editor defaults to the speed graph, while for temporal properties such as Opacity, the Graph
Editor defaults to the value graph.

5   The white graph line represents the speed at which the property values change. It is
     currently a straight line, meaning that the property's change in value is constant. Notice
     that the keyframes on this speed graph correspond with the Position property's value
     keyframes in the layer bar display.

     The keyframes (represented by the white anchor points on the graph line) in this graph
     use linear interpolation, and each possesses one direction handle (to control the curvature
     of the graph line) each.

Linear keyframes produce a constant change in speed and may appear to create stiff animation.

Click on the first keyframe, hold the Shift key on your keyboard, and drag the keyframe to the zero px/sec position on the value graph.

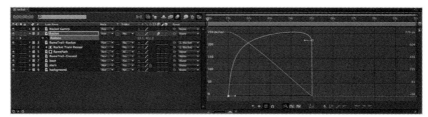

As you move keyframes vertically in the Graph Editor, the Timeline display automatically adjusts to make them all visible.

6 RAM preview the animation. The rocket now seems to accelerate suddenly and then the speed tapers off and remains relatively constant; this is due to the shape of the graph. The first keyframe on the speed graph has a value of zero px/sec. The graph rapidly increases in value toward the beginning of the animation and then levels off approximately halfway through. You can adjust this by moving the second keyframe up. Click on the second keyframe, hold the Shift key on your keyboard, and drag the keyframe to the 600 px/sec position on the value graph.

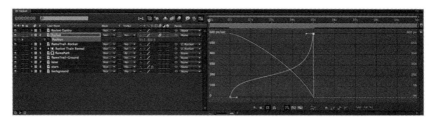

The Graph Editor automatically scrolls as you move a keyframe vertically and then adjusts to keep all your keyframes in view after you complete the movement because the Auto-zoom graph height button is enabled.

7 The keyframes are now in the proper position for the type of acceleration that you want, but you need to adjust the curvature of the graph line so that the rocket is picking up speed as it rises into the air. Click on the direction handle of the second keyframe and drag it to the left until the graph line resembles the one below.

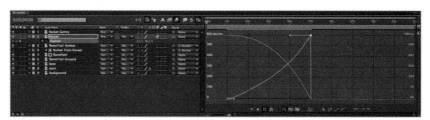

The direction handles adjust a property of the speed graph's keyframes called Influence.

8   RAM preview the animation. The rocket should now pick up speed as it rises. If you want a greater acceleration, you can always adjust the vertical position of the second keyframe so that the rocket is traveling at a speed greater than 600 px/sec when the animation completes.

Choose File > Save As and navigate to the ae09lessons folder. Rename the project **Creating Acceleration with the Graph Editor-complete.aep** and click the Save button. You may now close this project, as you are finished with it.

If you prefer, you can set the speed and influence values for a keyframe numerically in a dialog box by double-clicking on that keyframe.

Create a strobing effect using hold interpolation

Whether using the linear method to create uniform changes or the Bézier method to vary the speed and create the impression of acceleration, the animation must still progress through every single value between the two keyframes. But what if an animation calls for a property to immediately change from one value to another? This is a time to use the hold interpolation method.

In this section of the lesson, you will change keyframe interpolation to produce an effect in which a light bulb blinks on and off.

1   Choose File > Open Project and navigate to the ae09lessons folder. Locate the project named Using Hold Interpolation.aep and double-click it to open this file.

RAM preview the lightBulb composition. As you can see, the light bulb fades up and then fades down again, but in this case a better animation would have the light simply blink on and off.

2   The animation in this project is due to the opacity keyframes on the Filament-Dark, Bulb Color-White, and Flare Effect layers. Converting them all to hold keyframes will produce the desired effect. Click on the Opacity property for the Filament-Dark layer to select all this property's keyframes.

Clicking on any property selects all keyframes for that property; you can then move or edit them simultaneously.

3   Hold the Shift key on your keyboard and click on the Opacity property for the Bulb Color-White and Flare Effect layers to select these keyframes as well.

4   Right-click on any one of the selected keyframes and choose Keyframe Interpolation from the menu that appears.

5   In the Keyframe Interpolation dialog box, change the Temporal Interpolation to Hold. This converts all the linear keyframes that you selected to hold keyframes. Click OK to close the dialog box.

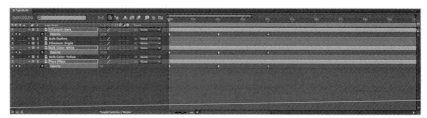

The Opacity property only has temporal keyframes.

6   RAM preview the animation. The light bulb now blinks on and off.

Choose File > Save As and navigate to the ae09lessons folder. Rename the project **Using Hold Interpolation–complete.aep** and click the Save button. You may now close this project, as you are finished with it.

Automating animation with expressions

What are expressions, you may ask? They are the scripting language built into After Effects and you can use them to automate some animation tasks that are otherwise tedious or time-consuming to complete. Expressions are not the answer to every problem you will face in the program, but they can be the solution to some of them. You can add them to any layer or effect property and they will either complement or replace (depending on which expressions you are using) the keyframes you have already set.

Expressions can be helpful to you in many ways. There are some effects that are virtually impossible to achieve using keyframes alone, while in other situations, such as when you want to loop an animation, they can simply cut down on the number of keyframes that you have to create. You can use expressions to link different properties on different layers together or force one layer to move or change in relation to another. Expressions are not the solution to every problem; in fact, sometimes it is easier to keyframe a series of actions than to try and create a complex expression to achieve the same effect. However, understanding when and how to use them can speed up your workflow.

Expressions are based on the JavaScript language, which is a very common language used in web site development, but you don't have to learn much code to take advantage of their power. If you are already interested in scripting, then you may choose to explore the full range of features available by writing your own expressions; however, most users really only need a general understanding of a few scripts that they can use to optimize their animation workflows.

It is important to note that script is very sensitive to spelling and capitalization errors. Any deviation from the proper spelling and capitalization of the language will cause the code to fail. Please be very careful when typing code into the Expression field.

Finding expressions

There are many sites on the Web where you can find additional expressions for use in After Effects. A Google search for the terms "After Effects" and "Expressions" is often a great place to start. The following is a short, annotated list of a few of the resources you may want to check out:

SITE NAME	SITE ADDRESS	NOTE
MotionScript.com	*www.motionscript.com*	The site of Dan Ebberts. Many of the scripts listed in the After Effects help files come from him.
Adobe User to User Forums	*http://forums.adobe.com/index.jspa*	The forums have message boards that specialize in expressions and scripting.
AE Enhancers	*www.aenhancers.com*	The site includes libraries, tutorials, and discussion forums on scripts and expressions.

Adding expressions to properties

When you add expressions to individual layer or effects properties, they only affect those specific properties. In Lesson 7, when you learned how to work with audio in After Effects, you created an expression to link two properties together using the pick whip. Now you will move beyond simply linking two properties to each other and add expressions that modify the value or behavior of keyframes in your composition.

When working with Expressions you must be very careful. The Expressions language, like all scripting languages, is very sensitive to both spelling and capitalization. You will want to make sure that you input the code exactly as it is seen here. Any error that is made when you are entering code will disable the code and open a warning dialog box to appear when you exit the Expressions window. Once the error is corrected, the Expressions will then be re-enabled.

In this section of the lesson, you will work with a pre-built After Effects project and add several common and simple scripts to enhance the overall design and avoid having to create extraneous keyframes.

1   Choose File > Open Project and navigate to the ae09lessons folder. Locate the project named Using Common Expressions.aep and double-click it to open this file.

RAM preview the Dark City composition. As you can see, this project is composed of several different pieces, most of which are currently static. In the course of this exercise, you will:

- Add an expression to the yellow wedge swinging in the background to allow it to loop forwards and backwards continuously.

- Add an expression to the three-pointed white stars in the background that allows them to blink on and off randomly.

- Add an expression to the cloudy background that adds a constantly increasing movement so it seems to oscillate continuously.

- Add an expression to the color fields on the cloudy background that allows them to vary their position frantically.

Using the LoopOut( ) expression

You use the LoopOut( ) expression to allow a keyframed animation to continue to play, even after the playhead has reached the last keyframe. In this case, you will set the type of loop to use a ping pong effect so that the animation will play forwards and backwards continuously. You will work with the flourishes-Spikes composition in this section of the lesson.

1   With the Using Common Expressions.aep project open, double-click on the flourishes-Spikes composition in the Project panel to reveal it and make it active.

2   RAM preview the flourishes-Spikes composition to see that it is a simple animation of a yellow wedge shape rotating from a vertical to a horizontal position.

Click on the Single Spike layer to highlight it and press the **R** key on your keyboard to reveal the Rotation property. Notice that there are two keyframes for the property: one at the beginning of the Timeline (0;00;00;00) and the other at 3 seconds (0;00;03;00).

3   Press and hold the Alt key on your keyboard and then click on the Time-Vary Stopwatch (●) for the Rotation property to add a Rotation expression to the Timeline.

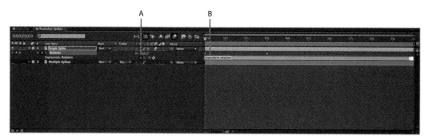

A. Expression interface. B. Expression field.

Adding an expression displays the expression interface, a series of buttons and menus for working with expressions and the expression field, which is a resizable text field that displays in the Timeline.

While editing expressions, previews are disabled.

4 Replace the placeholder text in the expression field with the following:

```
loopOut();
```

Click in any empty area of the Timeline to exit the expression field and then scrub the playhead from the beginning of the timeline to the end, to preview the animation. As you scrub the playhead past the second keyframe, notice that the wedge jumps back to the starting position and the animation repeats; this type of looping is called a cycle. It will continue to do this for the duration of the composition.

5 While the default behavior of a loop function is to cycle, you can change this by modifying the line of code you created in the previous step. Click in the expression field to make it editable and change the code you previously added, to the following:

```
loopOut(type="pingpong");
```

Click in any empty area of the Timeline to exit the expression field and again scrub the playhead from the beginning of the timeline to the end, to preview the animation. Notice that the wedge now swings down and then back up, playing forwards and backwards much like a ping-pong ball being hit back and forth across a table.

6 Double-click on the Dark City composition in the Project panel to return to the main composition, and RAM preview it to see the effect.

Choose File > Save As and navigate to the ae09lessons folder. Rename the project **Using Common Expressions-working.aep** and click the Save button. Do not close this file, as you will need it in the next part of this lesson.

Using the Random( ) expression

It can be difficult to create the impression of randomness in animation using keyframes alone. In situations where you need to create a sense that something is occurring randomly, you can always turn to the random function. In this section of the lesson, you will add randomness to the white, three-pointed stars to make them blink on and off haphazardly. To accomplish this, you will apply the expression to a single layer first and then copy that expression to other layers.

1 With the Using Common Expressions-working.aep project open, double-click on the Star Outlines composition in the Project panel to reveal it and make it active. This composition consists of a series of concentric three-pointed stars.

2 Click on the layer at the top of the layer stack to select it and press the **T** key on the keyboard to reveal the Opacity property.

Not all expressions act upon existing keyframes, some like the random function can be used to create animation.

3 Click on the Opacity property to select it, choose Animation > Add Expression, and in the expression field that appears, replace the placeholder text with the following code:

```
random(0,100);
```

This randomizes the Opacity property by choosing a random number using 0 (zero) as the minimum possible value and 100 as the maximum.

4 Click on the Opacity property again to confirm that it is selected, and choose Edit > Copy Expression Only. This doesn't copy the actual layer — only expressions written onto it.

5 Click on the second layer in the stacking order, press and hold the Shift key on your keyboard, click on the last layer to select all them, and then choose Edit > Paste.

This effectively replicates the code onto each selected layer, giving each a random opacity animation. Tap the **E** key on your keyboard twice in rapid succession to see the expressions that have been added to all the layers.

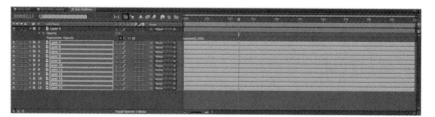

It is important to remember to choose the Copy Expression Only command; otherwise, After Effects will copy and paste the actual layer.

  To hide all the properties on all selected layers, you can hold down the Ctrl key on your keyboard and press the tilde (~) key.

6   Double-click on the Dark City composition in the Project panel to return to the main composition, and RAM preview it to see the effect.

Choose File > Save to commit these changes to your After Effects project. Do not close the file, as you will need it again in the next part of the lesson.

Using the Time property with expressions

The Time property is the value of the composition time at the playhead's current position. So if the playhead is at the 3 second (0;00;03;00) mark on the Timeline, the Time property's value is 3, and if it is at the 10 second (0;00;10;00) mark, the value is 10. Because the time property constantly changes, it can be a great way of making a property increase in value without having to create additional keyframes.

1   With the Using Common Expressions-working.aep project open, double-click on the Dark City composition in the Project panel to select it and make it active in the Timeline panel.

2   Click on the clouds shape layer to select it, and then click on the solo switch to the left of the layer name to hide every other layer. Press the **E** key on your keyboard to reveal the effects on this layer.

Soloing a layer is very helpful when you want to hide every other layer. Only layers with their solo switch enabled will display.

3   Double-click on the Fractal Noise effect beneath the layer name to reveal the Effect Controls panel. Then, in the panel, right-click on the Evolution property and choose Reveal in Timeline from the menu that appears.

4   Now that the Evolution property has been revealed in the Timeline, you can add an expression to it. This property uses progressive revolutions that continue to change the image with each added revolution and you can use it to specify how much the noise evolves over a period of time. With a little imagination, you can use the Time property to create an ever-increasing Evolution effect. Hold down the Alt key on your keyboard and click on the time-vary stopwatch for the Evolution property.

5   Click on the Expression language menu button in the expression interface, and choose Global > time from the menu that appears.

The Expression language menu provides a convenient way to add expressions to your property and can save you a great deal of typing time.

This replaces the placeholder text in the expression field with the Time property.

6   Click in the expression field after the Time property and add the following code:

```
*200;
```

The completed expression should look like this:

```
time*200;
```

7   Disable the cloud layer's solo switch and then RAM preview the animation to see the effect of the expression. The cloud layer is now in constant motion.

8   Choose File > Save to commit these changes to your After Effects project. Do not close the file, as you will need it again in the next part of the lesson.

Using the Wiggle( ) expression

Earlier in this lesson you used the Wiggler panel to add frantic movement to a layer; a side effect of using the Wiggler was the creation of a bunch of extra keyframes. The wiggle() function allows you to create the same effect but doesn't add any keyframes to the Timeline; as a result, adjusting the effect is much easier once you have applied it. In this part of the lesson, you will apply a wiggle function to the gradient fill on the orange, green, and blue shape layers in the Dark City composition. It is the gradient on these layers that gives the black-and-white cloud layer its color tinting.

1   With the Using Common Expressions-working.aep project open, enable the solo switches for the shape layers named orange, green, and red.

2   Click the reveal triangle to the left of the orange layer's layer name. Then click the reveal triangles in the following order—Contents > Rectangle 1 > Gradient Fill 1—until you see the gradient fill's Start Point property.

The Start Point property controls where the gradient fill begins, while the End Point property controls where it stops.

3   Hold down the Alt key on your keyboard and click on the time-vary stopwatch to the left of the Start Point property to add an expression to it.

4   Replace the placeholder text with the following code:

```
wiggle(10,50);
```

The wiggle function above has two parameters: The first parameter specifies the frequency, the number of wiggles per second. The second parameter sets the amplitude, the maximum amount of variation applied to the property the wiggle function is affecting. The amplitude uses the unit of measure of the property that you apply it to.

5   Click the reveal triangle to the left of the orange layer to hide all its properties.

Then click the reveal triangle to the left of the green layer's layer name. Again click the reveal triangles in the following order—Contents > Rectangle 1 > Gradient Fill 1—until you see the gradient fill's Start Point property.

6   Hold down the Alt key on your keyboard and click on the time-vary stopwatch to the left of the Start Point property to add an expression to it. Replace the placeholder text in the expression field with the following code:

```
wiggle(15,20);
```

Then click the reveal triangle to the left of the green layer to hide all its properties.

7   Click the reveal triangle to the left of the red layer's layer name. Then once again click the reveal triangles in the following order—Contents > Rectangle 1 > Gradient Fill 1—until you see the gradient fill's Start Point property.

8   Hold down the Alt key on your keyboard and click on the time-vary stopwatch to the left of the Start Point property to add an expression to it. Replace the placeholder text in the expression field with the following code:

```
wiggle(5,30);
```

Then click the reveal triangle to the left of the red layer to hide all its properties as well.

9 Disable the solo switches for all three layers and reveal the entire composition. RAM preview the animation to see the effect of your work with expressions.

10 Choose File > Save to commit these changes to your After Effects project. You may now close this project, as you are finished with it.

Working with scripts

You may not be familiar with scripts yet, but in many cases you can use them to make your workflow less tedious and more efficient, and they can often enhance the animation features of After Effects. A script is a group of programmatic commands that tell a program to perform a series of actions. Most Adobe applications have built-in support for running scripts to automate repetitive tasks, and some even offer scripting support for functions that are not supported in the program's interface. In After Effects, scripts are created using the Adobe ExtendScript language, a variation of the JavaScript language, which is often used in the development of web pages.

Scripts should not be confused with expressions, which use the internal scripting language of After Effects. While expressions are intended to assist in repetitive or difficult animation tasks, the scripts written in the ExtendScript language are intended to alter the actual application. They can add functionality that is usually lacking, or may currently require multiple menus or commands to run, such as scaling an entire composition or finding and replacing text in a comp.

Installing and running scripts

When After Effects starts up, it automatically loads scripts from the Scripts folder. Several scripts come pre-installed with After Effects and are automatically installed in the Scripts folder in the application folder on your hard drive. Loaded scripts are available from the File > Scripts menu. You can run scripts even if they have not already been loaded by choosing File > Scripts > Run Script File. Some scripts are intended to add additional panels to the program interface. These are installed into the ScriptUI Panels folder and are available from the bottom of the Window menu.

Creating scripts

If you are familiar with other scripting languages such as JavaScript or ActionScript, then you may want to explore the options available to you in writing your own scripts. You can write your own After Effects scripts using the Script Editor, which is part of the ExtendScript Toolkit. To start the Script Editor, choose File > Scripts > Open Script Editor.

Finding additional scripts

There are many sites on the Web where you can find additional scripts for After Effects or the other applications in the Adobe Creative Suite. Many scripts are given away for free, while others are provided for a fee similar to plugins, and still others are available with a voluntary donation. The following is an annotated list of some of the sources available to you:

SITE NAME	SITE ADDRESS	NOTE
Adobe Exchange	*www.adobe.com/cfusion/exchange*	Includes a wide variety of content for a range of programs in the Creative Suite.
AE Scripts	*www.aescripts.com*	Includes both free and for-purchase scripts.
AE Enhancers	*www.aenhancers.com*	Includes libraries, tutorials, and discussion forums on scripts and expressions.
Adobe User to User Forums	*http://forums.adobe.com/index.jspa*	The forums have message boards that specialize in expressions and scripting.

Additional resources for scripting in After Effects, including helpful sites for tutorials and script downloads on the Web, is available through the Adobe Help application by searching for the word "Scripts."

Using and applying scripts

To complete this section of the lesson, you will need to download and install a script from a third-party developer. If you do not currently have access to the Internet, cannot add scripts to the After Effects folder, or don't feel comfortable doing this at the current time, you should skip this section.

In this section of the lesson, you will use the Ease and Wizz script created by Ian Haigh. Ease and Wizz is a script-based panel that improves upon the functionality provided by using the built-in Easy Ease commands. The Ease and Wizz script is available for a voluntary donation from the AE Scripts web site listed above. Information on installing and using the script, along with a few sample animations, is available at Ian's web site, *www.ianhaigh.com/easeandwizz/*.

To install the Ease and Wizz script, copy the Ease and wizz.jsx file and easingExpressions folder into the ScriptUI Panels folder inside the After Effects folder on your hard drive. You can find the scripts folder in the following locations:

On the Windows OS: Program Files/Adobe/Adobe After Effects CS5/Support Files

On the Mac OS: Applications/Adobe After Effects CS5

Once you have copied the files to the appropriate folder you will have to change a preference to allow the script to create a new panel.

In the General category of the Preferences panel enable the switch that says; **Allow Scripts to Write Files and Access Network**.

Once the script has been copied to the ScriptsUI folder and the preference changed, you must restart After Effects so that the Ease and Wizz panel is accessible through the Window menu just like any other panel.

1   Choose File > Open Project and navigate to the ae09lessons folder. Locate the project named SecretOfSuccess-Animated.aep and double-click it to open this file.

RAM preview the SecretOfSuccess composition. As you can see, this is the same animation that you worked on in Lesson 8 where you worked with the 3D features of After Effects.

2   Choose Window > Ease and Wizz.jsx to open the Ease and Wizz panel. It opens as a very large panel with a great deal of empty space. Resize it by clicking and dragging on the lower-right corner of the panel to make it more manageable.

Many scripts exist that simply add additional panels to the After Effects interface.

The Ease and Wizz panel has four parameters that you can adjust:

Easing: Selects the type of easing algorithm to use. Enabling the curvaceous option below will limit the available choices somewhat.

Type: Specifies whether the easing algorithm is applied to the keyframe so that it sets easing in, out, or both.

Keys: Sets which keyframes for the selected property the Ease and Wizz effect is applied to. You can choose to affect all a layer's keyframes, only the start and end keyframes, or only the starting keyframe.

Curvaceous: A switch that has several different functions. When applied to keyframes of the Position property, it allows the animated object to follow a Bézier motion path. Additionally, this switch allows you to use the Ease and Wizz script on Mask Path keyframes.

3   Click on the Spot Light 1 layer to select it and press the **U** key on your keyboard to reveal its animated properties.

Click on property name; Point of Interest, to select all the keyframes for that property.

4 Right-click on the first highlighted keyframe and from the menu that appears choose Keyframe Assistant > Easy Ease.

This will add Easing to both highlighted keyframes so that the movement of the Spot Light 1's Point of Interest is no longer constant.

5 RAM preview the animation. The spotlight's Point of Interest now seems to pick up speed as it moves to complete its motion. As you learned when you worked with it earlier, the built in Easy Easing functions can be very helpful for making quick animation where things accelerate and decelerate. But what if you would like to be more creative with your easing? This is where the Ease and Wizz panel comes in.

6 With the Spot Light 1 layer selected, hold down the Ctrl key on your keyboard and press the tilde (~) key to hide all the layer's properties. Then lock the layer by clicking the lock switch to the left of the layer name.

Choose Edit > Select All to select the remaining seven layers and then press the **R** key on your keyboard to reveal their Rotation properties. These keyframes are what you will adjust to create a more visually engaging animation.

7 Each text layer has either the Y Rotation or X Rotation property animated. Click on the animated Rotation property of the layer named THE, hold down the Shift key, and then click on the animated Rotation property of the remaining six layers.

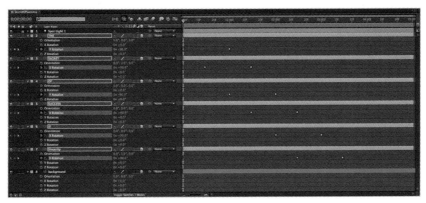

Holding down the Shift key and clicking on a property name allows you to select multiple properties at the same time.

When using the Shift key to select multiple layer properties, it is necessary to click on each property that you wold like to select. This is completely different from when you use the Shift key to select layers in sequence, where you only have to click on the first and last layer to select all the layers in between them.

In the Ease and Wizz dialog box, set the following parameters:

- Easing: Bounce
- Type: In
- Key: All
- Curvaceous: Disabled (checked off)

Click the Apply button.

If you select multiple keyframes for multiple properties, then you can apply the Ease and Wizz effect simultaneously to all them.

8   RAM preview the animation. The animation now seems more dynamic and engaging.

Choose File > Save As and navigate to the ae09lessons folder. Rename the project **SecretOfSuccess-Animated-complete.aep** and click Save. You may now close this project, as you are finished with it.

Congratulations! You have completed the lesson.

Self study

Now that you have learned some of the more advanced concepts and tools for creating animation in After Effects, you can try them out on your own. You should experiment with adding some of the expressions you have learned here to enhance the animations you have created in earlier lessons in this book.

Review

Questions

1   What is the advantage of creating your own animation presets?

2   Why would you want to use Motion Sketch?

3   What are expressions and why would you use them?

Answers

1   Animation presets allow you to quickly reuse animations you have created, and because their properties are editable once you apply them, you can adjust settings to match the specific needs of each project.

2   Motion Sketch offers a more intuitive solution to animating positional changes in After Effects. It allows an artist to draw motion paths onscreen and apply them to objects in the Timeline.

3   Expressions are the scripting language built into After Effects, and you can use them to automate some animation tasks that are otherwise tedious or time-consuming to complete. There are some effects that are virtually impossible to achieve using keyframes alone, while in other situations, such as when you want to loop an animation, they can simply cut down on the number of keyframes that you have to create.

What you'll learn in this lesson:

- Adding compositions to the Render Queue

- Adjusting render and output module settings

- Creating render template to speed repetitive tasks

Outputting After Effects Projects

Creating your animations in After Effects is only a part of producing a complete project. Once that task is complete you must still output your composition to a usable format by rendering it. Rendering creates a video file from the content on the Timeline.

Starting up

You will work with several files from the ae10lessons folder in this lesson. Make sure that you have loaded the aelessons folder onto your hard drive from the supplied DVD. See "Loading lesson files" on page 4.

See Lesson 10 in action!

Use the accompanying video to gain a better understanding of how to use some of the features shown in this lesson. The video tutorial for this lesson can be found on the included DVD.

Setting up

As you work in After Effects, you will open and close many panels depending on the type of project you are creating. When working through the remaining projects in this book, it is important to have an interface that matches the lessons. To this end, you should always reset your workspace to the preset Standard configuration.

1   Choose Window > Workspace > Standard to set your current workspace configuration.

2   Choose Window > Workspace > Reset "Standard" to reset the standard workspace in case you have modified it at some point.

Rendering files for output

Rendering is the process of creating the frames of a video file from an After Effects composition. Rendering an individual frame creates a single image by combining all the layers, channels, effects, and other elements together to form a composite image. When you render the entire composition, After Effects renders the individual frames and combines them into a single video file or image sequence. After Effects offers a wide variety of format and compression choices when rendering your project. The settings you choose for your project depend on how you plan to use it.

After Effects supports output to the following video, audio, and still image formats:

SUPPORTED FORMATS		
3GPP (3GP)	FLV, F4V	H.264 and H.264 Blu-ray*
MPEG-2, MPEG-2 DVD, MPEG-2 Blu-ray**	MPEG-4	QuickTime
SWF	Video for Windows (AVI)***	Windows Media****
Audio Interchange File Format	MP3	WAV

*The H.264 Blu-ray format splits the audio and video portions of a composition into different files.

**The MPEG-2 DVD and MPEG-2 Blu-ray formats split the audio and video portions of a composition into different files.

***Exporting video to the AVI format is a Windows-only feature.

****Exporting video to the Windows Media format is a Windows-only feature.

If you use Adobe Premiere Pro to edit video, there is no need to render your After Effects compositions. You can use Adobe Dynamic Link to import unrendered comps directly to the Premiere Pro Timeline.

Understanding the Render Queue

The Render Queue panel is the main interface for rendering and exporting files in After Effects. Multiple render items, each with its own output settings, can be managed simultaneously. You can create and apply templates for rendering and output settings in the Render Queue to aid productivity. The Render Queue has two sets of options that you must configure:

Render Settings: These options set characteristics for the output file such as resolution, frame rate, and duration.

Output Module: These options specify such settings as output format and compression. The Output Module also includes a section called Output To, which allows you to select a folder location and name for the output file.

Together, you use Render Settings and Output Module to control every aspect of your final rendered file.

Adding compositions to the Render Queue

Compositions that have been added to the Render Queue are known as *render items*. The queue can contain multiple render items at the same time, and once you initiate this process by clicking the Render button, After Effects renders them all sequentially, unsupervised.

In this exercise, you will open an existing project that contains multiple compositions and add one of them to the Render Queue to output a file for integration into a video editing application such as Premiere Pro.

1   Choose File > Open Project, navigate to the ae10lessons folder, and double-click on Adding Comps to the Render Queue.aep to open it.

    This composition contains two of the text animations that you completed in Lesson 6, with the curtain background that is taken from the Animation Presets > Backgrounds in the Effects & Presets panel.

2   In the Project panel, double-click on the Jabberwocky composition to select that comp and make it active in the Composition panel.

3   Choose Composition > Add to Render Queue to open the Render Queue panel and add the composition as a render item.

The Render Queue panel is the main interface for outputting the work you create in After Effects.

A composition needs to be active in either the Project or Composition panel for the Composition > Add to Render Queue command to work.

4 Click on the reveal triangles to the left of Render Settings and Output Module to show the current settings for each set of options. By default, the Render Queue assigns the highest-quality rendering templates to the render item based on the composition's properties.

By default, the Render Queue is set to output the highest-quality file for use in a video editing application.

In this case, the Project settings will produce a file for progressive display.

5 Click on the downward-facing triangle to the right of Render Settings to select a new template to use in rendering this item. From the list that appears, choose DV Settings. This will change how the item is rendered to produce an interlaced video file that matches the settings of a standard-definition NTSC video file.

6 Click the downward-facing triangle to the right of Output Module to select a new output template. From the list that appears, choose QuickTime DV NTSC 48 kHz to create a file that is compatible with the NTSC standard for digital video.

The built-in output templates provide a starting point for producing a video file that matches the established broadcast video standards.

If you are working on a PC, the equivalent template to QuickTime DV NTSC 48 kHz is named Windows DV NTSC 48 kHz.

7 Click the downward-facing triangle to the right of Output To and select Comp Name from the menu that appears; this opens a dialog box named Open.

In the dialog box, navigate to the ae10lessons project folder and click the Open button in the lower-right corner of the dialog box to choose a location to save the output file.

8 The status of this render item is now set to Queued, meaning that this file will be included when the next render operation occurs. Click the Render button in the upper-right corner of the panel to initiate a rendering. This renders every item in the queue with its status set to Queued.

The time it takes to render will vary, sometimes significantly, from file to file and computer to computer. Rendering is a very processor-intensive activity, and while After Effects is rendering, you cannot use it for any other purpose. You can use the status indicator at the top of the Render Queue panel to review the estimated time to completion. When the render is complete, a chime sounds.

9 Notice that once the rendering process is complete, the items remain in the queue but they now have a status of Done. This is to allow you to duplicate render jobs without having to send a composition to the queue again. Click the reveal triangles to the left of Project Settings and Output Module to collapse the property display.

10 Choose File > Save As and navigate to the ae10lessons folder. Rename the file **Adding Comps to the Render Queue-working.aep** and click the Save button. Do not close the file, as you will need it for the next section.

Adjusting render settings

Although the built-in Project Setting and Output Module templates can be very helpful in many situations, for more specific rendering needs, you will have to make adjustments to the individual settings. In this section, you will add another composition from the Adding Comps to the Render Queue project. This time, you will output the file in a format compatible with mobile devices and the Internet.

1 With the Adding Comps to the Render Queue-working.aep file still open, double-click on the Seneca–on speed composition to make it active. Choose Composition > Add to Render Queue. This adds the composition as the second render item in the queue.

2   Click on the words *Best Settings* to the right of the Render Settings label; this opens the Render Settings dialog box.

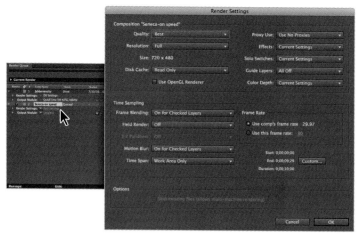

In the Render Queue panel the text labels function as buttons.

There are many settings in this dialog box that you will probably never want to change from their default values. However, in the Time Sampling section, there are two properties that you should become familiar with: Field Rendering and Time Span. You use the Field Rendering drop-down menu when you must switch from progressive to interlaced rendering, and the Time Span drop-down menu to control what part of the Timeline is rendered. You can specify either the entire Timeline or an area defined by the work area bar, or set custom In and Out points for the composition.

3   The animation in the composition ends at the 5 second (0;00;05;00) mark on the Timeline, so you will specify a custom duration for the output file to reduce both the file size and render time.

Click the button labeled Custom, located at the bottom-right corner of the dialog box, to open the Custom Time Span dialog box. You use this dialog box to override the default duration of the render item.

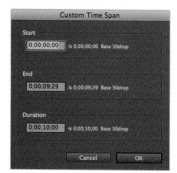

Setting custom in and out points for your render are also helpful if you need to preview part of an overall project.

4 Leave the value for the Start timecode set to 0;00;00;00 and change the End value to **0;00;06;29**. This changes the duration to **7** seconds (**0;00;07;00**). Click OK to close this dialog box and return to the Render Settings dialog box. Click OK in the Render Settings dialog box to return to the Render Queue panel.

When counting with timecode, you always begin at the number zero, so one second in duration on the Timeline would be at 0;00;00;29 and not 0;00;01;00.

5 Click on the word *Lossless* to the right of the Output Module label; this opens the Output Module Settings dialog box.

The default Output Module setting Lossless is intended to produce a high quality video file.

The Output Module controls everything about the final output file, from its format and compression to whether or not you include an alpha channel in the render. From this dialog box, you can also adjust the size of the output video by resizing or cropping it and also adjust the audio output settings.

6 From the format drop-down menu, choose H.264. This creates an MP4 file that is compatible with modern digital devices and display on the Web. Click OK to return to the Render Queue panel.

7 The status of this render item is now set to Queued, meaning that this file will be included when the next render operation occurs. Click the Render button in the upper-right corner of the panel to initiate a rendering.

8 Choose File > Save. Do not close this file; you will need it in the next section where you will duplicate the render job and create multiple Output Modules for it.

Duplicating jobs in the Render Queue

While it is possible to duplicate render items in the queue by choosing the Edit > Duplicate command, it isn't necessarily the most efficient way to work. An advantage of having the After Effects Render Queue is the ability to output a single render item with different Render Module settings. Instead of sending a composition to the Render Queue multiple times, you can simply assign multiple output modules to the item.

In this section, you will duplicate a render item and add multiple Output Modules to it with the intention of creating a QuickTime file for digital distribution and a low-resolution sample file for review purposes.

If you need to re-render an item that has already been rendered or output files with different Project Settings. For example, where one format requires interlacing and another requires progressive display—it is necessary to duplicate the entire item to make these changes.

1   With the Adding Comps to the Render Queue-working.aep file still open, click on the Jabberwocky render item in the Render Queue panel to highlight it.

2   Choose Edit > Duplicate to make a copy of the item. This adds a third render item to the panel with the same Render Settings and Output Module settings as the original, but with a different filename. You can also use a keyboard, Ctrl+D (Windows) or Command+D (Mac OS), in place of the menu command.

Duplicate the render item.

If you intend to use the new render item to replace the original, it is better to choose Edit > Duplicate with File Name when creating the new item.

3   From the Render Settings Templates menu, choose Best Settings.

4   Open the Output Module Settings dialog box by clicking on QuickTime DV NTSC, and then click on the Format Options button on the right. In the QuickTime Options dialog box, click the Video tab to view and adjust the video settings, then choose MPEG-4 Video from the Video Codec drop-down menu and click the OK button at the bottom of the panel to return to the previous dialog box.

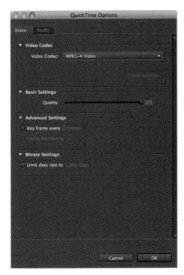

QuickTime is a common interchange format for video in many professional production settings.

5   Because this file lacks an audio component, uncheck the Audio switch at the bottom of the Output Module Settings dialog box. Confirm that all other settings match the example below and click OK to return to the Render Queue panel.

When render items are duplicated, all the settings of the original are transferred to the copy.

6   Click on the filename located to the right of Output To, and in the Output Movie To dialog box, change the filename to **Jabberwocky-large mobile.mov**. Click Save to commit the name change and close the dialog box.

7   Click the plus sign located to the left of Output To in order to add another Render Module to this item.

Adding additional Render Modules is an alternative to duplicating an entire render item.

8   Open the Output Module Settings dialog box by clicking on "Lossless" and click on the Format Options button on the right. In the QuickTime Options dialog box, choose MPEG-4 Video from the Video Codec drop-down menu and change the Quality slider to **80**. Click the OK button at the bottom of the panel.

Click the Resize checkbox to allow you to change the output dimensions of the video file, and with the Lock Aspect Ratio checkbox enabled, change the Resize to width to **360**. Click OK to return to the Render Queue panel.

When resizing video reducing the size is usually fine but increasing it will result in a loss of quality.

Because Lock Aspect Ratio is enabled, changing the width will also automatically change the height once you click outside of the numerical field. When using the Resize option, it is okay to decrease the size of the After Effects composition, but increasing it will result in a loss of image quality.

9   Click on the filename located to the right of Output To, and in the Output Movie To dialog box, change the filename to **Jabberwocky-small mobile.mov**. Click Save to commit the name change and close the dialog box.

10   The status of this render item is now set to Queued, meaning that this file will be included when the next render operation occurs. Because the render queue is now going to effectively render two files sequentially, this may take some time to complete. You can skip the render phase of this exercise if you choose.

If you would like to render the two video files, click the Render button in the upper-right corner of the panel to initiate a rendering.

11   Choose File > Save. You may now close the file.

Creating render templates

Render templates allow you to streamline the output process. They can be created for both Render Settings and Output Modules and then applied to the render items in the queue.

Next, you will create a Render Settings template for low-resolution previews and an Output Module template for QuickTime files that would be suitable for outputting these previews.

1   With a new untitled project open, choose Edit > Templates > Render Settings to open the Render Settings Templates dialog box.

2 Click the New button in the Settings section of the dialog box to open the Render Settings dialog box.

Set the Resolution drop-down menu to Half. This produces a file that is half the size of the initial composition because only every other pixel will be rendered.

When working with video resolution, it is sometimes used when talking about the pixel dimensions of a file which is why adjusting the menu in this situation reduces the size.

Click OK to return to the previous dialog box.

3 Type **Low resolution preview** into the Settings Name field and click the OK button at the bottom of the dialog box.

This template is now accessible from the Render Settings Template menu in the render queue.

4 Choose Edit > Templates > Output Module to open the Output Module Templates dialog box. Notice that it is set up almost exactly like the Render Settings Templates dialog box was.

5 Click the New button in the Settings section of the dialog box to open the Output Module Settings dialog box. Click on the Format Options button on the right.

In the QuickTime Options dialog box, choose MPEG-4 Video from the Video Codec drop-down menu and change the Quality slider to 80. Click the OK button at the bottom of the dialog box to return to the previous dialog box. Again click the OK button to return to the Output Module Templates dialog box.

6 Type **QuickTime–MPEG4 Medium Quality** into the Settings Name field and click the OK button at the bottom of the dialog box. This template is now accessible from the Output Module Template menu in the render queue. Templates are automatically saved with the application whenever they are made, and you can use them in any After Effects project you create on your computer.

If you need to share templates between users of different computers, you can do so using the Save All command found in both the Project Settings and Output Module Templates dialog boxes. After Effects saves the files in the .ars and .aom formats respectively, and they can then be loaded by another user through the Load command found in each dialog box.

Exporting a project file

While the render queue is indeed the main interface for outputting your After Effects work, it is not the only one. If you are developing content for deployment online or through digital devices, you may need to bring your work into Adobe Flash. A workflow that takes advantage of both programs allows you to build highly engaging visual content in After Effects and then add interactivity in Flash using the ActionScript language. If Flash is your intended destination, you will use the Export command found in the File menu to create an Adobe Flash Professional (XFL) project file. An XFL file is essentially an XML-based equivalent of the native Flash project file (.fla). When you export a composition to XFL format, the program attempts to create as accurate a conversion as possible by preserving as much data as possible, thus maintaining the integrity of individual layers and keyframes.

Now, you will export an After Effects project as a Flash XFL project.

There is a second project file format that you can export. An alternative workflow for video may involve exporting an After Effects composition as an Adobe Premiere Pro project (PRPROJ). Though viable, this isn't the most commonly used option, as users of Premiere Pro are more likely to opt for importing After Effects elements using the Adobe Dynamic Link feature, which allows unrendered content to be used on the Timeline.

1 Choose File > Open Project, navigate to the Lesson 10 folder, and double-click on Exporting to Flash.aep to open this project. This is a scaled-down version of one of the files you worked with in Lesson 6.

2 Double-click on the From word to deed composition in the Project panel to make it active.

3 Choose File > Export > Adobe Flash Professional (XFL) to open the Export Settings dialog box.

4 Not all layer types and effects are supported when the composition is converted to an XFL file. Unsupported features must be either rasterized (as a video or PNG sequence) or ignored. Choose the radio button for Rasterize To and make sure the Format drop-down menu is set to FLV. This converts all unsupported layers to Flash video files.

If you choose to rasterize unsupported content, you must choose to convert it to either an FLV (flash video) file or a PNG image sequence.

Click OK.

5 In the Export As dialog box, navigate to the ae10lessons folder. By default, the filename simply copies the composition name; leave it as is and click the Save button to complete the export operation.

The file is now ready to be taken into Flash. You can open it by simply using the File > Open command in Adobe Flash Professional. Flash Professional cannot save an XFL file, so you will have to create a Flash Document (.fla) from this exported file.

6 Because the export process does not affect the project file, there is no need to save it. Choose File > Close Project. If the Save Changes dialog box appears, simply choose Don't Save to close it.

Trimming and cropping compositions

When you create new compositions, you must specify their dimensions and durations, and it often seems perfectly reasonable to do so by just copying the settings of your current comp. But what happens when your project settings change? You may now need to trim a composition down to fit a new specification from your client or because you changed the length of your animation. Perhaps you have scaled down the content of a comp and want to reduce the dimensions to match. The ability to crop and trim layers is especially helpful when using the Pre-compose command, as it simply copies the duration and dimensions of your current comp. In this section, you will work with a pre-built project file where you will trim a composition's duration to eliminate excess time and you will crop it to fit the physical space that the animation occupies. In order to trim and crop a composition, you will use other features of the program as intermediaries to accomplish your goal. To trim you will use the work area bar to define the area to trim to, and to crop you will use the Region of Interest.

1   Choose File > Open Project, navigate to the ae10lessons folder, and double-click on Trimming and Cropping Comps.aep to open this project.

2   In the Project panel, double-click on the Creativity composition to make it active in the Timeline panel.

3   Click on the layer numbered 1 (the text layer) to select it and press the **U** key on the keyboard. This reveals all the properties on this layer that have animation enabled.

As you can see, this composition has a duration of 10 seconds (0;00;10;00), though the animation only lasts for the first 5 seconds. Additionally, its dimensions are the full DV NTSC size of 720 × 480, though it is intended for use inside of another comp and needs to be a fraction of that size.

4   Move the playhead to the 6 second (0;00;06;00) mark of the Timeline. This is one second after the animation is complete; adding a little time at the end of the animation gives the viewer time to absorb what they are seeing on screen. If you plan on importing your animation into a video editing application such as Adobe Premiere Pro, this extra space after the animation, which is sometimes called a handle, makes it easier for the editor to work with.

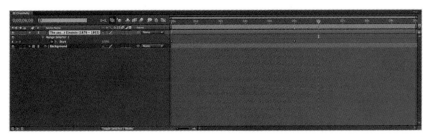

Adding handles to the beginning and/or end of your compositions make it easier for an editor to integrate your animation into a video project.

5   Press and hold the Shift key on your keyboard and in the time ruler at the top of the Timeline, click on the end marker of the work area bar and drag it toward the playhead. Because you are holding down the Shift key, the marker snaps to the playhead.

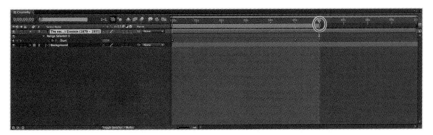

You can adjust the work area bar by clicking and dragging either its start or end marker.

*There are keyboard commands for setting the position of both the start and end of the work area bar. Pressing the **B** key on your keyboard moves the start of the work area bar to the playhead, while pressing **N** moves the end of the work area to the current position of the playhead.*

6 Right-click on the work area bar and choose Trim Comp to Work Area from the menu that appears. This command changes the duration of the composition to only include the area the work area bar currently spans.

7 In the Composition panel, click on the Grid and Guide Options button and choose Proportional Grid. This grid is a great tool when you need to have a general sense of the positioning of content in your composition but don't need to be as exact as the rulers and guides allow.

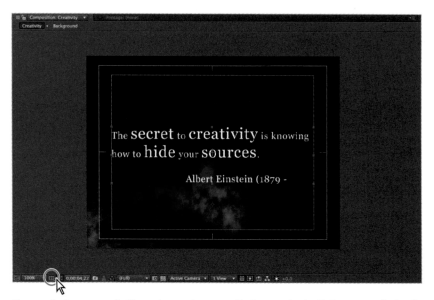

You can only show one set of grids at a time, so when you enable the proportional grid, the action- and title-safe margins are disabled.

8   Click on the Region of Interest button at the bottom of the Composition panel. This
changes the cursor into a cross–hair icon and disables the layer display.

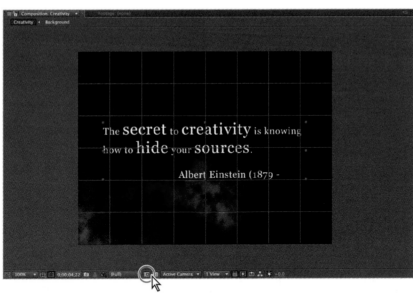

*Since the layer display is disabled when using the Region of Interest tool it is important to set up either the grid
or guides before hand.*

9   With the Region of Interest tool active, click and drag over the middle two rows of the
grid. This completely encompasses the text so that it is visible.

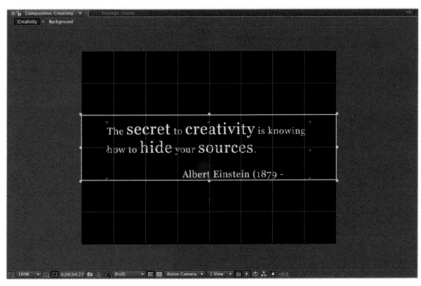

*The Region of Interest tool is also helpful if you want to preview only a portion of the composition panel because
only the area inside it will preview during rendering.*

You can remove the Region of Interest by holding down the Alt (Windows) or Option (Mac OS) key on your keyboard and clicking on the Region of Interest button.

10 Choose Composition > Crop Comp to Region of Interest. This changes the composition's dimensions to match the size of the Region of Interest.

Technically, this command doesn't delete the area outside the Region of Interest; it simply adjusts the comp size so that it isn't displayed. For example, you can still move the background layer around if you want to show a different portion of it.

11 Click on the Grid and Guide Options button and choose Proportional Grid from the menu to disable it.

Choose File > Save As and navigate to the Lesson 10 folder. Rename the file **Trimming and Cropping Comps-small.aep** and click the Save button. Do not close this file, as you will need it in the next section.

Rendering an individual frame

Sometimes you do not want to render an entire composition. Perhaps you want to render a single frame in order to use it as a template or visual guide. This can be a very useful tool if you must create content in another application such as Photoshop or Illustrator and you need to set its position relative to content in your After Effects comp. It can also be helpful for creating freeze-frame effects to hold a single frame of video in place, or if you need to make a still image to use as a thumbnail or preview image.

After Effects can output the following still-image formats:

OUTPUTTING FORMATS		
Photoshop (PSD)	Bitmap (BMP, RLE)*	Cineon (CIN, DPX)
Graphic Interchange Format (GIF)*	Maya IFF (IFF; 16 bpc)	JPEG (JPG, JPE)
OpenEXR (EXR)	PNG (PNG; 16 bpc)	Radiance (HDR, RGBE, XYZE)
SGI (SGI, BW, RGB)	Targa (TGA, VBA, ICB, VST)	TIFF (TIF)

*These formats can only be exported from a Windows-based computer.

1   With the Trimming and Cropping Comps-small.aep file still open, move the playhead to the end of the Creativity composition.

2   Choose Composition > Save Frame As > File. This opens the render queue and adds the current comp to it. In the render queue, the Render Settings field is set to Current Settings. Because you used the Save Frame As command, the current settings are to output the file as a single frame.

    The Output Module defaults to a Photoshop file and you can adjust it by editing the module's settings. In many cases, you will want to bring the image files that you output into Photoshop for additional processing, so it makes a good default format here.

3   Click on the text to the right of the Output To field, Creativity (0;00;06;00).psd, to open the Output Frame To dialog box. Navigate to the ae10lessons folder, change the filename to Creativity thumbnail, and click the Save button to commit your changes.

While the Photoshop format is the default for the Save Thumbnail As command, you can choose another format by editing the Output Module Settings.

4   Click the Render button at the top of the Render Queue panel to render the file.

    This may take a few minutes, but when the render is complete, the files will be ready for editing in Photoshop or another application that will open this image format.

5   Choose File > Save to commit your changes to the file. You may now close this project.

Self study

Experiment with rendering the sample project provided on the DVD as well as your own project in different video formats and with different codecs. You will find that the final output file's size varies, depending on the codec and the actual content of the file you are attempting to compress.

Review

Questions

1   How do the files produced with H.264 Blu-ray and MPEG-2 DVD output settings differ from the standard H.264 and MPEG-2 output?

2   What are the two project file types that can be exported from After Effects using the File > Export command?

3   What is the default image format when rendering an individual frame from a composition?

Answers

1   The H.264 Blu-ray and MPEG-2 DVD output settings produce two separate files, one for the audio portion of the composition and another for the video. This is so that they can be used in a DVD or Blu-ray disk authoring application such as Adobe Encore, as components in a multilingual disk.

2   The two project file types that can be exported from After Effects using the File > Export command are XFL for use in Adobe Flash Professional and PRPROJ for use in Adobe Premiere Pro.

3   Photoshop is the default image format when rendering an individual frame.

Appendix A

After Effects Secondary panels

In Lesson 2, "Understanding the After Effects Interface," the primary panels of After Effects are introduced in detail. This appendix is presented to provide reference of the remaining panels with which you may need to work.

Align

You use the Align panel to quickly align and distribute selected layers in your composition. The align commands line up selected layers in your composition either horizontally or vertically, while you use the distribute commands to even out the spacing between the anchor points of your layers. In order to use the Align commands two or more layers must be selected while to use the Distribute commands three or more layers must be selected.

The Align panel.

Audio (Ctrl + 4)

You use the Audio panel to display and adjust the volume of audio in your composition. During previews, the panel's VU (Volume Unit) meter dynamically displays the changing volume in your composition.

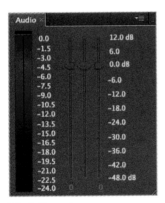

The Audio panel.

Brushes (Ctrl + 9)

When using a Paint tool (Brush, Clone Stamp, or Eraser), you can use the Brushes panel to set the brush tip shape, diameter, roundness, angle, hardness, and dynamic options. Brushes in After Effects are vector based and their shapes can be animated as an effect.

The Brushes panel.

Character and Paragraph

When working with text, the Character panel sets the properties of individual characters such as font, style, size, and tracking. The Paragraph panel sets the properties such as text alignment, indentation, and the space before and after each paragraph. Text in After Effects is very similar to the way you work with text in Illustrator, Photoshop or InDesign.

The Character and Paragraph panels.

Effects & Presets

The Effects & Presets panel is a library for both the built-in and add-on effects that are currently installed on your system. This panel also displays both the pre-installed animation presets and any custom presets that you have created. You can apply both effects and presets to layers in your composition from this panel either by dragging and dropping the preset name onto a destination layer or by double-clicking on the preset with a target layer highlighted in the Timeline panel.

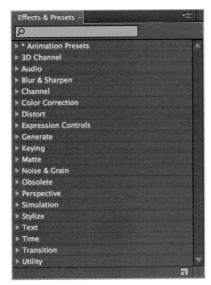

The Effects and Preset panel.

Info

Similar to the standard Info panel in other Adobe applications, (Illustrator, Photoshop, InDesign) this panel tells you the color value (RGBA) at the cursor's current position, as well as the coordinates of its current position. If you have a footage item highlighted, the Info panel displays its name and other related information.

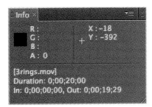

The Info panel.

Mask Interpolation

The Mask Interpolation panel allows you to automatically create new mask keyframes and speed the animation of mask shapes. This interpolation provides a high level of control for creating animation of mask path keyframes that have smooth and realistic motion. After you have selected the mask path keyframes that you want to interpolate, the mask interpolation panel is used to create intermediate keyframes based on the settings you specify.

The Mask Interpolation panel.

Metadata

In addition to the normal, audio-visual information that a media file can contain, some file types can also have metadata attached to them. This metadata can hold information about the type of camera that took a photograph, or perhaps hold Timeline markers for video or audio. The Metadata panel allows you to view the metadata associated with imported files.

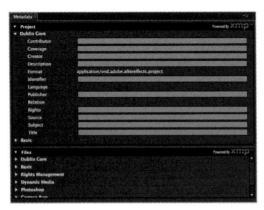

The Metadata panel.

Motion Sketch

The Motion Sketch panel gives you a more intuitive way to create animation by using your mouse or graphic tablet to draw a path for motion. It allows you to quickly create very complex and detailed motion animations. Many After Effects artists find it beneficial to use this panel to create motion paths that are natural or fluid.

The Motion Sketch panel.

Paint

When working with the Paint tools (Brush, Clone Stamp, and Eraser), you can use the Paint panel to set the color of the brush, as well as its other properties, such as opacity, mode, and duration. The controls of the Paint panel are similar to those found in other painting programs such as Photoshop and can be used to vary the appearance of painted strokes.

The Paint panel.

Tools

The Tools panel contains the various tools that you use in After Effects. Each tool performs a specific function, such as moving or rotating objects or creating shapes and masks.

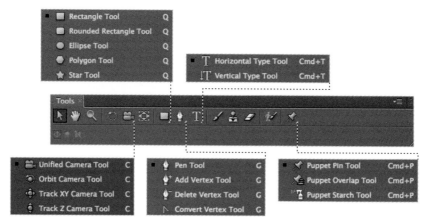

The Tools panel.

Preview

You use the Preview panel to control the playback and options of both Timeline and RAM previews. You can use the transport controls to move the position playhead around the Timeline or to initiate previews, while the switches control playback options, such as frame rate and resolution.

The Preview panel.

Smoother

You use the Smoother panel to adjust an animation by reducing the number of keyframes for a selected property. Removing extraneous keyframes based on the tolerance setting (use a higher value for greater smoothing) produces a softer animation. You can apply the effects to either a spatial property, such as position or a temporal one such as scale or opacity.

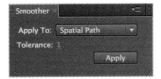

The Smoother panel.

Tracker

The Tracker panel contains the tools for both tracking and stabilizing video footage. Both tracking and stabilization work by analyzing the position of pixels on the screen and repurposing that information to either determine how the camera that took the footage was moving, or follow the movement of a point in the footage.

The Tracker panel.

Wiggler

The Wiggler panel performs the opposite function of Smoother. Instead of reducing the number of keyframes for a property, the Wiggler increases the number based on the frequency and magnitude settings that you input. You can use the Wiggler to add randomness and frenetic motion to animations.

The Wiggler panel.

Appendix B

Importable media formats

Some After Effects artists only work with one type of media; for example, they may specialize in animating still images built in Photoshop or Illustrator. But most users will be called upon to handle a wide variety of different media, and thanks to the integrated environment of the Adobe Creative Suite, this is easier than ever. Most standard and many esoteric media types can be imported into After Effects.

Video and audio

Prerecorded video and audio media are often imported into After Effects for enhancement or to be used to accompany an animation. You can import video files, video files that contain audio, or audio files independently.

After Effects CS5 supports importing the video formats in the following table.

FILE FORMATS	FILE TYPE EXTENSION	NOTES
Animated GIF	GIF	
DV	MOV, AVI, DV	DV footage can be in either an MOV or AVI container, or the DV stream format.
Electric Image	IMG, EI	EIZ files are also supported.
Material eXchange Format	MXF	After Effects can only import some kinds of data contained within MXF files.
MPEG-1, MPEG-2, and MPEG-4	MPEG, MPE, MPG, M2V, MPA, MP2, M2A, MPV, M2P, M2T, M2TS (AVCHD), AC3, MP4, M4V, M4A	Some MPEG formats are stored inside container formats with file extensions that After Effects cannot understand, such as VOB. In some cases, merely replacing these extensions with one of the recognized extensions can help.
Photoshop Document	PSD	Importing PSD video layers requires that the QuickTime Player be installed on your computer.
QuickTime	MOV	The QuickTime Player is required.
RED	R3D	

FILE FORMATS	FILE TYPE EXTENSION	NOTES
Flash Movie	SWF	The SWF file's alpha channel is retained, though its audio and interactive content are not.
Video for Windows	AVI	The QuickTime Player is required for Mac OS.
Windows Media File	WMV, WMA, ASF	This can only be imported into the Windows version of After Effects.
XDCAM HD and XDCAM EX		Uses either MPEG-2 or MPEG-4 file extensions.

After Effects CS5 supports importing the audio formats in the following table.

FILE FORMATS	FILE TYPE EXTENSION	NOTES
Adobe Sound Document	ASND	Multi-track files are imported as a single, merged track.
Advanced Audio Coding	AAC, M4A	
Audio Interchange File Format	AIF, AIFF	
MP3	MP3, MPEG, MPG, MPA, MPE	
Windows Waveform	WAV	

Still images and image sequences

You can import individual still images into Adobe After Effects or import a sequentially numbered group of images as a sequence. The After Effects environment uses only the RGB color space, though it will convert CMYK images to RGB on import. When working with programs such as Photoshop and Illustrator, it is always best to create images in the RGB color mode for use in video, film, mobile devices, and other non–print based displays.

After Effects CS5 supports importing the image formats in the following table.

FILE FORMATS	FILE TYPE EXTENSION	NOTES
Adobe Illustrator	AI, AI4, AI5, EPS	
Adobe PDF	PDF	Only the first page of multipage PDF files is imported.
Adobe Photoshop	PSD	PSD Video and 3D layers are supported.
Bitmap	BMP, RLE, DIB	

FILE FORMATS	FILE TYPE EXTENSION	NOTES
Camera Raw	TIF, CRW, NEF, RAF, ORF, MRW, DCR, MOS, RAW, PEF, SRF, DNG, X3F, CR2, ERF	
Cineon/DPX	CIN, DPX	
Discreet RLA/RPF	RLA, RPF	Embedded camera data is imported.
Encapsulated PostScript	EPS	
Joint Photographic Experts Group	JPG, JPEG	
Maya camera data and Maya IFF	MA and IFF, TDI	
OpenEXR	EXR, SXR, MXR	
PICT	PCT	
Portable Network Graphics	PNG	
Silicon Graphics Image	SGI, BW, RGB	
Tagged Image File Format	TIFF, TIF	

Project formats

In addition to still images, video, and audio files, you can import a select number of native project files into After Effects CS5 from applications such as older versions of After Effects, Premiere Pro, and Apple Motion.

PROJECT FORMATS	FILE TYPE EXTENSION	NOTES
Adobe Premiere Pro	PRPROJ	Versions supported: 1.0, 1.5, 2.0, CS3, CS4, CS5. Versions 1.0, 1.5, and 2.0, Windows only
Adobe After Effects 6.0 and later	AEP, AET	
Adobe After Effects CS4 and later XML projects	AEPX	
Photoshop Vanishing Point Data	VPE	
Apple Motion Project	MOTN	Imports as a QuickTime file with an alpha channel premultiplied with black.

Appendix C

Understanding formats and codecs

There is a great deal of confusion among novice video makers about the differences between codecs and video formats. Most computer users are probably familiar with the term format when used to describe files. If you come from a design background, you are probably used to dealing with files of different formats such as JPEG or TIFF, and even casual computer users may be familiar with formats such as Word DOC or PowerPoint PPT files. However, when working with video, understanding the format isn't enough. Video formats such as QuickTime, AVI, Windows Media Video, and Flash Video are containers, much like a briefcase or a backpack that is filled with content. This is the relationship between formats and codecs: formats are the containers but the codecs are the language in which the contents are written.

Codec is a combination of the words "compressor" and "decompressor." Codecs are mathematical algorithms that are used to shrink audio and video files down to manageable sizes. It is important to understand that video files are very large; for example, 20 minutes of NTSC DV video (from a standard-definition MiniDV camcorder) are over 4GB in size. That is about the capacity of one single-layer DVD. Without codecs, not only would it be much harder to store and save video footage that you want to archive, but it would also never be small enough to watch online, send through e-mail, or view on a mobile device. In order to view an audio or video file, not only must you have a player that is compatible with the format, but you must also have the same codec that was used to compress it, available on your computer so that you can decompress it.

Here is a quick scenario: your friend shoots a short video of his dog doing a back flip. He edits it a little, maybe adds some background music and sound effects, and then creates a QuickTime movie using the H.264 codec and e-mails it to you. In order to view your friend's video of the wonder dog, you open the movie in the latest version of QuickTime Player or VLC Media Player or one of several other media players that support QuickTime files, and it plays. No fuss; it just works. Now most people never actually think about why it works, they're just happy and sometimes surprised that it does. The reason it works is because not only do you have a player that is compatible with the QuickTime Movie format, but you also have the H.264 codec installed.

When working with video editing and animation programs, there are times when a format incompatibility will cause a problem where you can't import a specific file type, but very often problems are caused by a codec that is either missing or unsupported by your software.

Understanding bit rate

Storing video takes up a lot of space on your hard drive, considerably more than text, images, or even audio files. If you tried to take these massive files and display them on the Internet or e-mail them to someone, it would never work, and this is the reason that codecs are used to shrink files. In general, there are two types of codecs: those that are intended for editing purposes and those that are intended to be used as a final delivery format.

When determining the quality of a digital video file, a major factor to consider is the file's bit rate. Bit rate is the amount of data that is allocated to each second of video. Usually the bit rate value is displayed as kbps (kilobytes per second); for example, the average bit rate of DVD video is 25,000 kbps. In general, the higher the bit rate of a video file, the better its quality will be. To get an idea of comparative bit rates, standard-definition DV 25 (MiniDV) footage is approximately 25,000 kbps, while DVD-quality video is approximately 5,000 kbps, and if you can recall videotapes, VHS has a bit rate of approximately 1,200 kbps. Understanding the relationship between a file's bit rate and its quality is important when choosing the export settings for your video project.

Understanding spatial and temporal compression

There are two types of compression that video codecs can use to shrink the size of files: spatial and temporal. While some codec use only one or the other, most use both compression types to reduce audio and video files to manageable sizes, thus allowing them to be easily shared.

Spatial compression is the easiest to understand because it is very similar to the compression used in image formats such as JPEG and GIF. This image compression is usually lossy, works on each frame in a video file individually, and is sometimes called intraframe compression. Another very powerful method of compression is called temporal or interframe compression. This type of compression compares each video frame to the one previous to it and only saves the data describing what has changed between them. This type of compression can experience problems if the original frames are removed or damaged.

All codecs employ one type of compression or the other, and many employ both methods. Codecs that only use spatial compression, such as the DV codec, are usually preferable for editing as each frame can stand alone. Codecs that employ temporal compression such as MPEG-2 tend to offer better compression ratios, but because of the interrelationship between frames, they can be problematic for editing.

Appendix D

Understanding Video Displays

When shooting and displaying your video or when preparing your graphics there are a few very important concepts you need to keep in mind:

What is the aspect ratio of your video?

What is the pixel aspect ratio of your video?

Will the video be displayed on an interlaced device or a progressive one?

Asking these questions before you begin your production will save time and effort when you are in the post production stage of editing, compositing and graphics creation. It will also avoid sometimes time-consuming errors that can occur when you output your final projects.

Understanding aspect ratio and pixel aspect ratio

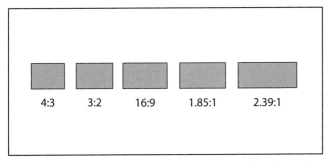

Differences in the aspect ratio of film and television are what cause letter boxing when films are shown on televisions.

Aspect ratio and pixel aspect ratio (called PAR) are two terms that can cause some confusion and frustration when working with video formats. The aspect ratio, also called image aspect ratio, is the proportion of the width of an image to its height. Usually this value is expressed as two numbers separated by a colon, as in 4:3 or 1.85:1, though sometimes it is referred to using more generic terms such as standard and widescreen mode. In videography, the two most common aspect ratios are 4:3 (sometimes denoted as 1.33:1) for standard-definition display and 16:9 (sometimes denoted as 1.78:1) for widescreen or high-definition formats. Film uses different aspect ratios than video and broadcast television, two notable ones being 1.85:1 and 2.39:1, to accommodate a wider vista and to better mimic human vision.

The differences in aspect ratio usually become apparent when video is displayed on a television screen with an aspect ratio different from that of the actual video. When displayed on a 4:3 television or computer monitor, widescreen video (16:9, 1.85:1, 2.39:1) such as that created when a film is transferred to DVD, is usually displayed at the full width of the screen with two black boxes at the top and bottom in a technique called letterboxing. Footage that is created using a 4:3 aspect ratio and then displayed on a widescreen device can appear with black bars to each side in a technique called pillarboxing. It is possible for a video image to be displayed with simultaneous letter- and pillarboxing, in a situation called windowboxing.

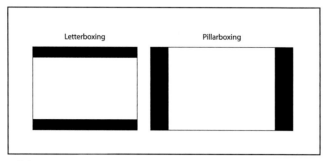

Pillarboxing is caused when 4:3 footage is shown on a widescreen device.

Often confused with aspect ratio, pixel aspect ratio is the proportion of the width of the pixels that make up a video or still image to their height. While many people know that a pixel is the smallest individual unit of a digital image, they sometimes don't realize that pixels can be different shapes and sizes. The pixels used by a computer monitor are square in shape and have a pixel aspect ratio (par) of 1:1 (1.0), while many of the standard video formats have rectangular pixels; for example, standard definition D1/DV NTSC footage has a par of 0.9:1 (.9), widescreen NTSC footage has a par of 1.21:1 (1.21), and high-definition HDV 1080 and DVCPRO HD 720 have a par of 1.33:1 (1.33).

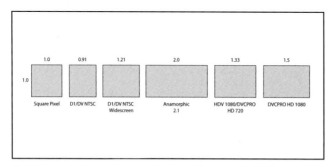

Pixel Aspect ratio distortion can cause video or graphics to seem stretched.

After Effects usually does a good job of mixing different types of source footage, though distortion can occur if the wrong par interpretation is used. When footage is interpreted incorrectly, it can appear either squashed or stretched, causing circular objects on screen to appear as ovals. Graphics programs such as Photoshop can only create content using square pixels but they have presets and previewing modes for video projects that provide a good representation of what your graphics will look like when displayed on a television monitor. When creating graphics in Photoshop and Illustrator, it is always best to use their provided video presets and choose the one that matches your After Effects project.

To change the pixel aspect ratio interpretation of a footage item, right-click on the item in the Project panel and choose File > Interpret Footage > Main. Choose the correct ratio from the Pixel Aspect Ratio menu and click OK.

Progressive display versus interlacing

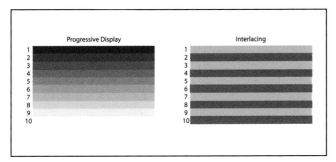

All video signals, whether broadcast or not, are either sent as a progressive or an interlaced signal.

Progressive display and interlacing are the two methods of displaying images on a video screen. In the United States, prior to the changeover to a digital broadcasting system, all television was sent as an interlaced signal in which every frame of video was actually made by combining two half-images called fields. Prior to the days of high-definition LCD and plasma screens, all televisions were made by wrapping a plastic or wooden frame around a large glass device called a cathode ray tube (CRT). These CRT television screens were made up of a series of even- and odd-numbered lines called scan lines, and each frame of video was displayed by illuminating these lines starting at the top of the screen. Interlacing was created to display video signals on this type of TV set and worked by illuminating one set (either the even or odd numbered) of lines first and then jumping back up to the top of the display to illuminate the other set. By the time the first set of lines began to fade, the display was already showing the second set, and the result formed one complete picture for the viewer. With NTSC broadcast television, this process happened 60 times per second. An alternative to interlacing, progressive display illuminates these scan lines sequentially, one after the other, from top to bottom.

Most modern televisions have the ability to display in both interlaced and progressive modes, and the ATSC includes broadcast standards for both, while all computer monitors use progressive display only. The difference between the two display methods carries over into video camera formats as well; while older NTSC or PAL cameras can only shoot interlaced video, many newer cameras offer a choice between both interlaced and progressive shooting modes such as 50i (25 fps), 60i (30 fps), 30p (30 fps), and 24p (24 fps). When working in After Effects, you will want to use project settings that match your intended output medium.

Index

A

Acceleration, 281–286
Accepts Lights option, 216
Accepts Shadows option, 216
Action-Safe margin, 153
Active Camera, 214, 233
Add or Remove Keyframe at Current Time button, 93, 174
Add property, of masks, 116
Add/Remove Keyframe switch, 123–124
Adjustment Layers, 77, 80
Adobe After Effects 10.0 MC Prefs, 3–4
Adobe After Effects CS5
    Prerequisites for, 1–2
    Starting, 2–3
    System requirements, 1–2
Adobe Bridge, 170–171
Adobe Creative Suite, 186
Adobe Exchange, 301
Adobe ExtendScript, 300
Adobe Flash Movie, 336
Adobe Flash Player
    Flash video, 13–14
    Viewing video tutorials with, 7
Adobe Flash Professional, 319
Adobe Illustrator
    Compositions, importing of, 72–73
    Description of, 14
    File extensions, 336
    Importing files, 55–58
    Vector paths, 121
    Work anchor point, 115
Adobe Marketplace & Exchange, 175
Adobe PDF, 336
Adobe Photoshop CS5
    Compositions, importing of, 72–73
    Description of, 14–15
    File extensions, 55, 335–336
    Importable 3D formats, 253
    Importing files, 55–58
    Live Photoshop 3D
        Importing effects, 248–250

        Working with, 248–257
    Repoussé effect, 253–254
    3D objects created in, 253
    Track mattes created from animated files, 137–139
    Vanishing Point Data, 337
    Work anchor point, 115
Adobe Premiere, 42
Adobe Premiere Pro, 308, 319, 337
Adobe Sound Document, 336
Adobe User to User Forums, 301
Advanced Audio Coding, 336
Advanced Television Systems Committee. see ATSC
AE Enhancers, 301
AE Scripts, 301
.ai, 55
Align panel, 33–34, 327
All Transform Properties, 168
Alpha, 22–23, 27, 135. see also Transparency
Alpha channels
    Changing the type of, 64
    Definition of, 14–15
    Revealing of, 21
    Transparent areas created with, 126
Ambient light, 221
Ambient option, 216
Amount (Range Selector), 169
Amplitude Modulation, 192
Anchor Point
    Bounding box, 120
    Definition of, 82, 168
    Illustration, 115
    Kinestasis creation by animating, 83–85
    Motion paths, 95
    3D Transform, 215
Anchor setting, 71
Animate In, 164
Animate Intro, 164

Animating
    Audio levels, 190–191
    Camera properties, 234–242
    Effects properties, 264–270
    Graphic Editor, 287–292
    Light properties, 227–231
    Masks, 121–125, 132–134
    Photoshop 3D compositions, 250–253
    Position, 90–97
    Rotation, 86–90
    3D layers, 217–220
Animation
    Compositions, 68–72
    Expressions used to automate. *see* Expressions
    Positional, 90–97
    Presets, saving, 268
    RAM preview for previewing, 210–211
    Simultaneous, 219
    Squash and stretch, 285–286
    Syncing, to composition markers, 199–203
    Text properties, 164–169
    Workflow, 68
Animation menu, 19
Animation workspace, 33
Animator group, 164
Animators. *see* Text animators
Aperture, 234
Appearance, 38
Apple Final Cut Pro, 42
Apple Motion Project, 337
Applications folder, 2
Apply Interpretation command, 63–64
Apply To pull-down menu, 276
Aspect ratio, 341–343
ATSC, 12, 344
Audio
    Composition markers added to
        Creating, 194–195
        Description of, 193–194

        Naming, 196–197
        Position, refining of, 198–199
        Syncing animation to, 199–203
    File formats, 182, 335–336
    Previewing, 50–51, 183–186
    Uncompressed formats, 182
Audio Amplitude layer, 205
Audio effects, 191–193
Audio files
    Adding to Timeline, 183–186
    Keyframes created from, 203–206
    Looping, 62–63, 188–190
    Metadata, 186–188
Audio Hardware, 38
Audio Interchange File Format, 336
Audio layers
    Adding effects to, 191–193
    Stacking order of, 189
Audio levels, animating, 190–191
Audio On/Off switch, 78
Audio Output Mapping, 38
Audio panel, 327
Auto Bézier interpolation, 280
Auto-Orientation dialog box, 231
Auto-Orient property, 275
Auto-Orient Towards Point of Interest, 231
Auto-Save, 38–40
Auto setting, 25
.avi, 336

B

Background Color dialog box, 69–70
Background color setting, 71
Background color swatch, 69
Based On (Range Selector), 169, 173
Baseline, 160
Baseline shift, 156
Bézier interpolation, 280, 291
Bézier vertices, 115, 125
Bitmap, 336
Bit rate, 340

Blending modes, 100–103
Blur
    Motion. *see* Motion blur
    Text properties, 168
Blur-in effect, 177–178
Blur Level, 234
Bounding box, 119–120
Bridge (Adobe), 170–171
Brushes panel, 328

C

Camera
    Active, 214, 233
    Animating properties of, 234–242
    Creating, 231–247
    Depth-of-field effect, 243–244
    Options, 234
    Point of Interest property, 231, 234, 241
    Rack Focus, 245–247
Camera layers
    Description of, 77
    Point of Interest property, 231, 234
Caps Lock key, 265
Capture Speed At, 273
Capturing motion, Motion Sketch for, 272–275
Cast Shadows option, 216, 221, 223–224, 227
Cathode ray tube television screens, 343
Character Offset, 168
Character panel, 156–157, 328
Character Range, 168
Character Value, 168
Choke, 147
Chroma key
    Creating, 144–146
    Garbage matte, 142–144
    Uses, 140–142Codecs, 339–340
Collapse Transformations/Continuously Rasterize switch, 79
Collect Files command, 64–65

Collect Files dialog box, 65
Color label, 79
Color of light, 227
Color Range effect, 145
Color Range Keying effect, 149
Column
    Contraction of, 80
    Expanding of, 80
Column displays, 46–47
Composition(s)
    Creating, 42, 68–70
    Cropping, 320–324
    Definition of, 42
    Double-clicking of, 74
    Illustrator, importing of, 72–73
    Importing, 60–61
    Importing file as, 56
    Layer sizes, 57
    Nested, 31, 42, 105–108, 211
    Photoshop, importing of, 72–73
    Photoshop 3D, animating, 250–253
    Previewing, 74
    Render Queue, 309–313
    Settings, 70–72
    Trimming, 320–324
Composition markers
    Creating, 194–195
    Description of, 193–194
    Naming, 196–197
    Position, refining of, 198–199
    Syncing animation to, 199–203
Composition menu, 19
Composition panel, 21–25, 32, 35–36, 119, 123, 322
Composition - Retain Layer Styles setting, 57
Composition setting, 57
Composition Setting dialog box, 70, 91, 99
Cone Angle, 227
Cone Feather, 227
Continuous Bézier interpolation, 280, 282

Convert Audio to Keyframes command, 205
Convert vertex tool, 130–131
Copying lesson files to hard drive, 4
Corner vertices, 115
Create New Folder button, 57–58
Creating
    Chroma key, 144–146
    Compositions, 42, 68–70
    Folders, 47–49
    Garbage matte, 142–144
    Lights, 221–231
    Masks, 117–118, 125–132
    Projects, 43
    Scripts, 300
    Subfolders, 47–49
    Text, 152–155
    Track mattes, 135–139
Creative Suite (Adobe), 186
Cropping compositions, 320–324
Current Time button, 52–53, 93
Current Time Indicator, 31
Custom text animators, 175–178
Custom Time Span dialog box, 312
Custom workspace, 37

D

Darken property, of masks, 116
Deceleration, 281–286
Depth-of-field effect, 243–244
Depth of Field option, 234
Deselecting
    Folders, 47
    Masks, 133
Desktop distribution graphics, 10
Dialog boxes
    Auto-Orientation, 231
    Background Color, 69–70
    Collect Files, 65
    Composition Setting, 70, 91, 99
    Custom Time Span, 312
    Fill Options, 101

Go to Time, 53
Import, 44–46, 58, 185
Import File, 59, 249
Import Multiple Files, 72–73
Import Options, 72
Interpret Footage, 62–64, 188
Keyframe Interpolation, 282
Light Options, 222
Mask Color, 130
Open Project, 175, 177–178, 235
Output Module Settings, 313, 315–316
Preferences, 38–39
QuickTime Options, 318
Replace Footage File, 61
Stroke Options, 102
Difference, 116
Diffuse option, 216
Digital video
    Basics of, 11–15
    Dimensions, 11
    Formats, 11–13
    Frame rate, 11, 13–14
    Pixel aspect ratio, 11, 71, 341–343
Directional handles, 96, 115, 130–131
Display, 38
Displays, video
    Aspect ratio, 341–343
    Interlacing, 343–344
    Pixel aspect ratio, 11, 71, 341–343
    Progressive display, 343–344
Docking panels, 33–34
Dragging
    Layers, 103
    Masks, 122
Drawing masks, 128–132
Drop shadow, 103–104
Drop zone, 33–34
Duration setting, 71
DV, 335
DV codec, 340

E

Ease and Wizz script, 301–302
Ease High (Range Selector), 169
Ease Low (Range Selector), 169
Easy Easing
  Acceleration created using, 281–286
  Deceleration created using, 281–286
  Keyframes, 283–284
Editing
  Layer, 43
  Text, 163
Edit menu, 19
Edit Original command, 49
Effect Controls panel, 25, 146, 255, 264–265, 267
Effect menu, 19
Effects
  Animating properties of, 264–270
  Applying to layers, 260–264
  Glow, 254–257, 266
  Lens Flare, 254–257
  Presets, applying and modifying, 268–270
  Shatter, 260–261, 268, 271
  Strobing, 291–292
Effects & Presets panel, 33, 171, 254, 260–261, 268, 329
Effects switch, 79
Electric Image, 335
Evolution property, 297
Exchange (Adobe), 301
Expand/Collapse button, 212
Expand or Collapse Transfer Controls Pane, 136
Expand Transfer Controls Pane button, 102, 106
Exporting a file, 319–320
Expressions
  Adding to properties, 293–294
  Definition of, 292
  Finding, 293
  JavaScript language, 292
  LoopOut(), 294–295
  Random(), 295–297
  Scripts versus, 300
  Spelling errors in, 293
  Time property with, 297–298
  wiggle(), 298–300
ExtendScript (Adobe), 300
Eyedropper tool, 145–146, 149

F

.f4v, 14
Fade-in, 110
Favorite effects, 175, 268. *see also* Presets
File(s)
  Collect Files command for consolidation of, 64–65
  Exporting, 319–320
  Illustrator, 55–58
  Mac OS, 5
  Missing, locating of, 61–62
  Multiple, importing of, 54–55
  Photoshop, 55–58
  Renaming, 49
File formats
  Audio, 182, 335–336
  Description of, 14, 44, 339
  Image sequences, 336–337
  Still images, 336–337
  Video, 11–13, 335–336
File menu, 19
File Path column, 46
Fill Options dialog box, 101
FireWire, 42
First line indent, 156
First Margin, 178
Flash Player (Adobe)
  Flash video, 13–14
  Viewing video tutorials with, 7
Flash Professional (Adobe), 319
Flowchart panel, 25
.flv, 14
Focus Distance, 234
Folder button, 47

Folders, creating, 47–49
Font size, 156
Font style, 156
Fonts used in book, 3
Footage, previewing, 49–53
Footage panel, 26–28, 49–50
Force Alignment, 178
Formatting individual text characters, 158–164
4:3 aspect ratio, 341–342
FPS, 52
Frame Blend switch, 80
Frame Rate, 210
Frame rate, 11, 13–14, 71
Frantic motion, Wiggler panel for, 277–279
Freeform masks, 125–132
From Current Time, 211
Full Screen, 211
Full-screen mode, 30

G

Garbage matte
    Creating, 142–144
    Refining, 147–149
General, 38
Geometric softness, 147
GIF, 335
Glow effect, 254–257, 266
Glow Intensity property, 271
Go to Time dialog box, 53
Graphic Editor, 31, 287–292
Graphics
    Television, 10
    Video, 10
Gray Level Softness, 147
Greenscreen, 141–142
Grid and Guide Options button, 322
Grid & Guides, 38

H

Handles
    Adding, 321
    Definition of, 51
    Directional, 96, 115, 130–131
Hand tool, 128, 232
Hard drive
    Copying lesson files to, 4
    Copying video tutorials to, 5
Height, 70
Help menu, 19
Hide Shy Layers Composition switch, 79, 194
Hiding panels, 32–33
High-definition television, 12, 341
Hold interpolation
    Description of, 280
    Strobing effect created using, 291–292
Horizontal scale, 156
Horizontal Type tool, 153

I

Illustrator (Adobe)
    Compositions, importing of, 72–73
    Description of, 14
    File extensions, 336
    Importing files, 55–58
    Vector paths, 121
    Work anchor point, 115
Image sequences
    File formats, 336–337
    Importing, 58–60
Import As drop-down menu, 56–57, 72
Import dialog box, 44–46, 58, 185
Import File command, 54
Import File dialog box, 59, 249
Import/importing
    Compositions, 60–61
    Description of, 38
    Illustrator files, 55–58
    Image sequences, 58–60

Keyboard shortcut for, 44, 54
Live Photoshop 3D effects, 248–250
Media files, 44–49
Photoshop files, 55–58
Import Multiple Files, 54
Import Multiple Files dialog box, 72–73
Import Options dialog box, 72
Info panel, 329
In Point, 127
Intensity, light, 227
Interlacing, 343–344
Internet devices, 10
Interpolation
    Auto Bézier, 280
    Bézier, 280, 291
    Continuous Bézier, 280, 282
    Hold
        Description of, 280
        Strobing effect created using, 291–292
    Keyframe, 280
    Linear, 280–281
    Spatial, 280–283
Interpret Footage dialog box, 62–64, 188
Intersect property, of masks, 116
Intraframe compression, 340

J

JavaScript language, 292, 300
Jumping between keyframes, 94

K

Karat symbol, 130
Kerning, 156, 159, 162
Keyboard shortcuts
    Beginning of work area, 265, 322
    Composition Settings dialog box, 91
    Deselecting all layers, 101
    End of work area, 265, 322
    Import, 44, 54, 185
    Interpret Footage dialog box, 63

Layer properties, 87, 108, 110
Moving playhead, 174
New camera layer, 223
New composition, 68
Opening a project, 235
Out Point, 127
Rotation properties, 217
Save, 25, 27, 49, 53
Save As, 46
Keyframe(s)
    Audio files used to create, 203–206
    Creating, 255
    Easing added to, 283–284
    Jumping between, 94
    Smoother panel for modifying, 276–277
Keyframe interpolation
    Spatial, 280–283
    Types of, 280
Keyframe Interpolation dialog box, 282
Kinestasis, 83–85

L

Labels, 38
Label switch, 79
Last Margin, 178
Layer(s)
    Adjustment, 77
    Audio
        Adding effects to, 191–193
        Stacking order of, 189
    Blending modes, 100–103
    Camera, 77
    Definition of, 19, 43
    Deselecting, 101
    Dragging of, 103
    Effects to, applying, 260–264
    Light, 77
    Names, changing, 81–82
    New camera, 223
    Null Object, 77
    Orientation, controlling, 275

Precomposing, 108–109
Properties of, 43, 82, 87, 303
Shape, 77
Solid, 77
Stacking order, 80–81
Styles, 103–104
Switches, 78–80
Text, 77, 158
Time-reversing, 270–271
Trimming, 201
　　Working with, 73–82
Layer bar mode, 31
Layer menu, 19
Layer panel, 28–29
Layer solids, 77
Layer/Source Name switch, 79
Leading, 156
Left margin, 156
Lens Flare effect, 254–257
Lesson files, 4
Letterboxing, 342
Levels of Undo, 39
Lighten property, of masks, 116
Light layers, 77
Light Options dialog box, 222
Lights
　　Animating properties of, 227–231
　　Creating, 221–231
　　Options, 227
　　Point of Interest property, 241
　　Using, 221–231
Light Transmission option, 216
Light Type, 227
Line Anchor, 168
Linear interpolation, 280–281
Line Spacing, 168
Live Photoshop 3D
　　Importing effects, 248–250
　　Working with, 248–257
Lock Aspect Ratio, 317
Lock button, 212
Lock switch, 78
Looping

Audio file, 62–63, 188–190
Video file, 62–63
LoopOut() expression, 294–295
Luminance, 135

M
Macintosh OS
　　Starting in, 2
　　Unlocking files, 5
Magnification drop-down menu, 27, 59, 93
Marketplace & Exchange (Adobe), 175
Mask(s)
　　Animating, 121–125, 132–134
　　Color, 129–130
　　Composition of, 114
　　Creating, 117–118, 125–132
　　Definition of, 114
　　Deselecting, 133
　　Dragging, 122
　　Drawing, 128–132
　　Freeform, 125–132
　　Manipulating, 118–121
　　Multiple, 120
　　Position, animating, 121–125
　　Properties, 116, 130
　　Selecting, 118–121
　　Shape, animating, 132–134
　　Shape tools for creating, 117–118
　　Stacking order, 115
　　Vertices, 114–115, 122, 132–134
　　Working with, 114–121
Mask Color dialog box, 130
Mask Expansion property, 116
Mask Feather property, 116
Mask Interpolation panel, 330
Mask Opacity property, 116
Mask Path property, 114, 116, 121, 123, 132
Material eXchange Format, 335
Matte Choker, 147–148
Mattes

Garbage, 142–144
Refining, 147–149
Traveling, 135–139
Media & Disk Cache, 38
Media files, importing, 44–49
Media management, 42
Memory and Multiprocessing, 38
Menus
Animation, 19
Composition, 19
Edit, 19
Effect, 19
File, 19
Help, 19
Layer, 19
Presets, 70
View, 19
Window, 19
Working with, 18
Metadata
Audio file, 186–188
Definition of, 186
Metadata panel, 330
Metal option, 216
Microsoft Zune, 13
Mini-Flowchart view, 204
Missing files, locating of, 61–62
Mobile devices, 10, 13
Mode (Range Selector), 169
Modulation Depth, 192
Modulation Rate, 192
Modulation Type, 192
Motif layer, 250
Motion Blur
Adjusting settings, 98–100
Definition, 72, 80, 97
Using of, 97–100
Motion Blur Comp button, 98
Motion Blur switch, 98, 286
Motion graphics
Defining, 10
Types of, 10
Motion path

Auto-Orient setting changed to
follow, 275
Changing the shape of, 282
Description of, 95–97
Motion Sketch panel, 272–275, 331
.mov, 14, 335
MP3, 336
MPEG-1, 335
MPEG-2, 335
MPEG-4, 335
Mute Audio, 210

N
Names
Composition markers, 196–197
Layer, 81–82
National Television Systems Committee.
see NTSC
Nested compositions, 31, 42, 105–108,
211
New camera layer, 223
New Composition button, 117, 126
None property, of masks, 116
NTSC, 12, 43, 342, 344
Null Object layers, 77
Null objects, 252
Number switch, 79

O
Offset (Range Selector), 169
1080i, 12
1080p, 12
Opacity, layer
Description of, 82, 296
Fade-in created by animating, 110
3D layers, 217
Opening a project, 18, 42, 235
Open Project dialog box, 175, 177–178,
235
Orientation property, 215
Orthographic view, 214, 218, 246

Outer glow, 103
Out Point, 127, 133
Output, 38
Output Module Settings dialog box, 313, 315–316
Outputting
    Exporting a project file, 319–320
    Rendering, 308–317
    Supported formats, 308, 324

P

Paint panel, 331
PAL, 13
Panels
    Align, 33–34, 327
    Audio, 327
    Brushes, 328
    Character, 156–157, 328
    Composition, 21–25, 31, 35–36, 119, 123, 322
    Description of, 20
    Docking, 33–34
    Drop zones, 33–34
    Effect Controls, 25, 146, 255, 264–265, 267
    Effects & Presets, 33, 171, 254, 260–261, 268, 329
    Flowchart, 25
    Footage, 26–28, 49–50
    Hiding, 32–33
    Info, 329
    Layer, 28–29
    Mask Interpolation, 330
    Metadata, 330
    Motion Sketch, 272–275, 331
    Paint, 331
    Paragraph, 154, 156–157, 328
    Preview, 332
    Primary, 21–32
    Project. *see* Project panel
    Render Queue, 30, 309
    Resizing, 35–36

    Smoother, 276–277, 333
    Timeline, 22, 25, 28, 31–32, 73, 75, 82, 171
    Tools, 332
    Tracker, 333
    Undocking, 33–34
    Uses, 21
    Viewing, 32–33
    Wiggler, 277–279, 334
Paragraph alignment, 156
Paragraph panel, 154, 156, 328
Paragraph text, 152, 155
Parallel light, 221
Parentheses, 25
Parenting
    Applications of, 88–90
    Definition of, 80
Path
    Creating Text on, 178–180
    Reverse, 178
Path Options property group, 179
Pen tool, 125, 128–132
Perpendicular to Path, 178
Phase alternating line, 13
Photoshop CS5 (Adobe)
    Compositions, importing of, 72–73
    Description of, 14–15
    File extensions, 55, 335–336
    Importable 3D formats, 253
    Importing files, 55–58
    Live Photoshop 3D
        Importing effects, 248–250
        Working with, 248–257
    Repoussé effect, 253–254
    3D objects created in, 253
    Track mattes created from animated files, 137–139
    Vanishing Point Data, 337
    Work anchor point, 115
Pillarboxing, 342
Pixel, 11
Pixel aspect ratio, 11, 71, 341–343
Playhead

Definition, 31
Moving, 92, 94, 121–122, 134, 174
Position, 270
Scrubbing the, 50, 138, 193, 198, 242
Point light, 221
Point of Interest property, 231, 234, 241
Point text, 152
Position
    Animating of, 90–97
    Text, 168
    3D Transform, 215
Position, layer, 82
Positional animation, 90–97
Precomposing layers, 108–109
Preferences
    Resetting of, 3–4
    Setting, 38–40
Preferences dialog box, 38–39
Premiere (Adobe), 42
Premiere Pro (Adobe), 308, 319, 337
Premultiplied – Matted With Color option, 64
Presentation graphics, 10
Preserve frame rate when nested or in render queue setting, 71
Preserve resolution when nested setting, 72
Presets
    Animation, saving, 268
    Definition, 268
    Description, 69–70
    Effects, applying and modifying, 268–270
    Text animators
        Applying, 170–172
        Browsing, 170–172
        Modifying, 172–175
        Saving as, 169–170
        Sharing of, 175
        Working with, 170–175
Presets menu, 70
Preset workspaces, 32
Preview, 38

Duration of, 61
Footage panel, 26–27
Quarter resolution, 24
RAM, 50–51, 61, 183, 186, 210–211, 274, 284, 287, 290, 303
Thumbnail, 29
Timeline, 332
Previewing
    Audio, 50–51, 183–186
    Compositions, 74
    Footage, 49–53
    Spacebar for, 60
    Stills, 50
    Video, 50
Preview panel, 332
Progressive display, 343–344
Project file, 42
Project panel
    Description of, 29–30, 45–46
    Folders, 47–48
    Renaming files, 49
    Tilde key for changing size of, 30, 45–46, 49
Projects
    Anatomy of, 43
    Creating, 43
    Formats, 337
    Multiple, 248
    New, 43
    Older versions, 20
    Opening, 18, 20, 42
    Schematic diagram of, 43
Proportional grid, 119, 128, 322
.psd, 55, 335

Q

Quality switch, 79
Quarter resolution, 24
QuickTime, 13–14, 335
QuickTime Options dialog box, 318

R

Rack Focus, 245–247
RAM, 39
RAM preview, 50–51, 61, 183, 186, 210–211, 274, 284, 287, 290, 303
RAM Preview button, 51
Random() expression, 295–297
Randomize Order (Range Selector), 169
Random Seed (Range Selector), 169
Range Selector properties, 169
Rectangle tool, 102, 120, 143
References, 29
Refining, matte, 147–149
Region of Interest button, 323
Remember Interpretation command, 63–64
Renaming files, 49
Rendering
    Definition, 61, 308, 311
    Individual frame, 324–325
Rendering plug-in setting, 71
Render items
    Definition of, 309
    Duplicating, 314–315
Render queue
    Compositions added to, 309–313
    Duplicating jobs in, 314–317
    Options, 309
    Settings, 311–313
Render Queue panel, 30, 309, 312, 314
Render templates, 317–319
Repetition, parenting for, 88–90
Replace Footage File dialog box, 61
Repoussé effect (Photoshop CS5), 253–254
Re-rendering, 314
Resetting
    Preferences, 3–4
    Workspace, 37, 182, 276
Resizing
    Columns, 46
    Panels, 35–36
Resolution

Description of, 13–14
Quarter, 24
RAM preview, 210
Setting, 71
Resolution/Down Sample Factor Popup button, 24–25, 265
Resource Central, 188
Resources, 8
Reveal
    Alpha channels, 21
    Columns, 46
Reverse Path, 178–179
RGBA mode, 14, 329
RGB mode, 14, 27
Right margin, 156
Rotation
    Animating, 86–90
    Keyboard shortcuts for, 217
    Layer, 82, 303
    Text, 168
Rotation tool, 239
Rulers composition, 21

S

Save As function, 46
Saving
    Custom workspace, 37
    Keyboard shortcuts, 25, 27, 49, 53
Scale, layer
    Description of, 82
    Fade-in created by animating, 110
Scale (Text), 168
Scale (3D Transform), 215
Script Editor, 300
Scripts
    Applying, 301–304
    Creating, 300
    Definition of, 300
    Expressions versus, 300
    Finding, 301
    Installing, 300
    Running, 300

Using, 301–304
Scrubbing the playhead, 50, 138, 193, 198, 242
Selection tool, 120, 122, 124, 127, 158, 229, 232
Select View Layout drop-down menu, 214, 236
Setting preferences, 38–40
720p, 12
Shadow Darkness, 227
Shadow Diffusion, 227
Shape Layers, 77
Shape (Range Selector), 169
Shape tools, 117–118
Shatter effect, 260–261, 268, 271
Shininess option, 216
Show Channel and Color Management Settings button, 23, 27
Shutter Angle, 98
Shutter Phase, 98
Shy switch, 79
Silverlight, 13
16:9 aspect ratio, 341
Skew (Text), 168
Skip, 210
Smoother panel, 276–277, 333
Smoothing, 273
Smoothness (Range Selector), 169
Software versions, 20
Solid layers, 77
Solo switch, 78
Source text, 155
Space after paragraph, 156
Spacebar, 60
Space before paragraph, 156
Spatial compression, 340
Spatial interpolation, 280–283
Spectral Background composition, 60
Specular option, 216
Spelling, 293
Spill Suppressor effect, 149
Spot light, 221
Squash and stretch, 285–286

Stacking order
    Audio layers, 189
    Layers, 80–81
    Masks, 115
Standard-definition television, 12–13, 341
Start and End (Range Selector), 169
Start Timecode setting, 71
Still images
    File formats, 336–337
    Previewing, 50
Strobing effect, 291–292
Stroke Options dialog box, 102
Stroke width, 156
Subfolders, 47–49
Subtract property, of masks, 116
Switches, layer, 78–80
Syncing animation to composition markers, 199–203

T

Tagged Image File Format, 14
Television
    High-definition, 12, 341
    Standard-definition, 12–13, 341
Television graphics, 10
Templates, render, 317–319
Temporal compression, 340
Text
    Character panel, 156–157
    Creating, 152–155
    Editing, 163
    Formatting individual characters, 158–164
    Margins, 153
    Paragraph, 152, 155
    Paragraph panel, 156–157
    On a path, 178–180
    Point, 152
    Properties
        Animating, 164–169
        Global, setting, 155, 157–164

List of, 168

Selecting, 158

Source, 155

Text animators

    Blur-in effect, 177–178

    Custom, 175–178

    Description of, 77

    Presets

        Applying, 170–172

        Browsing, 170–172

        Modifying, 172–175

        Saving as, 169–170

        Sharing of, 175

        Working with, 170–175

    Types of, 164, 168

    Typewriter effect, 175–176

Text layer

    Animating properties of, 164

    Description of, 77

    Double-clicking to select text, 158

.tga, 14

3D layers

    Animating, 217–220

    Creating, 211–212

Material Options, 216

    Multiple viewports for, 213–215

    Photoshop CS5 creation of, 253

3D Layer switch, 80

3D Transform, 215

Thumbnail preview, 29

.tiff, 14

Tilde key, 30, 45–46, 49, 188, 192, 296

Time code, 52, 71, 313

Timeline

    Audio files added to, 183–186

    Composition markers added to, 195

    Previews, 332

Timeline panel, 22, 25, 28, 31–32, 73, 75, 82, 171

Time Marker, 26

Time property with expressions, 297–298

Time-reversing, 270–271

Time Ruler, 26, 31

Time-Vary Stopwatch, 85, 87–88, 104, 133, 166, 174, 176, 179, 217, 228, 230, 237, 267, 271, 285

Title-Safe margin, 153

Tolerance property, 276

Tools

    Convert vertex, 130–131

    Eyedropper, 145–146, 149

    Hand, 128, 232

    Horizontal Type, 153

    Pen, 125, 128–132

    Rectangle, 102, 120, 143

    Rotation, 239

    Selection, 120, 122, 124, 127, 158, 229, 232

    Type, 158–160

Tools panel, 332

Tracker panel, 333

Tracking, 156, 159, 162

Track mattes, 135–139

Transfer Controls pane, 138

Transformation point, 82

Transparency. *see also* Alpha

    Description of, 14

    Masks. *see* Masks

    Opacity, 82

Trimming

    Compositions, 320–324

    Layers, 201

    Video clips, 51–53

Truevision Advanced Raster Graphics Adapter, 14

Tsume, 156

Typeface, 156, 161

Type tool, 158–160

Typewriter effect, 175–176

U

Uncompressed audio formats, 182

Undo, Levels of, 39

Undocked Panels workspace, 33

Undocking panels, 33–34
Units (Range Selector), 169
USB 2.0, 42

V

Vector paths (Adobe Illustrator), 121
Vertical scale, 156
Vertices, masks, 114–115
Video
    Digital. *see* Digital video
    Formats, 335–336
    Previewing, 50
Video clips, trimming, 51–53
Video displays
    Aspect ratio, 341–343
    Interlacing, 343–344
    Pixel aspect ratio, 11, 71, 341–343
    Progressive display, 343–344
Video files, looping of, 62–63
Video graphics, 10
Video On/Off switch, 78
Video Preview, 38
Video tutorials, 6–7
Viewing Panel, 32–33
View menu, 19
Volume Unit meter, 327

W

Web video, 13
Widescreen
    NTSC, 12
    PAL, 13
Width, 70
wiggle() expression, 298–300
Wiggler panel, 277–279, 334
Windowboxing, 342
Window menu, 19
Windows Media File, 336
Windows Media Video, 13
Windows operating system, 2
Windows Waveform, 336

Wireframe switch, 273
Workspace
    Animation, 33
    Custom, saving of, 37
    Definition of, 32
    Illustration of, 20
    Preset, 32
    Resetting, 37, 182, 276
    Understanding of, 32
    Undocked Panels, 33
    Viewing and hiding panels on, 32–33

X

XFL file, 319
X Rotation, 168, 215, 240

Y

Y Rotation, 168, 215, 240

Z

Z-axis, 243
Zoom, 25, 234
Z Rotation, 168, 215, 240

Wiley Publishing, Inc.
End-User License Agreement

READ THIS. You should carefully read these terms and conditions before opening the software packet(s) included with this book "Book". This is a license agreement "Agreement" between you and Wiley Publishing, Inc. "WPI". By opening the accompanying software packet(s), you acknowledge that you have read and accept the following terms and conditions. If you do not agree and do not want to be bound by such terms and conditions, promptly return the Book and the unopened software packet(s) to the place you obtained them for a full refund.

1. **License Grant.** WPI grants to you (either an individual or entity) a nonexclusive license to use one copy of the enclosed software program(s) (collectively, the "Software") solely for your own personal or business purposes on a single computer (whether a standard computer or a workstation component of a multi-user network). The Software is in use on a computer when it is loaded into temporary memory (RAM) or installed into permanent memory (hard disk, CD-ROM, or other storage device). WPI reserves all rights not expressly granted herein.

2. **Ownership.** WPI is the owner of all right, title, and interest, including copyright, in and to the compilation of the Software recorded on the physical packet included with this Book "Software Media". Copyright to the individual programs recorded on the Software Media is owned by the author or other authorized copyright owner of each program. Ownership of the Software and all proprietary rights relating thereto remain with WPI and its licensers.

3. **Restrictions on Use and Transfer.**

    (a) You may only (i) make one copy of the Software for backup or archival purposes, or (ii) transfer the Software to a single hard disk, provided that you keep the original for backup or archival purposes. You may not (i) rent or lease the Software, (ii) copy or reproduce the Software through a LAN or other network system or through any computer subscriber system or bulletin-board system, or (iii) modify, adapt, or create derivative works based on the Software.

    (b) You may not reverse engineer, decompile, or disassemble the Software. You may transfer the Software and user documentation on a permanent basis, provided that the transferee agrees to accept the terms and conditions of this Agreement and you retain no copies. If the Software is an update or has been updated, any transfer must include the most recent update and all prior versions.

4. **Restrictions on Use of Individual Programs.** You must follow the individual requirements and restrictions detailed for each individual program in the "About the CD" appendix of this Book or on the Software Media. These limitations are also contained in the individual license agreements recorded on the Software Media. These limitations may include a requirement that after using the program for a specified period of time, the user must pay a registration fee or discontinue use. By opening the Software packet(s), you agree to abide by the licenses and restrictions for these individual programs that are detailed in the "About the CD" appendix and/or on the Software Media. None of the material on this Software Media or listed in this Book may ever be redistributed, in original or modified form, for commercial purposes.

5. **Limited Warranty.**

    (a) WPI warrants that the Software and Software Media are free from defects in materials and workmanship under normal use for a period of sixty (60) days from the date of purchase of this Book. If WPI receives notification within the warranty period of defects in materials or workmanship, WPI will replace the defective Software Media.

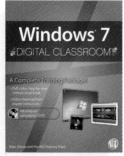